READINGS IN
MARKETING MANAGEMENT

Strategy and Action

Jerry L. Thomas, Ph.D., M.B.A.

College of Business
San Jose State University

Revised Edition, 2011

Readings in Marking Management

ISBN-13: 978-1467940900
ISBN-10: 1467940909

Library of Congress Cataloging in Publication Data

Appendix
Problem Set
Glossary
Index
End Notes
Test Bank

1. Marketing.   2. Organization.   3. Communication.
4. Statistics.

Printed in Charleston, SC

First published by South-Western Publishing Company
ISBN: 0-538-82819-6

TABLE OF CONTENTS

Acknowledgments

I would like to thank many San Jose State University faculty as well as other university faculty who have contributed to the completion of the articles in this book: Dr. Bill Campsey, Professor Accounting and Finance, who evaluated my early writings in the Lease-Purchase area; Dr. Joe Giglierano, Associate Dean of the College of Business, who encouraged a sabbatical leave to develop the Market Communications sections. For the time I was fortunate to spend with Dr. Jagdish Sheth at the University of Illinois and the Bell Laboratories; also, in memory of now past mentors—Dr. Robert Loewer, Professor Emeritus and Director of the Master of Business Administration Program; Dr. Jim Harper, Associate Dean Emeritus; Dr. Otto Butz, President of Golden Gate University and Dr. Ramon P. Heimerl, Dean Emeritus, College of Business, University of Northern Colorado.

I would like to thank a wide range of corporate decision makers who made invaluable contributions and suggestions at conferences of the Retail Merchants Association, New York; Direct Mail Marketing Association, Los Angeles; and Association of Retail Management Information Systems, Los Angeles. A particular thanks to Mr. Rod Sturm, Vice President Sales (Ret.), and Mr. D. Lance Cooper, Vice President New Ventures (Ret.) of American Telephone and Telegraph Company, as well as Ms. Anne Perlman, Past Vice President of Marketing, Tandem Computers, Inc. for generously adding their professional remarks.

Gratefully, I extend appreciation to several of my past and present students: Mr. Kurt Rohrs, Ms. Theodosia Foley, Ms. Nancy Escoto, and Mr. Robert Fetter (Master of Business Administration candidates); Mr. Anthony DeMaria, Ms. Salley

Faber, Mr. Richard Trifo, Ms. Heidemarie Heroldt, and Ms. Karrine Kleinbort, (Bachelor of Science students) for their stellar assistance researching, refreshing, formatting, and proofing articles and appendix material.

Thank you all.

Preface

The following articles are dedicated to the concept that effective marketing requires the practitioner to be conversant in each of four strategic and applied areas: **Statistic and Quantitative Methods, Market Research, Management of Markets, and Marketing Communications.**

Why Read This Book?

Readings in Marketing Management is an anthology of articles from the many published academic/trade journal articles, conference proceedings, industry white papers, and two other books written by Dr. Thomas as well as his substantial teaching and consulting experience. The articles included have been used regularly in business professional development programs and in the courses he teaches in marketing at San Jose State University's College of Business. The following pages offer examples, skills, and practical techniques to develop competitive advantage.

Introductory undergraduate through graduate and a few post-graduate remarks are presented in readings, articles, appendices, a glossary, and index, allowing the reader to follow logically the materials of most interest to him or her.

Who Should Read This Book?

The collection of writings is not intended to be eclectic, but, rather, introductory, intellectual, and practical "bait" to students, practitioners, and observers of today's corporate market milieu. The amassing of marketing facts (which is simply memorization and recall) is useful, but it is a dead-end venture unless combined with thinking and reasoning skills to solve real-life marketing tasks. Remember, memory is both defective and selective (*e.g.,* first, we rarely remember things as they truly are, and, second, we remember what we want to remember).

As you can quickly see, the recall of marketing concepts is only a quick and perfunctory beginning in the solution of marketing tasks. For example, suppose your task on the job is to determine if a viable market segment exists in a particular market. The first step, of course, is to recall the definition of "market segment." This step involves merely recall of a marketing definition. *A profiled subset or target of a mass market.* The next step requires the understanding of a skill, a somewhat more advanced ability: the three specific tests used to determine an actual market segment.

At this point, the marketer must add thinking and reasoning skills to apply and evaluate the *identifiability, accessibility,* and *substantiability* measures regarding the segment in question. The steps of skill and then application may take hours to perhaps days, or weeks.

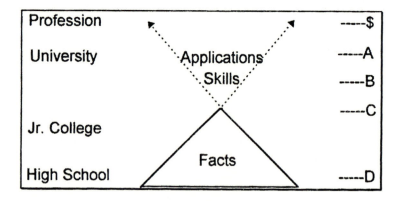

Unfortunately, we tend to get "stuck" in the memorization of marketing concepts. Without an understanding of what lies beyond in real-world practice, we often see the goal of a marketing course as merely a memorization process. As you can see from the preceding graphic, the memorization of marketing facts is really only the beginning. Marketing concepts and facts build the needed foundation, but, as concepts go, they are very limited until brought to bear on an application, with the addition of logic and reasoning skills. In business, knowing facts, using skills, and developing applications create marketing successes and are highly rewarded.

Whether we are students or practitioners, how effective we are to move from memorizing facts (average) to processing those facts into skills (above average) and on to their appropriate applications (excellence) will be the true measure of our competence. This intellectual evolution is the greatest competitive advantage that can be developed in the profession of marketing management.

The pages that follow should stimulate the novice's understanding of terms through relevance and bring applied acumen to the more advanced observer/practitioner through analytical involvement and value-added applications. It is fair to say that certain readers will wish that there were fewer numbers and less attention paid to quantitative method in the pages that follow.

These persons will most likely be the individuals who most need to observe the fundamental relationship between nominal understanding of market theory and the quantitative competitive edge required to "win" in the day-to-day practice of contemporary market management. Further, the foundation of these readings assumes a functional understanding of basic business English, statistics, economics, and accounting principles. Therefore, the treatments that are developed should not bore the reader but, rather, "move right along."

Throughout this writing, considerable effort has been made to present fundamentals of the most relevant market issues. A few theoretical underpinnings and definitions were necessary, but then on to practical applications. These applications should encourage a more robust understanding of the basic concepts while, at the same time, challenging the more advanced observer or practitioner. The articles included in each part differ in sophistication and allow the reader to "support," by example, the concepts at the level of his or her individual interest and ability.

A liberal number of references have been made to real-time "war stories" and their resulting "scar tissue." Some of these anecdotes are humorous, others nostalgic; several are ethical/political, a few are damning, but each is revealing and a part of the market lexicon of grit found inextricable in the migration from academic courseware to the realities of business and industry practice—THE REAL WORLD (or the difference between reading from the Adventures of Pooh and avoiding stepping in it). "Intelligence [education/professional development] is important only in that it allows you to play the game. Without intelligence, you don't even have a ticket to enter the competition."[1]

Remember, the objective of capable marketers should be to remain in the significant one-third of John Munzer's "Dummy Theorem." The dummy theorem states that in any group of n people, k of them are dummies, and the ratio of k over n is a constant greater than or equal to 2/3. That is, in any group of people, two-thirds of them will be dummies.[2] Put another way, don't be an "in-duh-vidual."[3]

The following are published remarks regarding books written by Jerry Thomas:

Psychographics of Telephone Shopping.
ISBN: 0-931290-70-8
"The [book] research is an impressive accomplishment."

—Institute of Retail Management

The Retail Lease versus Purchase Decision.
ISBN: 0-931290-86-4

"This work will serve well as a basic reference for considering high-technology options."

—Mr. R.W. Sturm (Ret.)
Vice President, Sales
AT&T

Readings in Practical Marketing Management.
ISBN: 1-866870-44-0

"An appreciation for understanding of...markets, forces, cultures, and business practices...."

—Anne Perlman
Vice President, Marketing
Tandem Computers, Inc.

Introduction

About the Author

 Dr. Thomas' academic research, consulting, and public speaking backgrounds are extensive. He has over 30 years of university teaching experience and is a full professor with tenure at San Jose State University's College of Business. He earned B.S., M.B.A., and Ph.D. degrees in Business. He has been Director of Graduate Programs at the College as well as Associate Dean. Likewise, he maintained a successful private consulting practice for 20 years which regularly advised over 25 Fortune 500 companies at their corporate levels, both domestically and internationally.

Among his clients have been Apple Computer, American Telephone and Telegraph Company, J.C. Penney, Macy's, Olivetti, Pacific Stock Exchange, Bank of America, Lockheed-Martin, Pacific Bell, Deloitte & Touche, Telefonos de Mexico, U.S. Chamber of Commerce, and USX (U.S. Steel, Inc.). Dr. Thomas' academic and professional specialty is the psychographic study of customer propensity in high technology voice/data communications markets.

His unique writing style and delivery are born out of real-world business experience, combined with extensive business education and the career teaching and training of over 10,000 students and business practitioners. His has been a rare privilege in both the boardroom and the classroom.

About the Approach

A Marketing colleague, Dr. Ed Laurie, once remarked that nearly anyone could be an Olympian if the high jump bar were lowered to three feet. George Ade put it even more directly: "Anybody can win unless there happens to be a second entrant." And, some years ago, Guerilla Marketing attacked standard "textbook" Marketing in favor of a more unabashed approach.

While much of the classical textbook market theory is sometimes not very useful in the day-to-day practice of marketing management, it is also true that "There are no exceptions; it's not possible to succeed without Marketing."[4]

The approach must be disciplined, but it must also be practical, applied, and add value to a "trench" solution (one that can be implemented, not just discussed). This book assumes the following learning objectives:

- to develop value added, do-it-yourself techniques
- to create logical, usable, pragmatic solutions
- to combine education, experience, and communication
- to build competitive advantage in your industry

Visit Dr. Thomas' university website at
www.cob.sjsu.edu/Thomas_J.

About the Book

"I appreciate that the book is relatively shorter and more concise than most traditional textbooks—no fluff or 'fun facts'"

—Gladys C. - Accounting Major

"This is one of those books I don't mind using to prepare for class.   It helps me see the application to real life."

—Krista S. - Advertising Major

"I don't think any book is perfect, but the text is excellent."

—Thomas L. - Accounting Major

"The book...gets right to the point.   I also like the fact that it is real world.   I have looked through other Marketing textbooks and am glad I have this book."

—Mathew K. - Public Relations Major

"What I really like about the book is the fact that Marketing materials are related to other courses such as Economics, Finance, Management, etc."

—Adan O. - Finance Major

"English is my second language and this...book is clear and provides explanations."

—Elsa G. - Accounting Major

"I wish all my classes had a book like this.   It's small, it's inexpensive, it's straight to the point...."

—Brandon S. - Marketing Major

Navigate to Succeed

Publications, prophecies, and deliveries in business today are made by pundits, many of whom have no real experience in business or have ever worked in a business setting or been personally responsible for a practical business deliverable of any kind. In fact, even many of those teaching in business colleges and providing professional development today don't hold advanced degrees in business or even bachelor's degrees in business, neither have they been responsible to produce any tangible business deliverable, or have succeeded in publishing in business forums.

This is not to say that these are not generally capable people with even very high I.Qs. But many do not have the requisite ability to be frank, direct and to the point, or discuss applications of theory—and, after all, in business we are paid to be practitioners of philosophy, having developed the skills to assess problems, develop strategies, and implement solutions rather than simply talk about them. *"Get smart"*—select the trainers, educators, and study materials most likely to help you succeed in your development effort.

"The Three-Legged Stool"

The ambition of this revised edition continues to be a pragmatic discussion of strategies and actions which, at the end of the day, will provoke curiosity, reason, and improve the ability to influence effective market decisions. Demand that the business professionals you study or train with have demonstrated the trilogy of professional skills to truly help you understand Marketing. Then strive to develop and hone these same personal competitive talents. You will proactively build your own career proficiency by similarly working toward these same goals. The "three-legged stool" rule applies here. One leg is relevant experience (responsibility for significant work product at management levels of business), another leg is relevant education (**earned degrees in business**), and the third leg is demonstrated communication ability (**extensive professional development**, and/or consulting, and publication deliveries).

No credible argument can be made that one of these legs is more important than another.   And all three are required in order that the "stool" remains stable, strong, and able to fulfill its function. Success in Marketing is all about creating an added value to business.   It is what we are ultimately paid for.   Each of our values to a business organization, indeed our own futures, will be measured in developing this relevant experience, education, and the ability to communicate them in effective ways.

> On Tuesdays when it hails and snows
> The feeling in me grows and grows
> That hardly anybody knows
> If these are these and those are those.
>
> —Winnie the Pooh

Part One

Statistics and
Quantitative Methods

This article was first published in Psychographics of Telephone Shopping *(Alchemy Press) and was entitled, "Sampling for Primary Data—Consumer Populations."*

Sampling

What must be understood is that there is an inextricable relationship between the effective practice of contemporary marketing management and qualitative and quantitative procedures. The synergy contributed by the combination provides a "competitive edge" required to "win" in the day-to-day practice of marketing. Complex markets of the twenty-first century demand a "first focus" on the customer— and that requires the application of both pragmatic theory and numerical practice.

The application of arithmetic algorithms can help the market manager to reduce the ambiguity of decision making. These techniques will not provide "fail safe" decision modules or solutions, but they will reduce a considerable amount of risk and increase the probability of richer, more capable solutions for the market manager. "Statistical thinking is distinct from everyday thinking.   It is a skill that is learned."[5]

Stay on the trail!!!

Applying capable methodology requires discipline. Stay "on the trail" and be tenacious to achieve valid results.

Descriptive and Inferential Statistics

Descriptive statistics consists of various procedures for presenting existing data. The main purpose of descriptive statistics is to organize, classify, summarize, and make more useful data which left in its existing form may be confusing, illogical, or, at best, difficult to understand. Examples of descriptive statistics are frequency distributions, measures of central tendency (mean, median, and mode calculations), measures of skew, frequency polygons, data arrays, charts, graphs, and other methods of non-probabilistic data analysis.

Inferential statistics are applied when we wish to use a "few" observations to represent, measure, and analyze the "many" observations of an entire group. Probability is used in these calculations. Examples of inferential statistic calculations include sampling applications, estimating measures of central tendency, testing hypotheses, forecasting, correlation, and others.

Measures of Central Tendency

The marketing manager will need to categorize market segments by specific characteristics. S/he will be observing and measuring demographic and psychographic characteristics among customers to be identified as existing markets or potential target markets. The first step in evaluating a customer base is to exhaust observation of all secondary data. If these data are insufficient to support the decisions which must be made, primary data collection will be required. No matter what type of data is collected (descriptive or inferential), its presentation can distort the true meaning of the information. Because of the large number of data required to evaluate target markets, averages are often used to help manage and "make sense" of the disaggregated data. The most common averages used in analysis of markets are the basic measures of central tendency: mean, median, mode and standard deviation.

Measures of central tendency find their underpinnings in the logic of the central limit theorem of statistics. The rudiments of this proof permit several very important concepts for the market researcher:

1. Proper collection methodology will permit sample results to be generalized to the larger (but not measured) population.

2. Samples collected n = or > 30 from populations which are normally distributed will also be normally distributed and will possess "central tendency." (Their mean, median, and mode values will equal or nearly equal each other.)

3. Samples collected n = or > 30 will be normally distributed with equal numbers of respondents represented both above and below the mean value.

Distributions are groups of raw data that help organize and classify market/consumer information by a specific characteristic. For example, if a sample of 30 customers from a group of 300 are asked their ages, these individually reported and unarranged numbers offer little help to explain age as a characteristic or factor regarding the 30 or the 300 in the original customer base. But a few fundamental measures of average help to clarify the data.

Normal Curve with Actual "n" of 30

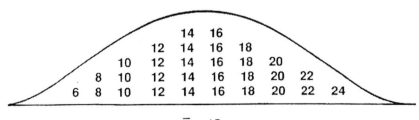

$$\overline{X} = 15$$

$$\bar{x} = \frac{\sum fx}{n}$$

where: $\bar{x}$ = mean of the distribution
                   f = frequency of x
                   x = observation of respondent
                   n = number of observations

Using the example of raw age data collected of 30 consumers, a calculation of the arithmetic mean ($\bar{x}$) age presents a central measure for comparison. (Notice that some ages in the sample occur more than once. These anomalies may appear in any natural combination.) While the mean of a distribution helps to show the average age, it is really a point estimate. In other words, the calculated mean stands for a representation of all 30 ages collected.

Why Sample?

Practitioners, researchers, and students/observers of the market milieu will agree that the valid understanding of customers is critical to the central strategy and tactics required for effective market decision making. But what is less understood is how to develop a sampling plan such that the findings are reliable, the fewest customers (potential customers) are polled, and, at the same time, the results produce a collection of consumer data which will accurately reflect the characteristics of all of the customers not questioned in the sample (the entire target market) as well as those respondents who were questioned. Even those who would argue that cost and [approximations] have a paramount role in sampling design must admit that much more precision is available when statistical concepts are applied to determine the sample size.[6]

Statistically, there is "correct data" (validity) and there is "incorrect data" (invalidity). The distance between the two is error.[7] Any time that a sample of a few customers is used to evaluate the many customers in the entire target market, error will exist—no matter how competent the research effort is. The focus of any capable sample plan should attempt to identify error and understand/explain its impact on the data results. It is important to remember that error can occur at any stage of examining consumer behavior and markets (*i.e.,* development of hypotheses, articulation of the test instrument, selection and application of the data collection methodology, or evaluation and enumeration of the study results). Each of these stages is important, but, if the sampling approach is flawed, the errors will promulgate throughout all successive stages and confound the entire data collection.

No matter how complicated or simple the data collection methodology[8] will be, correct sampling is critical. Market managers have been criticized for using inferential statistics (particularly psychographics) to evaluate consumer behavior because measurement is not precise. Remember, while this criticism may be accurate, the competent business analyst does not fear error but rather searches it out, accounts for it, and controls/documents the data results to reflect the impact of the discrepancy.

When the population of consumers to be studied is small, a census may be used rather than a sample. A census evaluates each and every consumer. This process does not require inferential statistics; however, the process is time-consuming and expensive.

Sampling is popular with the marketing analyst because most consumer populations are large and time is critical, not only for the data collection but also to the ultimate deployment ("market roll-out") of the product or service. This concept may be thought of as a "strategic window."[9] Because the business market is dynamic and not static, the opportunities for a successful product or service pass the "window" quickly. Sampling helps to provide necessary data for market decision-making while this information is still relevant.[10]

Sampling Elements

The market manager is faced with the evaluation of four characteristics in order to collect a sample of appropriate size:

1. Confidence level
2. Standard deviation
3. Error (or confidence) interval around the mean
4. Resource budget

Confidence level is the probability that when the sample is drawn from the larger population of consumers that the actual data parameters (*i.e.,* mean, standard deviation, etc.) of the entire group will actually be among the sample data collected. This probability is expressed as a percent and is determined based on the risk profile of the manager, organization or business climate. Classical levels of confidence are 90%, 95%, and 99%. In many business applications, the analyst may choose a lower percentage. The logic of this choice will be shown in the actual sample size formula to follow. It is important to note here that the sample size formula requires converting the percent of confidence to the statistical measure of the Z value.

Z is used to determine the critical value of confidence. For most studies, the sample size needed will be large enough (and "n" greater than or equal to 30) that standardized values of area under the normal curve will prove accurate.[11]

The Z value for any percentage probability may be found simply by looking up a brief calculation on a table for the areas under the normal curve (found in the last pages of any basic statistics text or Appendix C of this book). Note that the leftmost column and the topmost row are Z values, and all other series of numbers internal to the table are probabilities. If the analyst chooses a confidence level of 95% when using a standard table, the equal and corresponding Z value is found by dividing the confidence level by two:

$$.95 / 2 = .4750$$

then locating the answer (.4750) in the body of the Z table.

Treating the table as a "matrix," find the number located in the leftmost column (1.9) and the corresponding number in the topmost row (.06), and add them together:

$$1.9 + .06 = 1.96$$

Therefore, the Z value for 95% confidence is 1.96. Z value and probability are like the same physical states of water in science. For example, H_2O may appear as a gas (steam) or a solid (ice). The concept of probability and Z score are similar—they are the same stochastically (probabilistically) but are represented in two different forms.

Standard Deviation is a measure of variability among the total market of the respondents. Specifically, standard deviation is a measurement of how far one consumer's opinion or data is above or below the average response among all consumers in the target population. This calculation is very important and must be made for each new target market of customers. Consumers have different opinions concerning different products, companies, etc. This fact (and variable in the sample size formula) is why there is no relationship between the size of the population to be sampled and the size of the sample to be drawn in behavioral research.

While it is true, for example, that in engineering, by using a "sampling distribution of sampling means," a matrix table can be devised which will yield a sample size based on confidence level and population size, this procedure <u>may</u> <u>not</u> be done in consumer behavior samples. Engineering testing permits many successive trials of the same measurement to be replicated and observed. In consumer behavior, a new respondent is observed for each sample, and, therefore, the variability (standard deviation) for each sample/population is not redundant and must be measured individually.

In order to accurately evaluate this characteristic of variability, a "pilot" sample of respondents must be drawn from the larger population of customers. At this point, it is important to do several things. First, always collect a minimum of 30 responses to a single principal hypothesis or question. Statistical significance will be assured for this measurement with an "n" equal to or greater than 30. Next, associate a random number with each potential respondent. (These can be water/gas/electric billing numbers, social security numbers, selective service numbers, etc.)

The important issue here is that each member of the population of customers has a similar identification. And, last, a random selection of the "n" > or = 30 must be made. Remember, there is nothing random about a telephone book (unless the numbers themselves are used with a random number table)—<u>do</u> <u>not</u> select any combination of names from a telephone directory and consider it a random selection. Use the identification number mentioned earlier; then, if the sample is small, use a random number table to make the selection. (Telephone directories are even more confounded with the now extensive use of cell phones.)

If the number selected for the pilot sample is larger, use a random number generator[12] (common software capable of selecting randomly by number). To test for random selection: every member in the entire population of consumers must have an equal chance of being selected, and the selection of any one respondent must not change the probability of any other respondent's being selected.

Once these "tests" have been met, responses to a single question are made and the results tabulated to yield the calculation of sample standard deviation (variability among the customers).

$$S = \sqrt{\frac{\sum f(x - \bar{x})^2}{n}} \quad \text{and} \quad \hat{\sigma} = s\sqrt{\frac{n}{n-1}}$$

where:

S	= Sample standard deviation
f	= Frequency of x
x	= Individual observation of the respondent
n	= Sample size of respondents
$\bar{x}$	= Mean of the sample respondents
$\hat{\sigma}$	= Estimate of the population standard deviation

Error interval must now be determined and is the third major element in the sample calculation. Similar to the decision of confidence level, the researcher/practitioner determines the interval of error which has been selected to be "tolerated" above or below the true population average response.

The market researcher must decide how large a sampling error to allow. Deciding the error interval ("margin of error") in the same way that confidence level was determined previously.[13]

For example, if the possible responses to the question asked are measured in utiles of agreement ([5] "strongly agree," [4] "agree," [3] undecided, [2] "disagree," and [1] "strongly disagree"), the marketing managers must select the amount of error that they wish to "tolerate" in the sample above or below the true mean response of all respondents (e = .10 would allow the sample mean calculation to deviate above or below the actual population mean by ± 1/10 utile).

The marketing manager establishes the interval of tolerable error s/he or the organization will tolerate. An intuitive sense, judgment, risk profile of the individual, and corporate risk aversion may be weighed in the confidence interval decision. Classical error intervals are: .01, .05, .10, and .20. In establishing initial confidence levels and error interval measures, the marketing manager should consider that when the error interval estimate is allowed to be too wide, the estimate will have no utility. Conversely, when these measures are too narrow, the sample size calculated may be too large to be effectively or efficiently collected.

The resource budget must now be considered because all marketing applications involve costs. The total number of consumers to be sampled may be so large that the data collection would be too expensive. The analyst can determine quickly by multiplying the cost of each individual interview times the required sample size, whether or not the budget will be a constraint. By observing the actual relationship of sampling characteristics in the formula once the formula is solved, the analyst can algebraically alter the confidence and error levels until the sample size does fit the budget allocation.[14]

$$ n = \frac{Z^2 \hat{\sigma}^2}{e^2} $$

n =   Sample size to be drawn from the total population
Z =   Confidence level (converted to Z score)
e=   Error interval selected
$\hat{\sigma}$ =   Estimated population standard deviation

In the earlier example, confidence level could be reduced to 90%, and the error interval could be increased to .20; "n" will then be reduced and may fall within the budget constraint. However, more error will have to be tolerated, and the confidence of the sample data emulating the population data is reduced. It is a tradeoff. (This approach is a form of "judgment" sampling.)

Similarly, if the variability among the individual consumers (standard deviation) is large, the required sample size will increase. If the consumer responses are nearly the same as one another, the standard deviation will be low, and the required sample size much smaller. At a point, as the responses become dissimilar, the marketing manager may conclude that the results of such a study will be sufficiently invalid or useless to continue statistically. Significant research must then be aborted. (Although each of the following population curves is symmetrical, the greater the deviation among respondents [the distance from the response to the mean], the larger the sample drawn must be.)

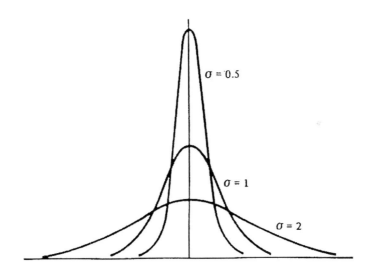

Implications

The marketing manager must understand the rudiments of sampling practice. S/he must remain confident in the face of criticism that these calculations are the best way to understand and enumerate error. Further, to not use this basic procedure is to relegate any inferential methodologies measuring business and industry environments to guesswork. Practical applications of sampling consumer behavior must be made with the fundamental understanding of inferential statistics and also the pragmatic assumption of error and risk. However, we are far better off to recognize statistical limitations than to ignore its usefulness. The human condition is to ignore these fundamental skills in sample applications. Indeed, many organizations as well as individuals either do not understand or choose to ignore these principles. Experience proves the 80/20 rule here: the 20% of the companies employing/demanding this level of research are making 80% of the money.

For sample study questions, see Appendix J.

This article was first published in the California Business Education Journal.

Forecasting for Market Management

A "wag" once explained history as, "Just one damn thing after another." However, to the market manager, there is a future value relationship between past performance and expectation. The concept of regression estimates unknown values of a variable based on past observations (history), and "linear" implies that a straight "trend" line may be calculated which will propagate the relationship.

Sir Francis Galton, around the turn of the 20th century, compared the heights of people to the heights of their parents. His major conclusion was that offspring of unusually tall persons tended to be shorter than their parents, while children of unusually short parents tended to be taller. The successive offspring from tall persons "regressed" downward toward the average population height, while the opposite was true of short families.[15]

This movement of outcomes toward an average is a basis for the "simple" two-variable regression model. The phenomenon allows the marketing manager to apply the principle of forecasting to obvious areas of concern such as future levels of sales, costs, wages, manpower, cost of capital, and others. The prudent manager can apply this technique to relationships unique to his own task, but for our own purpose, we will consider a sales revenue example to explore the practical value of this quantitative tool.

Because of the complex nature of the marketer's environment, s/he may wish to correlate several observations at a time. To accommodate this measure, multivariate regression analysis is valuable but much too cumbersome for mechanical calculation. For this reason, multiple regression will be more specifically dealt with later in this presentation but does deserve brief description here.

Multivariate regression— $\hat{Y}$ = a + b1X1 + b2X2 +...+ BkXk— should be considered by those administrators and managers who wish to correlate more than one independent variable (X) with the dependent variable (Y). Computer routines are available for this purpose.

Bivariate Regression

While not as sophisticated as multiple regression, bivariate linear regression $\hat{Y}$ = a + b(X) is a relatively simple way to enumerate values of two variables and determine future forecasts or predictive outcomes. [16] The variable to be predicted is called the dependent variable (y), and the predictor is the independent variable (x).

A simple problem concerning levels of sales in a small/medium-sized department will be used to examine the regression procedure. This analysis will be accomplished manually in tableau form. It should be mentioned that if large numbers of observations are desired, computer routines in different languages are available on almost any statistical software package. [17]

Figure 3 is a sales problem run on a program of Information Science Systems' Time Share Library. A number of sophisticated hand-held calculators can manage regression. The formulae used in this presentation are the same as those which Hewlett-Packard chose to program into its model HP30S.

Suppose that the marketing manager knows that annual historical sales demands for a product were as follows:

2007 9,250   2008 10,000
2009 10,500   2010 14,000
2011 15,500

S/he could first plot a "scatter" diagram of the data by positioning the observations on a graph:

Figure 1
X,Y Scatter Plot

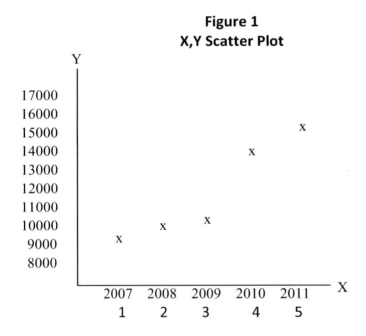

These data are valuable in a visual sense, but they do not allow accurate future predictions to be made. If, however, the manager now applies regression analysis to "best fit" a straight line through the scatter, such that the summed squares of distances between the observed points above the line are equal to the summed squares of distances of observations below the line, we say that the best fit has been made. This line, then, allows future forecasts of potential levels of sales demand.

The dependent variable (sales) is plotted on the Y axis, and the independent variable (time) is plotted on the X axis. In order to

Page 23

draw the straight prediction line, the market manager must determine only two points, $\hat{Y}$, then the laws of geometry will allow him or her to approximate the line. Once the two points have been joined at the estimate for 2007 and the estimate for 2011 (the "Y actual" data may or may not fall on the line), a forecast solution for 2012 is possible. Called a "secular trend line," geometry will allow the extension of a line between two points. Figure 2 shows this graphic solution of the estimated demand for 2012. The following tableau procedure will calculate the two values:

Year	X	Y	XY	X^2	$\hat{Y}$
2007	(1)	9250	9250	1	8550
2008	(2)	10000	20000	4	
2009	(3)	10500	31500	9	
2010	(4)	14000	56000	16	
2011	(5)	15500	77500	25	15150
Σ	(15)	59250	194250	55	

Figure 2
X,Y Correlation Schematic

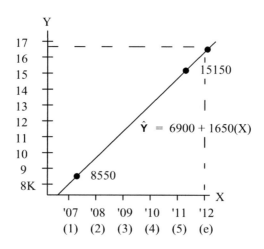

$$\hat{Y} = 6900 + 1650(X)$$

The $\hat{Y}$ value or the estimate of a Y observation (sales) at a value of X (time) is determined by formula.[18]

$$\hat{Y}=a+b(X)$$

where:

$$a \quad = \quad \frac{(\sum Y)(\sum X^2)-(\sum X)(\sum XY)}{N(\sum X^2)-(\sum X)^2}$$

$$= \quad \frac{(59{,}250)\,(55) - (15)\,(194{,}250)}{(5)\,(55) - (225)} = 6{,}900$$

$$b \quad = \quad \frac{N(\sum XY)-(\sum X)(\sum Y)}{N(\sum X^2)-(\sum X)^2}$$

$$= \quad \frac{(5)\,(194{,}250) - (15)\,(59{,}250)}{(5)\,(55) - (225)} \quad = 1{,}650$$

Figure 3
Linear Regression Software Routine

DESCRIPTION: COMPUTES THE SLOPE & OTHER STATISTICS FOR SIMPLE LINEAR REGRESSION WITH ONE DEPENDENT VARIABLE Y. INSTRUCTION: ENTER YOUR DATA USING DATA STATEMENTS.

USE THE FORMAT DATA 1,30,2,40,3,50

NUMBERS 1, 2, & 3 ARE YOUR X VALUES; 30, 40, & 50 ARE THE CORRESPONDING Y VALUES.

HOW MANY DATA PAIRS (X,Y) DO YOU HAVE? 5
DATA 1,9250,2,10000,3,10500,4,14000,5,15500
RUN

**********DATA ANALYSIS*********
NUMBER OF OBSERVATIONS 5 SLOPE 1650
MEAN OF X 3
MEAN OF Y 11850
Y-INTERCEPT 6900
R = .95

As my students say, "The crank has now been turned." With the work complete, it is simple to plot two points and draw the regression line.

$\hat{Y} = a + b(x)$

$2007 = [6900 + 1650 (1)]$ or when x = 1
$\qquad \hat{Y} = \$8550$
$2011 = [6900 + 1650 (5)]$ or when x = 5
$\qquad \hat{Y} = \$15,150$

$2012 = [6900 + 1650 (6)]$ or when x = 6
$\qquad \hat{Y} = \$16,800$

With regression analysis complete, the marketer can predict that in 2012 the rate of sales demand will approximate $16,800. While the actual process as presented in this simple example is manageable, the computer routine generates in a matter of seconds the values necessary to determine the line coordinates. Note that "a" and "b" values are identical to their computer counterparts. Further, it is conceptually important to distinguish between "Y" values (actual historical observations) and "$\hat{Y}$" values (estimates).

This discussion of forecasting for market managers is a rudimentary presentation of the model. Whether called "least sum of squares" or two-variable regression, this valuable tool is a quantitative technique that adapts well to the myriad of forecasts which the business manager must assume. Linear regression is a probabilistic expectation of forward values based on sound quantitative principles statistically capable of establishing a future secular trend line from historical data. Uncertainty and the need for prediction are required in virtually every aspect of market management. Regression is one solution.

Multivariate Regression

Now let's take a look at a bit more sophisticated application of linear regression where it is possible to look at the contribution of several independent variables when attempting to explain or forecast the dependent variable. If, as in the prior example, we wished to predict the demand for a product but believed that there were reasons other than time which influenced customers, we could set the regression equation as follows:

$$\hat{Y} = a + b_1 X_1 + b_2 X_2 + ... + b_k X_k$$

where:

$\hat{Y}$	=	The dependent variable (estimated)
X	=	An independent variable
a	=	An intercept constant added to each case
b	=	The regression coefficient

A prudent marketing manager would expect that not only time but also other characteristics might influence the customers' propensity to purchase the product.

A competent methodology, to be relevant, would probably include geo-demographic issues of age, sex, income, and location. Further, psychographic elements such as prestige or social acceptability may influence demand.

If we are investigating a unique market segment that has *a priori* knowledge about the product (behavioristic segment), then perhaps technical variables such as beta test results or performance criteria might be collected. In any event, the linear relationships between each of these independent characteristics and the dependent variable (demand) could be measured, compared, and evaluated.

Because the linear algebra required to solve the equation becomes more iterative with the addition of each succeeding variable, regression calculations are tedious by hand, but are a superb application for computer technology. In our example, each characteristic to be measured is now named as an independent (predictor) variable. (As we have previously discussed, X_1 has been set equal to "time.")

X_2 = Age X_6 = Prestige Influence

X_3 = Sex X_7 = Social Class

X_4 = Income X_8 = Product Test Results

X_5 = Location X_9 = Product Performance Expectation

or

$$\hat{Y} = a + b_1X_1 + b_2X_2 + b_3X_3 + b_4X_4 + b_5X_5 + b_6X_6 + b_7X_7 + b_8X_8 + b_9X_9$$

This equation is useful because it not only permits the evaluation and impact of several independent variables (X) simultaneously, but the process also provides for the examination and comparison of a regression coefficient (b) for each independent variable as well.

Look back to our earlier sales problem. Even though the solution is only bivariate, we observe the relationship among the dependent (Y), independent (X), and the regression coefficient (b) variables. Look specifically at the ******DATA

ANALYSIS****** section for the year 2007. The constant or ("a") value is calculated to be 6900, the X value is (1), and the slope of the regression line (the regression coefficient or "b") is calculated to be 1650. Therefore, the estimate of Y ($\hat{Y}$) for the year 2007 equals $8,550.

By observing the specific relationship between the independent variable (X) and the regression coefficient (b), the marketing manager can determine the influence that the independent variable will have in "explaining" the dependent variable. In the first example, the (b) value estimates the amount of influence that TIME will have on SALES. In a simple bivariate regression application, this relationship is useful and interesting but not particularly exciting or profound. However, when we consider the relationship in a multivariate regression model, the importance becomes readily apparent.

The solution to such an application indicates the "relative" importance among the independent variables by not only displaying the relationship between the respective independent variable and the dependent variable being predicted, but also the (b) values associated with each independent variable can be compared to "weight" the influence of each (X) in predicting (Y).

Let's consider the implications of such a multivariate solution. First, there is now a forecast of demand; second, we can determine how important each individual variable (or combination of variables) is in the explanation of the dependent variable; and, third, (based on the "relative" size of each "b" coefficient) we can determine the issues most capable to use in the promotional strategy to influence future sales.[19]

The descriptions of regression in this article are rudimentary; however, even in its simplest form, implications of regression analysis cannot be considered seriously without one additional measure of the data solution—R value. R value in concept is fairly simple to understand. It is similar in principle to standard deviation in the measure of central tendency. Remember that in central tendency measures, the smaller the standard deviation (the closer the observations are to the mean line), the greater the confidence in the calculation of the mean.

R value is the measure of the "scatter plot" of data located above and below the regression line. (See Figure One—the graphic solution of the sales demand example.) The linear algebra and calculus required to solve a regression problem "best fits" a line through the observations of (X) data such that the square of the sum of distances above the line are equal to the square of the sum of the distances below the line.

"R" is a measure calculated to indicate how much dispersion (distance) there is from the observed data and the regression line itself. If the plotted (X) values are a great distance from the line, its R value will be close to zero. If the plotted (X) values are close to the regression line, the R value will be further away from zero (R values range from 0 to 1.0 for a positive correlation, or, for a negative correlation, from 0 to -1.0).

R = Sample Correlation Coefficient[20] =

$$\frac{[(n)(\sum xy)] - [(\sum x)(\sum y)]}{\sqrt{[n\sum x^2 - (\sum x)^2][n\sum y^2 - (\sum y)^2]}}$$

By extending the sales data tableau to include a column y^2, we can easily determine $\sum y^2$ to equal 732,062,500. Now the sample correlation coefficient calculation can be completed:

$$\frac{[(5)(194,250)] - [(15)(59,250)]}{\sqrt{[(5)(55) - (15)^2][(5)(732,062,500) - (59,250)^2]}}$$

OR

$$\frac{(971,250) - (888,750)}{\sqrt{[(275) - (225)][(3,660,312,500) - (3,510,562,500)]}}$$

OR

$$R = \frac{82,500}{86,530} = .95$$

Comparing the statistical result of the "R" calculation from the previous sales example with the scatter plot (Figure 1) and the correlation schematic (Figure 2), we can see that the distance, or variation among (X) variables, is very low. And, the "R" calculation verifies this observation with a measure of total dispersion around the regression line being very close to 1.0. (Note: The coefficient of determination for the sales problem would be $r^2 = .90$.)

In conclusion, it is important to recognize that there are many criticisms of regression analysis. The major ones are: first, all independent variables considered for study in the model must have a linear relationship to the dependent variable; second, the model relies on historical data to predict the future; and, third, it is sometimes difficult to distinguish discrete contributions of each independent variable. (This phenomenon is called multicollinearity.) Where to go from here? The advanced student and practitioner will want to study the quantitative techniques and possible applications of canonical multivariate method (examining relationships among independent variables and more than one dependent variable simultaneously).

For sample study questions, see Appendix J.

This article was first developed as an industry white paper for the American Telephone and Telegraph Company and was entitled, "Multiple Regression and Factor Analysis in Psychographic Research."

Multiple Regression and Factor Analysis

The objective of the methodology which follows is not to suggest a quantitative "overkill" of statistical minutiae, although it does include marginally sophisticated applications of multivariate techniques. In fact, this approach by comparison to others in the field of classical propensity measurement is modest in calculation and classical acuity. The methodology is, however, practical, applied, and useful. It has also been effectively executed in numerous Fortune 500 regional and national business and industry psychographic studies.

The procedure includes psycholinguistic scaling, inferential sampling, measures of central tendency, regression analysis, "F" statistic comparison (ANOVA), factor and communality analysis techniques, and evaluation of eigenvalues.

Regression Model

Regression analysis is a statistical technique that can be used to develop a mathematical equation showing how variables are related.[21] This "least sum of squares" process of best fitting a regression line through a field of data can be expanded beyond the common "time-series" bivariate method. Bivariate regression analysis often used by example in cursory econometric or market product demand forecasts of relative changes in sales (the criterion or dependent variable) and time (the independent or predictor variable). The bivariate formula, $\hat{Y} = a + bX$ may be expanded to accommodate observing the relationship of one dependent variable and several independent variables.

$$\hat{Y} = a + bX$$

where:

$\hat{Y}$	=	the dependent or criterion variable
a	=	a variable intercept constant added to each case
b	=	the regression coefficient
X	=	independent variable

and:

$$\hat{Y} = a + b_1 X_1 + b_2 X_2 + ... + b_k X_k$$

These equations are both theoretically and practically important. "$\hat{Y}$" stands for the criterion or dependent variable. "a" is the intercept constant used to adjust the calculated values produced by substituting appropriate values added to each case in the equation. "X_1" and "X_2" stand for values or scores on the two independent variables. "b_1" and "b_2" are the regression coefficients. They express the relative weights of the independent variables in the prediction.[22]

The X's, X_1 and X_2, are scores on variables one and two. A (b) coefficient expresses how much weight a particular independent variable has in the regression solution. The term $b_1 X_1$ means that any score on independent variable number one is weighted (multiplied) by b_1. A low coefficient means that the variable to which the coefficient is attached is given less weight in the equation to explain or predict the dependent variable Y. A high coefficient has the opposite effect.[23]

Psychographic Model

While the following formulae may appear rather clinical and exacting, it must be recognized that market/consumer data collected and analyzed in behavioral science are considerably more fallible than most data in natural science. Errors of prediction are both larger and more conspicuous in analysis.[24] This is not to say that application of these techniques is spurious—it is to say that inferential statistics by its very nature has inherent error. The task of the psychographic market researcher is not to be deterred by error but, rather, to find, expose, explain, and account for its existence in evaluating psychographic behavioral intent and propensity toward buying goods and services.

It must be remembered that there is no axiom or proof providing for perfect explanation of the relationship among attitude, behavioral intent, and propensity. What has been demonstrated is the practical fiscal success enjoyed by business principals over the past decade who have used the following psychographic model to determine markets, penetration, pricing, and promotional strategies that take advantage of *a priori* customer profiles other than demographic.

A common definition of psychographics has not been generally accepted or adopted among academic and research experts. A review of some 24 articles on psychographics contained 32 different definitions of the term.[25] These definitions included behavioral, attitudinal, and lifestyle elements. This diversity seems to imply that behavior, attitude, and lifestyle characteristics are inextricably bound to any study of psychographics. Development of psychographic measurement has not yet become sufficiently exacting to isolate each of these three characteristics' contribution to psychographic explanation.

It is, therefore, dangerous to attempt to "clinically" differentiate these inner-related characteristics (although there are many studies which have attempted to go far beyond the basic relationships among attitude objects, belief measurements, and evaluative aspects: [26] —none have demonstrated any significant contribution [explained solution] to the traditional model).

Companies have developed a richer, practical understanding of their customers' attitude profile by adopting a more broad view of psychographics in their applied methodology. Certainly even considering error, the relatively "loose" definition of variables, and metric/artificial scaling of responses required by psychographic data collection, it is clear that these evaluations more capably explain the plethora of heterogeneous buyer behaviors not revealed by demographic enumeration.

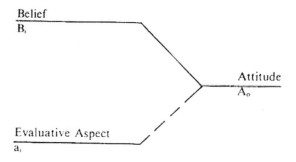

Belief
B_i

Attitude
A_o

Evaluative Aspect
a_i

Scaling Methodology

In order to format and code primary attitude data such that the linear algebra algorithm of regression is compatible to the prediction model mentioned earlier (see Footnote 4), A_o is set equal to propensity—the criterion variable, and each Bi is set equal to a predictor variable, and each a_i is set equal to a second predictor variable of the same X characteristic. (The "a_i" is gathered and regressed against the same single criterion [dependent] variable for comparative validity of the "B$_i$" variable only.) While it is also possible to develop canonical methodology (more than one dependent variable), it is not required and is beyond the scope of this discussion.

The actual data is formatted on an agree/disagree scale ("A$_o$" and "B$_i$ variables) and on a good/bad scale (a$_i$ variables). These bi-polar scales are possible by first utilizing the Likert-type (but not summated) rating scale. These contain a set of responses which are considered approximately equal in attitude or value loading. If a variable has categories that are mutually exclusive and can be ordered but also have a known distance between their scores (midpoints), the variable is an interval variable.[27]

"The subject responds with varying degrees of intensity on a scale (interval) ranging between extremes such as agree/disagree, like/dislike, accept/reject, good/bad."[28] This scaling methodology is based on the "psycholinguistics" approach of combining two methods of studying human behavior. First, there is the psychological approach, where attempts are made to sense or discover human motivation (Likert). Then there is the linguistic approach where attempts are made to discover patterns in language use and meaning (Osgood).[29]

It is important to point out that the scale discussed in this article, while Rensis Likert in type, is <u>not summated</u>. Scale positions represent discrete numerical values. Each potential scale position or response is equidistant from the next choice above or below it on the "pole" of choices. The resulting measures are consistent with traditional statistical hypotheses tests and measures of significance.[30] What makes multiple regression so capable psychographically is that its very premise is to analyze the data such that the squared errors of prediction are minimized where:[31]

$$\Sigma (Y_i - \hat{Y}_i)^2$$

Regression models for prediction are often useful even when the assumptions are moderately violated.[32] Additionally, since the loose data values may produce error, evaluative regression statistics such as R (sample correlation coefficient) and F-statistics of similarity among means of the distributions of consumer responses to each independent variable (ANOVA) provide much additional corroboration to the prediction.

Measures of Significance

Correlation Coefficient

While the beta value associated with each independent variable indicates the relative importance of that "X" in explaining any change in "Y," the quality of the "fit" of the responses to the regression line is unknown. Therefore, what appears to be a high level of prediction can be mitigated by high variability about the mean of "Y" (the regression line). This concept or phenomenon is theoretically similar to standard deviation about the mean in measures of central tendency. The "R" value then gives a measure of how much the respondents' answers to a given independent "X" question varied above or below the regression line.

Calculations for "R" are of the form:[33]

$$R = \frac{\sum \text{of squared errors explained by regression}}{\sum \text{of squared errors about the average}}$$

or

$$R = \frac{\text{SSreg}}{\text{SSt}}$$

Various dispersion or "scatter plot" about the regression line (Y) are demonstrated in the following regression schematic.[34] It is not necessary to discuss the mathematics and linear algebra required of computer software. It is sufficient for a firm, if an intuitive grasp of the principles is achieved.

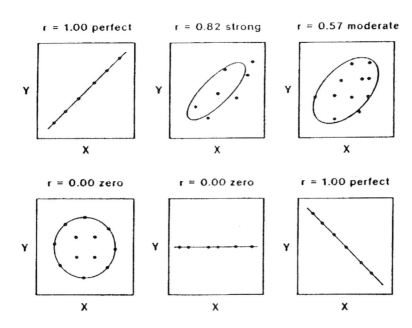

It is not necessary to discuss the mathematics and linear algebra required of computer software. It is sufficient for a firm, if an intuitive grasp of the principles is achieved.

F-Statistic

The more important issues of practical multivariate interpretation in market research come from the "art" of experience required to move from the traditional acceptance or rejection of a correlation based solely on the correlation coefficient being extremely high. Classical methodological parameters would suggest rejection of data that fall lower than an "R" of .8 or so. The psychographic researcher must train to observe that almost all multivariate data is valuable—the question is, how valuable? The answer lies in the pragmatic evaluation of all influence statistics. [35] The study and comparison of these measures permit the market researcher to further credit or discredit the ultimate value of the independent predictions toward propensity, or, in effect, establish a "discount" rate for certain data in the final analysis, recommendation, and conclusions drawn.

Among the measures yet to be discussed are F statistics, "Q" and "R" factor analysis, eigenvalue and communality analysis. The F statistic may be calculated where:[36]

$$F = \frac{k}{N - k - 1}$$

and:

k = the number of independent variables
N = total number of observations

"F critical" can be observed or compared to the "F calculated" F statistic by finding the value in the matrix tableau of the table, values of "F" for the F distribution by using the previous formula (also found in any basic statistics text or in Appendix B of this book). The "F-test" is used here as an analysis of variance (ANOVA) to test the null hypothesis among the distribution means of each regressed variable against Type I error.[37]

where:

Null Hypothesis: There is no significant statistical difference in means across group means.

Type I error: Probability of rejecting the null hypothesis when it should be accepted (concluding two means are significantly different when in fact they are the same).

If the "F calculated" is greater than the "F critical" value, there is no significant difference among the mean responses to the independent psychographic variables being evaluated.

The Analysis of Factors

Factor analysis is a statistical data reduction routine which can be used to evaluate relationships among large numbers of variables and then summarize these many variables in terms of common dimensions (factors). A graduate student of mine once made the analogy of factor analysis to sorting laundry. A machine (factor analysis) would identify all socks of similar color by pigment—canary, sunflower, gold, or, perhaps, burgundy, scarlet, cherry, etc. and sort them in piles of shades of a similar color (a factor). The researcher would then observe the outcome of piles and name each pile as a factor; *i.e.,* "yellow" or "red."

Each factor consisting of socks ranging in the various pigments is similar, then, to "factor loadings." Following the same analogy, factor analysis might sort factors of "size" or "fabric" or other similarities for evaluation as well as "color." This method can be extremely useful to help minimize two evaluation dilemmas of the regression solution. First, the potential for collinear explanations of the dependent variable in regression is demonstrated. That is when the common effect on the change in the regression "Y" is indistinguishable from two or more "X" variables. "Q" factor analysis permits the market researcher to summarize the variables common to a particular dimension and then evaluate their aggregate effect on the total explained solution. In this way, collinearity is not extracted, but rather permitted to summate similar variable influences to a common factor.

The second useful element of factor analysis in psychographic market research is to help explain independent regression variables which originally had relatively low correlation coefficients. A factor solution can expose combinations of variables which together may show cumulative explanations of significance when alone each was not impressive. The statistics provided by a software factor solution will include a correlation matrix (similar to regression analysis), associating a factor loading (the correlation between the original variables and the factor). These factor loadings or "scores" in the matrix indicate what amount of the variance in an original variable is explained by the factor.

In order to determine the appropriateness of a factor analysis for a particular set of data, examine the relative eigenvalues and communality scores provided by the algorithm. There should be at least one departure among an eigenvalue from the others. Without this "break" or "spike" evident, the market researcher should question the application. Likewise, if communality and correlation coefficients are all low, the procedures should be suspect. While there are more sophisticated tests of factor analysis appropriateness, eigenvalue and communality observations should satisfy the market researcher of procedural stability.

A distinction between the two major types of factor analysis should be made here. The R technique where relationships among items or variables are examined, and the "Q" technique, where relationships among persons or observations are examined. In other words, using the "Q" technique, factors are loaded by persons, indices of association are computed across variables, and the data are collected on one occasion. The factors obtained in the "R" mode are dimensions along which attributes may differ; the factors of "Q" analysis are dimensions along which persons may differ.

There are three criticisms (or abuses) of "Q" factor analysis in market research applications. First, sampling methods which collect data by variables is required; second, "Q" factor analysis correlates dimensions not types of people; and, third, use of "Q" factor analysis with large numbers of observations and small numbers of variables is questionable.[38] The first and second criticisms are not in conflict with the methodology proposed in this work. In fact, each is a major underpinning of the procedure.

The third issue, however, is a disagreement of classical research method and practical and applied experience, or "scar tissue." Practically and judiciously applied "Q" (principal component) factor analysis performs admirably for psychographic market research segmentation by dimension. It is agreed, however, that many practitioning analysts have attempted to segment types of respondents rather than dimensions of attitudes using the Q method—they were wrong. But "Q" factor analysis is capable of reliably classifying respondents into relatively small numbers of homogeneous groups based on psychographic data (dimensions).[39]

Interpreting a Factor Matrix[40]

Factor loadings greater than +.30 are considered significant. Loadings of +.40 are considered important; and, if loadings are +.50 or greater, they are considered very significant. The larger the absolute size of the factor loading, the more significant it is in interpreting the factor matrix. Each column of numbers represents a different factor.

1. Start with the first variable on the first factor in the matrix and move horizontally from left to right looking for the highest loading for that variable on any one factor. (Continue this procedure for each variable.) There may be variables that are not sufficiently significant to load on any factor. In this case interpret the solution as it is and simply ignore the variables without significant loading.

2. Name or label the factor by the variables which have the highest loadings. The name is not derived or assigned by the computer software. It must be intuitively developed by the

market researcher to represent the varying contributions of each loaded variable.

3. Now evaluate the eigenvalues for each of the factors. These indicate the relative importance of each factor in the total factor solution. There will also be an eigenvalue associated with the communality scores. (See step 4.) A pragmatic but crude evaluation of each factor's contribution to the solution may be obtained by dividing each respective factor eigenvalue by the communality eigenvalue.

$$\frac{\text{discrete factor eigenvalue}}{\text{communality eigenvalue}} = \text{\% of explained factor solution}$$

4. Last, observe the communality value for each variable. These figures show the amount of variance in a variable that is accounted for by all factors taken together. The size of the communality is a useful index for assessing how much variance in a particular variable is accounted for by the factor solution. Large communalities indicate that a large amount of the variance in a variable has been extracted by the factor solution. Small communalities show that a substantial portion of the variance in a variable is unaccounted for by the factors.

Summary

The past decade has made clear the migration of markets (both consumer and industrial) from mass demographic segments to heterogeneous psychographic niches. The organizations most capable to compete under these "new rules" are the ones which attempt to explain the customers' will to purchase goods and services by observing and explaining the motivational and behavioral correlation among their independent and dependent psychographic profile characteristics.

The rudimentary descriptive statistics traditionally used to categorize demographic responses are no longer sufficient to explain today's consumer buying behavior. However, by combining basic empirical frequency and measures of central tendency together with more advanced multivariate analysis techniques, the market researcher can begin to succeed in understanding not only "who" the potential target market is, but also "why" they make the choices they do.

Conclusion

The disciplined collection and multivariate evaluation of regression and factor analyzed data can provide the following:

1. Preliminary empirical frequency and central tendency of customer responses to business/industry hypotheses (later useful to help validate or discredit multivariate analysis).

2. Relative evaluation of independent psychographic characteristics which help to explain the propensity of the consumer to purchase.

3. "F" tests (ANOVA) of similarity among customer mean responses to the different questions which predict customer will to purchase.

4. Factor analysis capable of determining major dimensions of influence which explain psychographic interests of potential customers.

5. Eigenvalue value and communality measures to help isolate the most powerful psychographic elements and focus the theme of promotional strategy and optimal pricing.

Remember, the basics for psychographic market success include evaluating and understanding the consumer mind to an "unfair" advantage,[41] that is, to know more about the reasons and will of potential customers than they themselves are aware.[42]

Where to go from here? Exercise ethical application of the opportunity.

For sample study questions, see Appendix J.

> Sometimes he thought sadly to himself, "Why?" And sometimes he thought, "Wherefore?" And sometimes he thought "Inasmuch as which."
>
> —Winnie the Pooh

Part Two

Market Research

This article was first published in Dividends.

Research: A Marketing Must

Market research can be appropriate, accurate, and affordable— sometimes it is not. But, as a wag once said, "Knowing something about your customer may be more important than knowing everything about your product." Many business organizations shy away from using this important resource because the very idea reminds them of lengthy surveys, complicated statistics, and expensive retainer fees.

Corporate Questions

According to Vice-President for New Ventures of AT&T, Mr. D. L. Cooper (also an alumnus of the SJSU College of Business and emeritus board member of the COB Alumni Association), the requirement among large and small companies for market knowledge does not stem from a series of major corporate life-threatening decisions. Rather, market knowledge is needed in the on-going process of attempting to understand, forecast, and promptly act on perceived opportunities to market a service or product.

These opportunities are usually formed into questions such as: "Should we change our credit policy?" "Do our customers want a greater variety of offerings within our chosen product/service line?" "What are our direct and indirect competitors providing to our customers that we should or should not offer to ensure our profitability?" These seemingly surface questions point to the areas where properly prepared and executed market research studies can be of the greatest value. The ability to knowledgeably respond to the tactical questions of "Should we or should we not do it?" and "How and when should we do it?"

is perhaps one of today's greatest marketing challenges. Making sense of this disaggregated information also includes the "...collection and informed interpretation of what might appear at first as a number of random, unrelated events."[43]

Research Accuracy

For every marketing opportunity, certain marketing research issues are immediately raised: How appropriate is it that we do market research for this product or service? How much accuracy can we afford to pay for? (Accuracy in market research is expensive.) These issues must obviously be addressed.

An issue related to accuracy but one which is not often addressed is the subject of error in market research. Unfortunately, the possibility of inaccuracies (or error) is inherent in virtually all of the stages of data gathering and interpreting. For example, questions may be inadvertently worded so as to be understood differently by different respondents; arithmetical errors may be made in analyzing the data; incorrect inferences may be made by researchers, among others, evaluating the data. Such problems of inaccuracy can occur in the most complex data collection as well as in the most unsophisticated—all will have error.

Error dilutes the accuracy of the evidence gathered; therefore, to create the most accurate and usable research results, the possibility of error must be accounted for openly, objectively, and quantifiably in the analysis of the research done. And yet, every piece of market information collected is valuable to a research effort and, ultimately, to a business decision. Certainly, a beginning to dealing with error in data collection is to exercise the research/analysis discipline to focus on this issue at all. Many very expensive and sophisticated projects undertaken by even the Fortune 500 companies have neglected to address this issue of probable error. Remember, if it is research, there will be an error factor to consider and to weigh as objectively as possible against the data results.

Secondary data are facts and figures that have already been recorded before the project at hand.[44] There are no specific rules or guidelines for determining the true value of a piece of secondary information. However, if we begin with the premise that the value of perfect information is 100%, we can evaluate it based on certain criteria: who did the research? How capable is the methodology? Are the questions in the test instrument suspect? Who published the results? The answers to each of these questions begin to define the "real" value of the data. For example, if a study is commissioned by the Milk Advisory Board and one of its findings is that there is no relationship between blood cholesterol levels and the consumption of milk products, we might question this conclusion. This does not necessarily mean that the finding is faulty, but certainly further evidence of this conclusion should be sought through disinterested sources to either corroborate or refute the study's finding.

The Discount Rate

At times we must "discount" the true value of the primary data collected before we make decisions based on it, if one or more of the following exists: (1) if primary data are to be collected at low confidence levels, (2) if there is a great deal of variability among the respondents (see Sampling for Primary Data Consumer Populations, Part One of this book), (3) if there is an unusually high level of non-response, or (4) if there are reasons to believe that the study suffers from sources of test instrument or interview invalidity (see "Interview Invalidity" in Part Two of this book). If, on the other hand, we are evaluating secondary research, we must ask who did the research, who published it, how long ago was the research done, were the respondents members of our customer or potential customer base etc. The answers to these and other questions may cause us to subtract considerably from a "value of perfect information" to conclude that the data is only 80%, 70%, or 60% accurate.

Estimating the Value of Research Information

Before the research approach can be selected, it is necessary to have some estimate of the value of the information, that is, the value of obtaining answers to the research questions.   Such an estimate will help determine how much, if anything, should be spent on the research. The value will depend on the importance of the decision as noted in the research purpose, the uncertainty that surrounds it, and the influence of the research information on the decision. If the decision is highly significant in terms of investment required or in terms of its impact upon the long-run success of the organization, then information may have a high value.   However, uncertainty that is meaningful to the decision must also exist for the information to have value. If the outcomes are already known with certainty or if the decision will not be affected by the research information, the research information will have no value.[45]

Low-Cost Avenues to Market Research

Although certain types of research are national in scope, complicated to collect, and require the assistance of expensive professionals, many other sources of useful data are available to you at very low cost.   Following is a list of readily available, inexpensive secondary sources of market information:

- trade journals
- reference texts (public or school libraries)
- academic journals
- public research studies
- trade association literature

- government printing office public documents
- demographic information (from local radio/television stations; local newspapers).

Each of these sources can be extremely important to your search for marketing information, but remember to adjust the results for possible error. Carefully consider the quality/accuracy of the editor, publisher, author, currency of the data used, organization or sponsor, and any other characteristic which you feel may have skewed the printed results. Clearly, some data has always been better researched, interpreted, and presented than others. Those publications usually have a widespread positive reputation. It is a good idea to get to know which publications these are. While studies abound, it is important to remember that much secondary research will not necessarily have a good fit with your specific research problem. If the study only partially addresses your research needs, the study's value to you will obviously be reduced.

Doing your Own Primary Research

Also available is the option to conduct or to hire your own research study. This approach is, of course, more difficult than collecting secondary data, requiring expertise and more time and money. However, doing your own primary research should not be overlooked. Data tailor-made for your specific problem can be very valuable in determining a particular marketing avenue to take.

It would be foolish to embark on a sophisticated market research design without the experience or counsel of seasoned research professionals; however, simpler questions may be addressed and analyzed by in-house marketing managers using newly developed computer technology. Even the smallest of organizations is in a position to afford a PC sophisticated enough to perform basic statistical modeling and analysis (Dell

XPS, 1000 GB hard drive, 8GB memory, and 1020 MB video memory, all for around $1,000).

Primary research designs in marketing can begin as simply as organizing a data base of demographics (age, income, sex, etc.). The data base can then be expanded to include consumer attitude and other data. Following are some additional basic market research investigations you may want to consider:

- tabulating demographics
- collecting percentage responses to questionnaires prepared by you
- measuring mean (average) response data
- measuring modal (highest frequency) responses
- measuring median (middlemost) responses

Remember, data is only as valuable as it is accurate. Therefore, consider the kinds of error you may have included in your data-gathering and interpreting when assessing the value of your results. Books, professors, courses at your local university, and consultants can assist you with your basic plan and strategy. One real advantage to being this involved in your company's research is that you become much more aware of the level of accuracy being achieved and the need to interpret the results accordingly.

It is not always easy to determine how much money should be invested in a research study. However, it is important to remember that saving research dollars only to perilously reduce the accuracy of the results or, worse, to promulgate a wrong conclusion can turn out to be more expensive than you ever feared.

More Advanced Research

Almost no limitations exist to the sophistication and statistical/quantitative machinations (and therefore cost) which can be included in the primary data collection procedure. When you want to measure attitude, behavioral intent, or willingness to purchase a particular good or service, some of the following mathematical routines may be required:

- standard deviation (can be used to measure relative differences among responses)
- regression analysis (can be used to forecast levels of possible sales)
- factor analysis (can be used to help determine elements for a promotional strategy).
- conjoint analysis (can be used to determine desirable product attributes)

These are only a few examples of mathematical routines used in sophisticated studies. If these advanced techniques are warranted, and they may be, it is time to get professional help.

When and How to Spend on Consultants

Hiring a competent market research professional who is familiar and experienced with market data collection and analysis can be expensive. The cost of a small market study using 500 respondents prepared to provide results which are 95% accurate (statistically), ignoring design costs, questionnaire preparation, sampling plan analysis and report preparation, can run between $15,000 and $25,000 simply to complete the interviews. Additionally, most first-rate consultants will charge $2,000 to $3,500 per day to perform the other necessary components just mentioned.

First, is such professional help really required? This question is best answered from a cost/benefit perspective and a consideration of the amount of error your organization can tolerate, should your company not receive the additional sales the study predicted. Clearly, issues to consider here are competition in the marketplace, market size, market share, age, and potential of the market.

Second, if professional help is necessary, could some of the work still be done in-house? Consider the parts of the research study: methodology, sample plan, questionnaire (or other test instrument), data collection, analysis, and report preparation. If you believe that your department or company could perform any part of the research, discuss this possibility with the prospective consultant. For instance, the consultant could construct the methodology and sample plan and analyze the data; your company could participate in questionnaire development, data collection, computer data entry, and word processing of the final report.

Many consultants welcome such a joint effort as just described because this approach frees the consultant from routine detail which may not be particularly challenging. Yet, significantly, this division of responsibilities can reduce your costs of the project by 20% to 50%.

Third, if you've decided that a consultant is warranted, whom should you hire? Begin with the premise that these professionals work for YOU. Ask them for a "discovery" meeting to discuss and evaluate your project. Remember—they are without a "job" unless you choose to hire them. Ask them for a professional vita or resume. Ask for references, publications, and copies of past research.

If consultants are competent, they will be pleased to share their successes and/or copies of previous non-proprietary works. Check with their schools of graduation and professional organizations to which they belong for references. Also, don't forget to trust your own best judgment. Consultants abound. Be certain to select the best ones for your needs, and use them when the payoff to your company could be significant.

Research Objective

The market purpose of research is to better understand current and potential customers, segment them effectively, and to position products and services competently.

Description➔Attitude➔ Behavioral Intent➔Propensity➔Sale

A knowledge of the "who" (demography), "where" (geography), "what" (behavioral), and "why" (psychographics) regarding buyer behavior research data are essential to the capable forecasting of market demand. We first collect beliefs and evaluations (description) concerning customers. These data lead to measures of attitude, then behavioral intent, on to propensity, and, hopefully, a close of the sale.

For sample study questions, see Appendix J.

This article, published as a reprint in California Medical Technologist Newsline; *it also appeared in the* Proceedings of the California Medical Technologist Association Conference.

Interview Invalidity

Good interview techniques include direct, indirect, stress, and patterned. The thrust of this article is not to define and analyze each technique, but, rather, to highlight validity and invalidity in the data collection process. Further, prescriptions for reducing invalidity are cited. These checks and balances may then be applied universally to interview techniques, adjusting the probability of error.

Interview invalidity stems from two sources—conscious error (deliberate) or unconscious error. The conscious error is the more serious because it indicates a willingness to distort and manipulate the interview outcome. Awareness of deliberate error is the keyword. However, most interview error is unconscious. The solution must stem initially from an exposure to the basic concepts, and, when conscious of the problems, a willingness to perform corrective actions to reduce the inaccuracies.

Validity is the extent to which a test measures what the researcher actually wishes to measure and that the differences found reflect the true differences among participants.[46]

The sources of internal invalidity are the primary focus for analysis. Gerald Zaltman and Philip Burger, in their discussion of research fundamentals and dynamics, enumerated eight basic sources of error which apply to collecting data from respondents.

Sources of Invalidity:
1. History
2. Maturation
3. Testing Effect (Sensitizing)
4. Instrumentation Decay
5. Evaluation Apprehension
6. Expectancy
7. Non-standard Measures
8. Interviewer Cheating

Three additional common sources of deviation are the Halo Effect, the Hawthorne Effect, and the "Self-fulfilling Prophecy."

History

History becomes a factor if there are to be several interviews over an extended period of time. The basis for history as an error is that questions and possible responses may distort or be invalid over time. The basic idea is that the world changes every day. The best corrective measure for history is to limit the time frame of the interview pattern.

Maturation

Maturation is similar to history; it affects only the experimental unit or, in this case, changes in the prospective respondent. Maturation could take place, for example, in a long interview, occurring as fatigue, frustration, illness, boredom, and others. In order to hold the respondent's attention, the interview must be short, to the point, and administered in just a few minutes.

Testing Effect

This error occurs when an individual is encouraged by cues, prestige biases, and any guidance to create a structured or unnatural frame of reference. The best corrective action is to reduce preliminary cues to answers and stay away from socially charged issues of prestige. For example, if an individual is asked if he or she drinks alcohol, he will most likely say, "socially, yes." If he is then asked what liquor he prefers, the answer will be "scotch." And if asked the brand, it will be "Chivas Regal." The impact of this example becomes apparent when it is found that not only is the individual a beer drinker, but also really buys "Horrible Hops Brand" at 89¢ a six-pack. Ask only those questions which will yield useful data to the collection.

Instrumentation Decay

Unlike its mechanical sound, instrumentation decay takes place when the interviewer himself begins to fail. Obviously, the interviewer is more alert, bright, and aggressive for his 8 a.m. interview than he will be for his 4 p.m. appointment. His ability to determine sources of error and his willingness to perform corrective action wanes as decay sets in. The best alternative to this source of error is to provide frequent breaks for the interviewer and reduce the number of contacts and hours. Also, a redistribution of the larger numbers of interviews to morning hours and fewer toward the end of the day will reduce error.

Evaluation Apprehension

Evaluation apprehension is a source of deviation when an individual anticipates the interview, *i.e.,* questions and acceptable responses. The anticipation of questions and answers in itself does not create invalidity; however, invalidity does occur when the prospective respondent does not answer his conscience but, rather, anticipates answering with the "appropriate or desired response." According to Zaltman and Burger, a reduction in apprehension error may be affected by reducing the distance or relative difference in social status or class between the interviewer and interviewee. Further, the authors suggest that all cues of good or poor response must be eliminated, and the interviewer must remain neutral to answers.

Expectancy

Expectancy is the same source of error as evaluation apprehension, except that it occurs with the interviewer. The interviewer anticipates the expected outcome and distorts (consciously or unconsciously) the results of the interview or even the questions themselves. For example, the interviewer may expect a tall, short, old, young, male, female, black, white, educated, or uneducated person to answer in a certain way. Here an open mind, free from preconception, must be maintained to eliminate or reduce error.

Nonstandard Measures

Non-standard measures affect reliability as the interviewer— due to fatigue, cheating, or other combinations of error— restates the question or test in differing forms to alternate candidates. These errors are among the most serious and most often committed. The interviewer must treat all respondents equally if the correlation among results is to be valid. Even the slightest differences in voice, gesture, or body language can cause respondents to change their responses.

Interviewer Cheating

Interviewer cheating is a source of conscious error. The interviewer distorts the question or result to his end. A number of reasons cause this action. First, the interviewer may feel poorly paid and "is getting back" at the system, or s/he may be frustrated or bored. Any number or combination of influences may affect the interview outcome. The best way to minimize interviewer cheating is to pay well, train, and educate the interviewers and make them "stakeholders" in the importance of a valid data collection.

Halo Effect

Stephen Isaac and William Michael in their analysis of research and evaluation describe the halo effect as an impression: it is a "valence" surrounding an irrelevant feature of a given situation which creates an invalid "polarity." A strong initial positive or negative impression is accepted which overwhelms all subsequent trials or responses. In other words, either the respondent can do "nothing wrong" or, conversely, "nothing right" after the first impression. Train interviewers not to develop initial impressions when collecting data, and halo effects will be eliminated.

Hawthorne Effect

Isaac and Michael further describe a classic source of error discovered by Elton Mayo in the Hawthorne Plant of Western Electric Company, Chicago, 1920. This error is generated by the fact that the interview is **not** a "non-event." The interview is a marked stimulus to the prospective employee as a (1) novelty, (2) participation, (3) diversion, and (4) staging or orchestration of daily activity. In short, the respondent reacts to questions in a biased manner because of the attention s/he receives. This effect can be reduced by making certain that the respondents know that you want only their "natural" opinion or observation.

Self-Fulfilling Prophecy

Dr. Robert Rosenthal of Harvard suggests that interviewers might experience still another error because of desires for particular outcomes. The interviewer directs the questions (more practically he conveniently ignores or forgets) and answers so that the result yields what s/he "expected or wanted to see," supporting his foregone conclusion. Remember when collecting data: collect the data without bias. Bias may change your predisposition to an incorrect conclusion.

Synopsis

The cumulative and most significant source of interview invalidity is ignorance. While it is true that conscious cheating and manipulation occur, the serious posture is one in which errors take place and go undetected and unresolved. The enumeration of error sources does not imply that all combinations take place simultaneously; however, combinations do occur. If the interviewer recognizes the potential pitfalls and is willing to expend effort to understand and neutralize interview error, deviations may be brought to an acceptable level. Reducing all sources of interview invalidity is impossible; the key is to reduce its level through recognition of and compliance with thoughtful application of sound interview technique.

Bibliography

Benjamin, Alfred, *The Helping Interview*, Houghton Mifflin, Company, New York.

Isaac, Stephen, and William B. Michael, *Handbook in Research and Evaluation*, Robert K. Knapp, Publisher, San Diego.

Richardson, Stephen A., Barbara Snell Dohrenwend and David Klien, *Interviewing: Its Forms and Functions*. Basic Books, Inc., New York.

Shurter, Robert C., J. Peter Williamson and Wayne G. Broehl, *Business Research and Report Writing*. Mc-Graw-Hill Book Company, New York.

Zaltman, Gerald and Philip C. Burger, *Marketing Research*. The Dryden Press, Hinsdale, IL.

For sample study questions, see Appendix J.

This study was first published as an industry white paper for a California-based operating telephone company (BOC).

A Primary Research (VMS) Application

THE ONACLOV TELEPHONE COMPANY

Foreword

You are about to read a market research study that was undertaken to help a company decide whether or not to offer a new service to its customer base. The company needed to have data regarding each of the market mix (product, price, place, promotion) elements in order to make an informed decision concerning market entry. The service the company was considering is voice mail.

While it is true that today voice mail services (VMS) are available nearly everywhere, this study was done at a time when VMS was very new. No telephone company had as yet offered services other than in a pilot sense, and only one company had done any significant primary research. That company was Pacific Telephone Company, and their research was being held as proprietary. Before reading the study, first consider what the Onaclov Telephone Company wanted to know about each of the four P's.

Product:
1. What features did the prospective service need to provide to the customer?

2. Could the cost from the supplying vendor be covered at a profit?

Price:
1. What return on the investment in the product was possible?
2. What would the customer's propensity be?
3. What price point would cause the customer to purchase?

Place:
1. Was the Onaclov customer base a viable location for such a product?
2. What were the attitudes of existing customers to receiving VMS applications?

Promotion:
1. Based on penetration and price point, how much promotion could be used?
2. What were the most important components of the product (relating to propensity) that the company could use as a promotional strategy?
3. How much initial advertising might be needed?

_____

For a more detailed discussion of the marketing mix, read "Marketing Mix: The Fundamentals."

VOICE MAIL:

A PRIMARY RESEARCH STUDY OF THE ONACLOV TELEPHONE COMPANY—THE REGULATED AND UNREGULATED BUSINESS SEGMENT

An Industry Study

Table of Contents

EXECUTIVE SUMMARY

INTRODUCTION

Statement of the Problem
Need for the Study
Nature and Purpose of the Study
Limitations of the Study

METHODOLOGY

Statistical Psychographic Model
Multivariate Regression Model
Population
Sampling Frame
Sample Size/Sample Method

FINDINGS

Empirical Findings
Regression Results

SUMMARY

CONCLUSIONS AND RECOMMENDATIONS

APPENDIX.   TEST INSTRUMENT/FINAL QUESTIONNAIRE
(A partial display)

Figures

FIGURE 1. Statistical Psychographic Model

FIGURE 2. Consumer Attitude Diagram

Executive Summary

This study consisted of over 2,340 analyzed pieces of data collected from the Onaclov Telephone Company business segment. Industry standard limitations of statistical error, limited number of variables, limited data base, and relationships between customer attitude and behavioral intent were considered in its preparation.

The methodology used to first analyze the raw data was a frequency (percentage) distribution of the responses to each question. Additionally, an analysis of customer propensity to subscribe to voice mail was used together with a correlation algorithm called "regression analysis." A validated questionnaire was developed consisting of one dependent variable (question) about customer propensity, and 12 independent variables (questions) about customer attitudes toward voice mail as a concept and their particular communication needs.

Using the Onaclov Telephone Company data base, a sample size calculation was made to determine statistically the number of businesses required to be sampled in order to maintain a 95% confidence level regarding all data to be collected. The sample size required was 124 businesses.

The results of the data collection indicated a very high (70-85%) agreement among Onaclov business customers to subscribe to a voice messaging service, if its cost would be equal to or less than 10% of their current monthly telephone bill.

Two analyses were completed—a frequency analysis and a regression analysis. The frequency analysis measures the percentage of respondents who answered questions similarly. The regression analysis measures the relationship between the way the respondents answered the questions and their willingness to subscribe to voice messaging.

Combining the most significant results of both the frequency analysis and the regression analysis, the following recommendations are made, consistent with the customer responses most likely to influence their willingness to subscribe to a voice mail service.

1. Offer a business voice mail application to the Onaclov Telephone Service Area.

2. Base the initial offering on voice messaging features.

3. Develop a promotional strategy which includes the characteristics of improved communication to those who conduct "important business" over the phone; improved customer service; and improved productivity.

4. Direct initial advertising toward small, service-oriented businesses (5 phone lines or less, and fewer than 25 employees).

5. Consider a voice messaging application for the residential market.

Introduction

Need for the Study

No primary research study of independent telephone companies has been made of voice messaging in the rural Western United States. Therefore, it was proposed that this initial data collection and analysis be undertaken. Following is the study of voice mail as a product offering to the regulated and unregulated markets.[47]

Voice mail can be considered the "umbrella" under which there are three major features: interactive, non-simultaneous voice messaging; call answering and processing; and information providing. VOICE MESSAGING IS THE APPLICATION/FEATURE FOR WHICH THIS STUDY WAS DESIGNED.

Voice mail is more than just a telephone call or a recording. Voice mail has combined the intelligence and sophistication of today's computer with modern telephone technology to produce an extremely powerful communications tool.[48,49] It provides the convenience of allowing people to communicate and control interpersonal communications and to improve efficiency in sending and receiving information.

Voice messaging, also sometimes referred to as "voice mail," or "electronic voice mailbox," allows a person to call a single telephone number from anywhere in the world and record a personally tailored message on a computer-fixed disk. This message is then retrieved from the system later by the intended receiver, saving valuable time and allowing one to selectively manage messaging activities to the highest possible degree of efficiency.[50]

The following are potential user benefits of VMS:

- Eliminate message taking

- Stop constant interruptions
- Assures 100% call completion
- Free up secretarial time
- Reduce office expenses
- Send messages to entire groups
- Confidential communication
- Improve customer service
- Indicate a reach number if necessary[51]

Nature and Purpose of the Study

This research study was designed to determine representative responses of business clients to voice message technology. This report represents the analysis of over 2,340 pieces of data collected from Onaclov Telephone business accounts. These Onaclov clients felt strongly enough about the voice mail concept to share a total of approximately 35 hours of their valuable business day. It should be recognized that this commitment alone suggests strong customer views.

Further, while these respondents were business clients, the residential market may prove to be even more fertile for the voice mail concept due to the relatively larger number of subscribers in that segment, many of whom already utilize home messaging devices.

Regrettably, the study required more time to complete than was earlier estimated. Data collection difficulties, questionnaire changes, and changes of data collection personnel, each contributed to the delay. However, despite delays, NO concessions to the quality or accuracy of this report were made. On the contrary, the results should provide valuable insight to the Board of Directors' voice mail decision. All of the findings which follow are statistically accurate and are presented at a 95% confidence level.

Limitations of the Study

Experimental research in the psychographic/propensity-to-consume area has specific limitations which are inherent in the basic research design. The following limitations are recognized here:

1. The direct relationship implied among consumer belief, attitude, and behavioral intent used in the methodology for this study is not an axiom or proof.

2. The methodology utilized in this study was based on inferential statistics (the use of a specially selected "few" to predict the "many," offset by a calculated probability of error).

3. The design measures only 13 variables and 9 hypotheses.

4. The existing body of primary research and knowledge about voice mail is extremely limited.

Methodology

Statistical Psychographic Model

The methodology used in this study was designed to measure customers' attitude toward voice mail and their propensity (willingness) to purchase the service. The approach used here is based on research which has shown a strong relationship between a consumer's attitude about a product or service and his propensity to buy that product or service in the future.

Specifically, a consumer's propensity to buy any product or service (such as voice mail) is a combination of the consumer's beliefs about the product or service and the consumer's evaluation of the "accuracy" of his or her belief. That is, in order to purchase, the consumer or customer must believe the product or service to be a desirable one and evaluate whether it is a good idea for them to purchase it or not.

Practically, then, consumer attitude toward voice mail can be measured by collecting relevant data from potential customers about their beliefs regarding voice mail and using this data to predict their willingness to purchase the product. This data can also be used to help develop a promotional strategy and general marketing plan to most effectively appeal to potential customers.

Figure 1
Statistical Psychographic Model[52]

$$A_o = \Sigma\ B_i, a_i$$
$$n = \quad 124$$

<u>where:</u>

A_o = the attitude toward a specific product or service[53,54]

B_i = the strength of the respondent's belief that the attitude object has a particular attribute

a_i = the positive or negative evaluative aspect of the respondent's attitude toward the product or service

n = the number of respondents studied

Figure 2
Consumer Attitude Diagram[55]

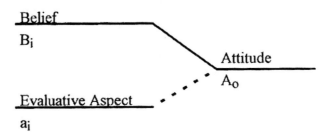

Multivariate Model

The data collected consisted of 12 independent or "predictor" variables, and one dependent variable (the propensity to purchase).[56] The independent variables are referred to as "X" and the dependent variable as "Y." Regression analysis, a mathematical tool used in this study, is a powerful statistical method which can help to identify the reasons a consumer will purchase. This type of analysis gives marketing managers data to intelligently predict the strength of customer preference and, therefore, likelihood of the customer's purchasing the product or service.

Regression analysis can also provide data with which to analyze the variables most likely to influence customer purchase (such as price, convenience, etc., depending on the variables specifically included in the questionnaire.) The equation used in regression analysis follows. This equation is both theoretically and practically useful because it is statistically accurate and it also may be applied to market forecasting. (Only two independent variables are shown here, in order to simplify an explanation of the concept.)

$$Y = a + b_1X_1 + b_2X_2 + ...+ B_kX_k \ ^{57}$$

<u>where:</u>

Y	=	the dependent variable (question 17)
a	=	a mathematical constant used to adjust the calculated values produced by adding it to each case.
X_1X_k	=	values or scores of the independent variables (questions 4 through 16)
b_2b_k	=	regression coefficients (used to explain the relative strength of the independent variables in the prediction of the customer's willingness to subscribe; the number expresses how much weight a particular independent variable has been given in the regression formula by the business person questioned). A "low coefficient" means that the variable to which the coefficient is attached is given less weight in the equation. A high coefficient has the opposite meaning.[58]

Population

The population used for this study consisted of all of Onaclov Communications Company's current business subscribers, including both regulated and nonregulated customers. The geographical areas included all or part of Olmsted, Daggett, Grand, and Box Elder counties and the Onaclov TELCO exchanges referred to as White Pine, Lincoln, Churchill, and Lander.

Sample Frame

Since it was financially prohibitive to poll the entire population of Onaclov business subscribers, a smaller group—a random sample statistically selected to represent the entire population of subscribers—was queried. But what sized group could be assumed to accurately represent the views of all subscribers? To be considered meaningful, this number had to be mathematically calculated using a statistical formula. Once this number was generated, customer names had to be randomly selected from the total pool of customers.

To make customer selection truly random (which it must be), a statistical routine was used called "stratified random sampling." Using the Onaclov data base of regulated and unregulated business customers and this statistical routine, two lists complete with replacement candidates were generated. (Replacement candidates were selected, should some of the original candidates not participate.) These sample respondents were selected proportionally from both the regulated and unregulated business segments.

Sample Size/Sample Method

To determine the size of the sample group to be questioned, a test was first given to 50 "pilot" respondents also selected from the same data base. These 50 individuals were asked to respond to the following statement (Hypothesis #8 and Question 17):

Q17: Onaclov business subscribers will subscribe to the voice mail product if the monthly charge is less than 10% of their current TELCO billing. Once the data from these 50 respondents was obtained, two important parameters had to be selected before the needed sample size could be determined: (1) a "confidence level"—a per cent probability that the actual average population response would be among the responses drawn from the sample group—and (2) a "point estimate error"—a parameter assuring that the average response or "mean" of the total population would not vary above or below that of the sample group by a certain amount.

The confidence level desired by Onaclov management for this study was 95%. They wanted to be 95% certain that the population mean would be among the sample responses. The point estimate error selected was 20%. This figure indicates that the actual mean response of the entire population would not vary more than 20% in agreement or disagreement above or below the sample mean.

Given the results **from the initial 50 pilot responses**, and using a 95% confidence level and a point estimate error of ±20%, the sample size (n = 124) was determined for the study.   Following is the **actual standard deviation and sample size calculation** using "real response" data (collected with the test instrument) of the 124 businesses sampled. This is an interesting "proof" that the central limit theorem is accurate in predicting population variability since the pilot sample standard deviation [n = 124] was so similar to the actual study standard deviation [n = 124.75] of Q17.

Figure 3
Questionnaire Results for Q17

RESPONSE	x	f	fx	$X - \overline{X}$	$(X - \overline{X})^2$	$f(X - \overline{X})^2$
Strongly Agree	5	39	195	1.16	1.35	52.65
Slightly Agree	4	50	200	.16	.03	1.50
Undecided	3	19	57	-.84	.71	13.49
Slightly Disagree	2	8	16	-1.84	3.39	27.12
Strongly Disagree	1	8	8	-2.84	8.07	64.56

$$n = \quad 124 \qquad\qquad \Sigma f(X - \overline{X})^2 = 159.32$$

$$\overline{X} = \frac{\Sigma\, fx}{n} = 3.84$$

$$S = \sqrt{\frac{\Sigma\, f(X - \overline{X})^2}{n}} = \sqrt{\frac{159.32}{124}} = 1.13$$

and

$$\hat{\sigma} = S\sqrt{\frac{n}{n-1}} = 1.14$$

Remember: once you have actually collected data in a study, now the collected or actual standard deviation can be calculated and compared to the pilot calculation for accuracy.

Figure 4
Sample Size Formula

$$n = \frac{Z^2\hat{\sigma}^2}{e^2} = \frac{(1.96)^2(1.14)^2}{(.20)^2} = \frac{(3.84)(1.30)}{.04} = \frac{4.99}{.04} = 124.75$$

<u>where</u>:

Z = the number of standard deviations from the mean

$\overline{X}$ = mean of the distribution of sample responses

$\hat{\sigma}$ = the population standard deviation estimate

e = the error about the point estimate of the population mean n = total number of respondents sampled

S = standard deviation of the sample

To get the same accuracy in both confidence level and point estimate error, it is necessary to take a larger sample from a population varying widely in their opinions than is necessary with a population which varies only slightly.

Given the relatively small variation in responses in this study, the original calculation was correct—that only 124 respondents would be needed to be interviewed to assure a 95% confidence level and a point error estimate of ±20%. (This "dispersion" is measured statistically in "standard deviation units"—see Figure 3. The calculation of standard deviation of the sample data for this survey was 1.13, a sufficiently low measure of dispersion, so that only 124 respondents were required for the study.)

Findings

The analysis which follows is based on an empirical frequency tabulation (percentages of respondents' answers) and a multivariate linear regression analysis (method of correlating responses) for the one dependent variable and the 12 independent belief variables regarding voice messaging in the Onaclov TELCO area. The presentation includes the results of 124 actual surveys taken. (Note that the sample size formula, figure 4, yielded "124.75." Since this number represents people to be polled, you may wish to round up or, as in this case, round down. The impact of either choice is statistically insignificant to study results.)

Empirical Findings

Attitudes. Figure 5, "Frequency Distribution by Response," shows in detail how Questions 4 through 17 were answered by all 124 businesses. Each interviewee was asked to select one of five possible responses to each question, such as "Strongly Agree," "Slightly Agree," "Undecided," "Slightly Disagree," or "Strongly Disagree."

After the data was collected, in order to tabulate it, numbers 1 through 5 were assigned to each of the five possible responses—a "Strongly Agree" response was given a "5," a "Strongly Disagree was given a "1." Column 1 in Figure 5 shows the responses to Questions 4 through 17 by number assigned (5 through l); column 2 shows the frequency of response—the number of individuals who said "1." (For example, "Strongly Disagree,"),"2," "3," etc.; and column 3 shows how the entire 124 answered, by percentage, in each category.

Results from Figure 5 show that the response to the concept of voice messaging was very favorable. Seventy percent (70%) of the respondents agreed with the dependent variable, question 17. (If the company could subscribe to a voice messaging service for less than 10% of its current monthly telephone bill, it would do so in the future.) It is also significant that an additional 15% indicated that although at this point they were uncertain about subscribing to the service, they thought that in the future they might. In other words, of the 124 Onaclov subscribers interviewed, between 70% and 85% indicated a willingness to subscribe to such a product offering—if the billing did not exceed 10% of their current monthly telephone charges.

Figure 5
Frequency Distribution by Response

Question Number	Response Choices	Customer Responses	Percentage of Total
Q4	Familiar with Voice Mail	29	23%
	Not Familiar with Voice Mail	95	77%
Q5	1 Not improve effectiveness	2	2%
	2	10	8%
	3	5	4%
	4	65	52%
	5 Improve Effectiveness	42	34%
Q6	1 Not Important Part	9	7%
	2	8	6%
	3	1	2%
	4	31	25%
	5 Important Part	75	60%
Q7	1 Not Simple Exchanges	24	19%
	2	13	10%
	3	5	5%
	4	43	35%
	5 Simple Exchanges	39	31%
Q8	1 Not Improve Customer Service	12	10%
	2	12	10%
	3	16	12%
	4	51	41%
	5 Improve Customer Service	33	27%

Q9	1 Not Improve Productivity	17	14%
	2	12	10%
	3	14	11%
	4	51	41%
	5 Improve Productivity	30	24%

Q10	1 Not Familiar with Options	86	69%
	2	17	14%
	3	3	3%
	4	8	6%
	5 Familiar with Options	10	8%

Q11	1 Not Improve Image	10	8%
	2	16	13%
	3	15	12%
	4	51	41%
	5 Improve Image	32	26%

Q12	1 Not Control Interruptions	6	5%
	2	8	6%
	3	7	6%
	4	55	44%
	5 Control Interruptions	48	39%

Q13	1 Not Important Feature	1	1%
	2	4	3%
	3	16	12%
	4	54	44%
	5 Important Feature	49	40%

Q14	1 0-25 Employees	122	98%
	2	2	2%
	3	0	0%

	4	0	0%
	5 201+ Employees	0	0%
Q15	1 Service-Based	113	91%
	2	0	0%
	3	5	4%
	4	2	2%
	5 Technology-Based	4	3%
Q16	1 0-25 Lines	100	100%
	2	0	0%
	3	0	0%
	4	0	0%
	5 201+ Lines	0	0%

DEPENDENT VARIABLE:

Q17	1 Disagree to Subscribe	7	6%
	2	11	9%
	3	19	15%
	4	51	41%
	5 Agree to Subscribe	36	29%

Certain of the independent variables also received very positive responses. Question number 5 ("Voice messaging could improve the effectiveness of communication in a business organization") and question number 6 ("An important part of your business is conducted over the phone") received, respectively, frequencies of agreement of 86 and 85 percent.

Two other variables were also regarded as having high belief agreements. Question number 13, ("Calls received by an operator is an important feature of voice messaging"), was rated at 84% and question number 12, ("voice messaging can control constant interruptions of your work day"), was agreed with 83% of the time by respondents. Questions number 8

("Voice messaging can improve customer service") and number 11 ("Voice messaging can improve the image of a company") received responses of agreement of 68% and 67%, respectively.

Variables which met with less favorable responses of agreement were question number 7 ("Many telephone calls are simple exchanges of information that do not require person-to-person discussions") and question number 9 ("Do you believe that voice messaging could improve productivity?") were agreed with 66% and 64% of the time, respectively.

Although percentages of 64% may not at first appear to be significant, they do represent well over half of the Onaclov business market—a significant number of potential subscribers to the voice mail product. Further, the significance becomes strongly evident when question number 4 ("Are you familiar with the concept of voice messaging?") received a response of 77% not familiar, and question number 10 ("How familiar are you with voice messaging options for routing your calls using a touch tone telephone?") also showed that 83% of the respondents were unfamiliar. The responses to these two variables imply that while the majority of customers were unfamiliar with voice messaging, they did feel that a business should subscribe to the service if it were made available at reasonable cost.

Generally when a sample of customers has favorable beliefs toward a product offering yet have little information about its specifics, an opportunity exists to even further increase their willingness to purchase the product through promoting, advertising, and providing greater awareness of its advantages.

Demographics. In addition to asking the customer base several belief or attitude questions, demographic data was also collected for analysis. Question number 14, ("How many employees does a business like yours usually employ?") determined that for the Onaclov service area, 98% of businesses had primarily fewer than 25 employees.

Question number 15, ("Your business can best be described as..."), indicated that nearly all Onaclov business customers (90%) perceived themselves as being service based. And, question number 16, ("How many telephone lines do you have?"), indicated that, overwhelmingly, 100% of the respondents had fewer than 25 lines—most had fewer than 5.

Additionally, question 18 offered the respondent the opportunity to add information which had not been asked for, but, that s/he felt was important. The most frequent issue raised was whether or not there was a possibility for voice messaging to be offered to residential service. Further interest in the subject was shown in the form of questions concerning logistics of the service, additional features, concerns for security, maintenance, and others were raised in much smaller proportion.

Regression Findings

Figures 6 and 7 and graphs Q4 through Q15 provide visual detail of the correlation between the businesses' willingness to subscribe to the voice mail product (the dependent variable, "Y") and the various attitude and demographic questions asked (the independent variables, "X's"). The numbers to pay particular attention to in Figure 6 are the "coefficient" and the "R value." The "coefficient" represents the strength that the consumer places on that question in terms of subscribing to voice mail.

The "R value" is a measure of how similarly other respondents answered the same question. Therefore, the higher the coefficient number, and the higher the R value, the more significant that question is in predicting the customer's willingness to subscribe to voice mail.

For example, the correlation between question number 8 (asking whether customer service could be improved with voice mail) and the dependent variable (always question number 17—the customer's willingness to subscribe to voice mail) is relatively high with an R value of 0.67. (One (l.0) is the highest possible R value for any correlation.)[59]

The interpretation of these numbers for question 8 is that a good deal of the reason that an Onaclov TELCO customer would subscribe to voice mail service is that s/he believed that it would improve their customer service.

Figure 6
Regression Analysis Output Matrix

Question	Constant	R Value	Coefficient
Q4	3.76	0.24	0.08
Q5	1.17	0.72	0.64
Q6	1.56	0.76	0.52
Q7	3.04	0.28	0.21
Q8	2.12	0.67	0.43
Q9	2.55	0.61	.035
Q10	3.74	0.23	0.02
Q11	2.52	0.38	0.35
Q12	2.61	0.27	0.29
Q13	2.92	0.35	0.21
Q14	4.070	0.23	−0.29
Q15	3.88	0.26	0.08

When analyzing a graph (see Figure 7 below) of the relationship between each of the questions (independent variables) and question number 17 (the dependent variable), note the following: the level of the respondent's belief about subscribing to the product is plotted on the "Y" axis, or the vertical line to the left; the level of the respondent's belief concerning the particular question being correlated on that graph is represented along the "X" axis, or the horizontal line toward the bottom of each graph. (The two axes together form an orthogonal or "L" shape.)

The values plotted on each axis refer to the "5, 4, 3, 2, 1" choices from the questionnaire. The "X" axis choices vary between 5 to 1 in order to show frequency of the respondents' choices. The slope (or slant) of the line that is plotted between the two axes indicates how strong the relationship is between that particular independent variable (question) and the dependent variable (question 17).

Figure 7
X,Y Regression Graph (Example)

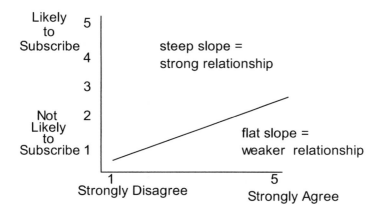

(#'s on this axis will vary to show the degree of the Rs' answers)

For example, the slope of the relationship in Figure 7 is not very steep. This flatter line indicates that little correlation existed between a customer's need for person-to-person discussions and their willingness to subscribe to voice mail. However, several of the other independent variables did prove to have a significant relationship concerning the business customer's willingness to use voice mail. Question number 5 (dealing with improved effectiveness using voice mail), and question 6 (measuring the importance of business conducted over the phone) had relatively high "R" values, 0.72 and 0.76, respectively.

This means that respondents who would subscribe to voice messaging would do so, to a great degree, because they believe that the service would improve their communication effectiveness and because a large part of their business is conducted over the phone.

Question number 8 (measuring the perception that voice mail could improve customer service), and question number 9 (measuring the customer's belief that voice mail could improve productivity) also indicated moderate correlations to the dependent variable (R=.67 and R=.61, respectively). This correlation should be interpreted to mean that of the 70% to 85% of Onaclov business customers who would subscribe to the voice mail service, much of the reason is due to their perception that voice mail could improve both productivity and customer service.

The remaining variables (questions 4, 7, 10, 11, 12, 13, 14, and 15) did not prove to contribute significantly to explaining the customers' willingness to subscribe to VMS. Each of their respective "R" values fell below .38, and, for that reason, will not be evaluated further with regression.

Summary

Background

Voice mail, the product, combines the intelligence and sophistication of today's computers with modern telephone technology. This study consisted of over 2,340 analyzed pieces of data collected from Onaclov Telephone Company's regulated and unregulated business customers regarding voice mail as a product. Over 124 business customers shared approximately 20 minutes each to give their opinions.

The following industry standard limitations were considered in the development of the research design: probable statistical error, limited number of variables, limited data base, and relationships between customer attitude and behavioral intent. The research findings are accurate to the 95% confidence level.

Methodology

The methodology used to first analyze the raw data was a frequency (percentage) analysis of each question. The statistical model used for this study was an application of psychographic consumer behavior attitude measurement. The data collected consisted of 12 independent or "predictor" variables and one dependent variable (propensity to purchase the voice mail service). Regression analysis was the algorithm used to determine the strengths of correlation among the variables, and to predict the likelihood of the customer's subscribing to the service.

The respondents for this study were selected by a method called "random stratified sampling," using the Onaclov TELCO business customer data base; both the regulated and the unregulated segments were included. Based on the respondents' answers to a question posed concerning the dependent variable in the pilot questionnaire, and using a confidence level of 95%, the sample size for the entire study was determined to be 124 businesses.

Frequency Results

Analysis of the frequency or percentage data indicate that between 70% and 85% of the Onaclov business customers questioned agreed that businesses like theirs would subscribe to voice mail, if the rate for that product was an amount less than 10% of their current TELCO monthly bill. Eighty-five percent (85%) of the respondents agreed that an important part of their business was conducted over the phone.

Eighty-six percent (86%) agreed that voice messaging could improve the effectiveness of business communication. Eighty-three percent (83%) of the respondents agreed that voice messaging could control constant interruptions during the workday. Sixty-eight percent (68%) believed that voice messaging could improve customer service. And, sixty-seven per cent (67%) believed that voice messaging could improve the image of a company.

Variables which met with less agreement dealt with questions which measured beliefs concerning person-to-person communication and productivity. An important characteristic to note from the frequency data is that between 77% and 83% of the respondents were unfamiliar with voice mail as a service, and yet felt that the opportunity for such a service was significant.

Study results indicated that, demographically, the business customers in the Onaclov service area who are most likely to subscribe have fewer than 25 employees, fewer than five telephone lines, and are primarily service-based.

Regression Results

The results of the regression analysis were statistically significant concerning five of the variables (questions). 70%-85% of the respondents agreed with subscription to the voice mail service (question 17) relative to benefits they perceived would accrue in the following four areas:

- Improved Effectiveness of Communication (Question 5)

- Conducting Important Business over the Phone (Question 6)

- Improved Customer Service (Question 8)

- Improved Productivity (Question 9)

These correlations are particularly useful to consider in the development of

—Selection of a Voice Mail Promotional Strategy

—Selection of a Voice Mail Advertising Campaign

—Selection of Voice Mail Target Markets

—Selection of Voice Mail Feature Offerings

Conclusions and Recommendations

Based on the findings and analysis of this data collection, several appropriate conclusions may be drawn:

1. The Onaclov business segment of consumers strongly favor the offering of voice mail as described in this research.

2. An indicated propensity to subscribe of 70% to 85% should be considered very high because consumers were asked to make their purchase analysis only after they were informed that the service would cost as much as 10% of their current telephone billing.

Further, respondents felt that

*an important part of their business was conducted over the phone (85%)
*voice messaging could improve the effectiveness of business communication (86%)
*voice messaging could control constant interruptions during the work day (83%)
*voice messaging could improve customer service (68%)
*voice messaging could improve the image of a company (67%)

These high percentages of agreement indicate features and applications of voice messaging which large numbers of Onaclov business customers agreed with. These certainly "add value" to the legitimacy of voice messaging for these potential consumers as a successful market segment. The most revealing and important conclusions may be drawn, however, from the regression results which correlate the percentage of customer agreement and THEIR PROPENSITY OR WILLINGNESS TO SUBSCRIBE to voice mail as a service. This combination of frequency and correlation to intended propensity substantiate the following recommendations.

1. Offer a business voice mail application to the Onaclov Telephone service area.

2. Base the initial offering on voice messaging features.

3. Develop a promotional campaign to include the benefits of improved communication to those who conduct "important business" over the phone, improved customer service, and improved productivity.

4. Direct initial advertising toward small service-oriented businesses (five phone lines or less and fewer than 25 employees).

5. Consider a voice messaging application for the residential market. This research makes no recommendation of hardware or software vendor or product. However, RFP (Request For Proposal) specifications should require that any technology under consideration easily provide the applications and features which the customer data suggests above. The vendor selected should also be capable of providing service for the number of current and future business subscribers as well as residential customers, in the event that segment is considered for service in the future.

This research makes no implication of break-even or return on investment analysis. The costs of acquisition, installation, and maintenance, together with revenue projections, should be developed by Onaclov Telephone Company with their vendor of choice.

APPENDIX

(This appendix is presented as a partial display of the original test instrument.

ONACLOV TELCO RESEARCH
VOICE MAIL NON-REGULATED BUSINESS SECTOR

Telephone #_____

KNOCKOUT QUESTIONS

Q1   May I speak to the person in charge of your communications?

Ko1   ____ _____

Yes   No

	Number of Call	Date	Hour
	2		
	3		
	4		
	5		

Never any answer _____
No eligible respondent _____
Refused to participate _____
Cannot reach communications manager _____

SCENARIO

S2   Hello, I'm _____, representing Dr. Jerry Thomas of San Jose State University. We are conducting a research study on a new telecommunications system. This study includes surveying 125 business executives who we feel can provide valuable information. We won't attempt to sell you anything, or call you back at any time.

Q3   Would you spend a few minutes to share your opinions?

Ko2

____   ____

Yes   No

         Abort Interview

PSYCHOGRAPHICS

Q4 Are you familiar with the concept of voice messaging?
Ho6

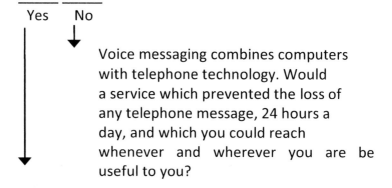

Yes   No

Voice messaging combines computers with telephone technology. Would a service which prevented the loss of any telephone message, 24 hours a day, and which you could reach whenever and wherever you are be useful to you?

The purpose of this study is to get YOUR opinion. There are no correct or incorrect answers. I will ask you to rate statements by agreeing or disagreeing with them.

Q5 Voice messaging could improve the effectiveness of communication Ho5 in a business organization.

Do you **agree** or **disagree** with this statement?

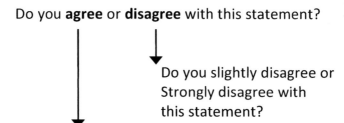

Do you slightly disagree or Strongly disagree with this statement?

Do you slightly agree or strongly agree with this statement?

Strongly Agree (5)	Slightly Agree (4)	Undecided (3)	Slightly Disagree (2)	Strongly Disagree (1)

Q6 An important part of your business is conducted over the telephone.
Ho1

Do you **agree** or **disagree** with this statement?

↓ Do you slightly disagree or strongly disagree with this statement?

Do you slightly agree or strongly agree with this statement?

Strongly Agree (5)	Slightly Agree (4)	Undecided (3)	Slightly Disagree (2)	Strongly Disagree (1)

Q7 Many telephone calls are simple exchanges of information
Ho7 that do not require person-to-person discussions.

Do you **agree** or **disagree** with this statement?

↓ Do you slightly disagree or strongly disagree with this statement?

Do you slightly agree or strongly agree with this statement?

Strongly Agree (5)	Slightly Agree (4)	Undecided (3)	Slightly Disagree (2)	Strongly Disagree (1)

Q8   Is it **good** or **bad** if an important part of your business is
Ho8   conducted over the telephone?

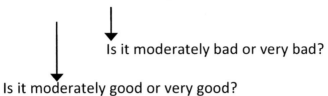

Is it moderately bad or very bad?

Is it moderately good or very good?

Very Good	Moderately Good	Undecided	Moderately Bad	Very Bad
(5)	(4)	(3)	(2)	(1)

For sample study questions, see Appendix J.

This presentation was first delivered as a professional development seminar to the Western Region United States Chamber of Commerce and was entitled, "Managerial Market Economics: The Fundamentals."

Managerial Market Economics

Sales Exchange

Marketing transactions can take place only when certain conditions are present. First, there must exist an object/service which has value to both parties; second, there must be some medium of exchange (*i.e.,* currency, barter, counter trade[60], labor, etc.); and, third, there must be a means to communicate the transaction (a common language of some sort). While these basic elements are straightforward enough, we must remember that they cannot exist in a vacuum.

The marketplace as we know it today exists and thrives within the catalyst of economics. At times, the economic milieu stimulates and encourages marketing activity. During other times, economic influences retard marketing transactions. The capable marketing manager recognizes that s/he cannot change the forces of the economic catalyst, but by clearly understanding the elements and relationships present, s/he <u>can</u> maintain efficient sales activity during economic fluctuations.

Classical Economics

Capitalism is the opposite of Karl Marx's philosophy of "organized collectivism," communism, and socialism.[61] Our propensity as a nation depends on the personal propensity of each of us as individuals.[62] It becomes easier to understand today's econometrics if first we examine its beginnings. Probably no one has made such a significant impact on the fundamental understanding of economic behavior than Adam Smith. Although he wrote *The Wealth of Nations* in 1776, three of his early theories are "alive and well" today. These fundamental theories <u>must</u> be the cornerstone of exel market management strategy and tactics.

The first of Smith's concepts that is operational today is the concept of an "invisible hand." According to Smith, this invisible hand stimulated competitive activity. For example, if a firm was successful producing a good at a high profit, a second firm would join that industry, reducing price (profit) and increasing quality to attract the consumers to the new product offering. Thus, "the invisible hand" would assure competition and, at the same time, keep prices down and quality up.

Next, the "rational economic man" theory, postulated by Smith and still operational, suggested that consumers opt to purchase the highest quality good at the lowest possible price; therefore, the most efficient producer would be compensated by attracting the largest market share in the industry or possibly have a total monopoly position.

The last Smith concept we will discuss here is the "dollar vote" theory. The message is simple, but the marketing result is critical: each consumer casts a "dollar vote" as s/he makes a product choice. Therefore, the consumer determines the organization's market share and ultimate business viability.

Remember that these early economic postulates consider pure competition and monopoly to be the objects of economic success. But it is also true that in the "good old days," laissez-faire government was a requirement of this system. Monopoly created unemployment. Low levels of return on capital investment provided no labor benefits, so some organizations regularly went bankrupt and convenience or time was not a factor in the consumer mind set.

Very simply stated, the basic market environment predictably reacted to a supply versus demand function: if supply went down, another manufacturer entered the market to produce until demand was met. And, if demand went down, the firm ceased to exist.

Contemporary Economics

By comparing the marketplace of today with classical competition, we quickly recognize the complication of our current mixed economy (competition, oligopoly, and monopoly). A growth economy develops many goods and services. Among these will be substitute goods and those products which have different elasticities. Consider first that if a company produces iceberg lettuce (for which demand is high), the company can charge a high price. However, if too high a price is charged, not only will demand go down, but customers will substitute spinach in their salad or sandwich. From this simple example, we learn that pricing and demand are functions not only of quality and pricing, but also of substitution.

It gets <u>more</u> complicated. Econometrics may be defined as the social science in which the tools of economic theory, mathematics, and statistical inference are applied to the analysis of economic phenomena.[63]

Now consider elasticity. Consumer demand (elasticity) for a product can be calculated as follows:

$$E = \frac{(Q_1 - Q_2) / (Q_1 + Q_2)}{(P_1 - P_2) / (P_1 + P_2)}$$

<u>where</u>:

$E =$ Elasticity
$P_1 =$ First Price

$P_2 =$ Price Change (second price)

$Q_1 =$ First Quantity

$Q_2 =$ Quantity Change (second quantity)

In the iceberg lettuce example, while consumers will continue to pay higher prices for the product, at a point, they will either not purchase it or will purchase a substitute. Therefore, this particular product is elastic (as price goes up, demand goes down).

Let's now consider petroleum products in the domestic U.S. market. During the 1970s oil embargo, prices of gasoline increased from $.60 per gallon to over $1.50 — a 150% change, and recently the price of gasoline fluctuated between $2.80 and $4.00 per gallon. Yet, demand remained relatively constant, and we continued to purchase fuel with only very modest changes in demand and usage patterns in both of these cases. This particular product in the domestic market has proved to be relatively inelastic. (As price goes up, demand remains constant or increases.)

Philip Kotler warns of 21st century "...turbulence, as defined as the unpredictable and swift changes in an organization's external or internal environment that affect its performance."[64] The change from a *laissez-faire* to a much more government-regulated economy has also seriously affected the market manager's decision freedom. While it is true that short-run pockets of monopoly are tolerated for new product development, only regulated monopolies are permitted as a long-term strategy (*i.e.,* natural gas and electric companies, water utilities, etc.). We only have to look toward the historic court breakup of American Telephone and Telegraph (AT&T) to see the catastrophic impact of government regulation on strategic marketing decisions.

Perhaps an iconic application of this type of impact was the decision of General Motors to factor the receivables of Chrysler to prevent that company's imminent bankruptcy in the early 1980's. Why would a competitor invest capital to save a rival? To prevent its industry oligopoly from appearing too close to monopoly and thereby inviting government regulation. The 21st century finds Microsoft as the government's current monopoly target. The following table lists some of the most common regulatory agencies that impact market management flexibility and their respective responsibilities:

AGENCY	RESPONSIBILITY
(FTC) Federal Trade Commission	Fair Business Practice
(FDA) Food and Drug Administration	Adulterated, Mis-Brand, Hazardous Products
(FCC) Federal Communications Commission	Wire, Radio, and Television
(EPA) Environmental Protection Agency	Environment Standards
(OCA) Office of Consumer Affairs	Consumer Complaints
The Justice Department	Monopoly

Gross National Product

There are probably as many definitions/explanations of the variables of GNP as there are economists (from [Milton Friedman] laissez-faire to [Kenneth Galbraith] controlled economy). The quarrel is not with the classical definition; the task here is to present an analysis that provides the marketing manager the necessary information to understand where his firm fits into the "equation."

$$GNP = C + I + G + S + NFI$$

where:

C   =   Consumption (consumer)
I   =   Investment (business and industry)

G	=	Government Spending
S	=	Savings
NFI	=	Net Foreign Investment

The left side of the equation is a country's aggregate production of all goods and services produced in one fiscal period. A fairly generally accepted broad definition of the variables on the right side of the equation is as follows: "consumption" is the total of all durable /non-durable goods and services consumed annually by the private sector. "Investment" includes all capital equipment, inventories, and business expenditure of industry.

The "government" variable includes government expenditure for all goods and services it purchases to provide for health, education, welfare, subsidies, transportation, defense, etc.). "Savings" is the total of funds set aside by the private sector in financial instruments to obtain a capital return. These instruments could include stocks, bonds, certificates of deposit, mutual funds, mortgages, treasury bills, etc.

"Net foreign investment" measures the positive or negative result of all goods and services which are imported or exported across our national border. Additional calculations are included here to account for inflows and outflow on international loans, incidental arbitrage occurring during international transactions, changes in gold and silver reserves, special drawing rights in the international monetary fund, etc.).

The three goals of the marketing or sales manager in relation to the economic picture should be to (1) determine the relationship between variable "s" and variable "c," (2) determine which of all the variables most impacts his or her industry and firm, and (3) apply a certain amount of skepticism to announced statistics, averages, and indexes.

For example, first, for every private sector "dollar vote" cast in savings, there is one less "dollar vote" to chase consumption of other goods or services. The effective marketing manager must maintain a vigil on the money supply (M_1, M_2, M_3) as well as other private-sector investments in order to forecast the velocity and magnitude of spending patterns which will impact dollars available for consumption in his particular industry.

Next, the total GNP figures which are generally announced are aggregated (the left side of the equation), as we see in the formula. Therefore, any changes in this amount only speak to a general well-being in the economy. As marketers, this value is important, but not nearly as critical as monitoring changes in the specific variable where our organization markets products. For example, McDonnell Douglas or Lockheed-Martin should be much more sensitive to the "G" [government] variable with regard to space shuttle product development than to general fluctuations in the aggregate GNP.

Third, be sensitive to what index number changes and announcements really mean to market decision making. I am reminded here of a political correspondent who observed during the Watergate break-in episode a great deal of political "double-speak." When remarking on the politicians involved, he said "I don't say that the men are liars—it's just that they have so much respect for the truth that they use it very sparingly."

Learn to be cautious of economic announcements and evaluate the format in which each is presented. For example, the difference between percent or real dollars can distort the actual meaning. Just as important is to evaluate the meaning of a particular index in terms of your own firm and the business it does. For example, the consumer price index is cited again and again as evidence for wage increases, the lowering of competitive price, contractual applications, and others.
But, remember, the consumer price index is comprised of a regular evaluation of the price of a consistent "basket of goods," and your product/service or those that your firm purchases may not be counted in the Consumer Price Index (CPI). If this is the case, then that particular index may have very little significance for any market decision in your industry.

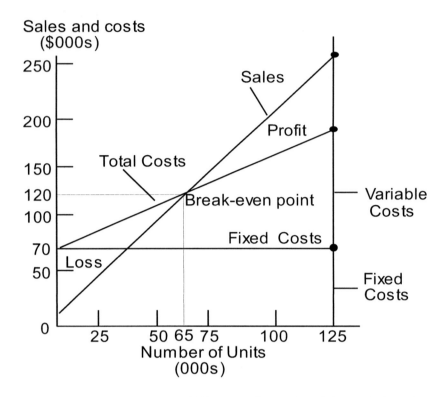

The preceding and following graphics display the relationship between sales and costs. The "bottom-line" for marketing managers, or as the wag once defined marketing, "the ability to separate the customer from his money," is a function of sound accounting and finance techniques applied to forecast where market penetration turns to profit, or, more pragmatically put, the point at which revenue equals total variable and fixed costs at a specified price. This calculation is often demonstrated graphically or with "break-even formulas." Appendix K (Marketing Arithmetic) contains formulas for determining break-even in dollars as well as determining break-even in units.[65]

Break-Even Analysis

Unit Price	Market Demand (units)	Total Revenue	Total Costs	Break-Even Points (units)	Expected Profits
$ 5	65,000	$325,000 (d')	$362,500	80,000 (d)	$ (37,500)
10	55,000	550,000 (c')	337,500	26,667 (c)	212,500
15	45,000	675,000 (b')	314,500	16,000 (b)	360,500
20	30,000	600,000 (a')	275,000	11,429 (a)	325,000

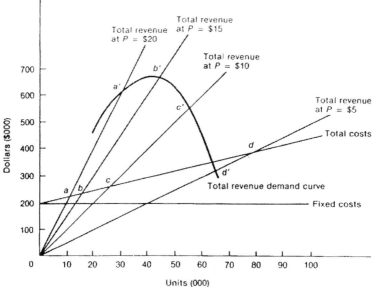

Following is the traditional break-even formula:

$$BEP = \frac{FC}{SP - VC}$$

or, including a hurdle rate of return (profit) on the investment, the formula would be:

$$BEP = \frac{FC + P}{SP - VC}$$

<u>where</u>:

FC = Fixed Costs	VC = Variable Cost
SP = Sales Price	P = Profit

Break-even is considered an obvious business analysis. However, effective rather than perfunctory application of the technique requires the market manager to recognize that the fundamental calculation is based on the assumption that both fixed and variable costs remain as estimated until break even is reached. The basic B/E algorithm is quite limited, unless changes in costs based on economies of scale, different customer demand levels (see previous B/E simulation), and various pricing strategies are considered.

The size of government and taxation are also serious variables in the strategic mix of management economic decisions. It is not a matter of Republican, Democrat, Conservative, or Liberal. The reality is that tax implications make serious parameters to capable business decisions. (For a more detailed discussion of taxation, see "Retail Lease Versus Purchase Decision" in this text.) The astonishingly rapid growth of government particularly (but not only) at the federal level over the last half-century has led many Americans to think of it as a recent development. In fact, with the exception of a couple of panics and depressions...U.S. Government spending has grown consistently in actual and per capital terms with every single [presidential] administration.[66] "Example: Records of taxes to GDP (gross domestic product), "Regan (1981-1988) 18.2%, Bush 41 (1989-1992) 17.9%, Clinton (1993-2000) 19%, Bush 43 (2001-2008) 17.6%."[67]

Summary

Applied managerial economics is not as simple as reading about "guns and butter." Nor is this presentation eclectic in terms of strategic, tactical success. But, the market/sales manager <u>can</u> establish a competitive advantage and efficiency in the market penetration process by applying systematic understanding and economic observation rigor in five major areas:

(1)   Sales exchange
(2)   Classical Economic Principles
(3)   Contemporary Economic Practice
(4)   Gross National Product
(5)   Break-Even Analysis

If economics is the proverbial dog "doing the wagging," let's make certain that we are at least (by calculated/capable economic understanding) "the tail," and our competition is relegated to being the "flea."

For sample study questions, see Appendix J.

Part Three

Management
of
Markets

This presentation was first delivered as a professional development seminar to Memorex Corporation and was entitled, "Reactive Versus Proactive Pricing: Strategies, Tactics, and Practices."

Pricing Strategies

Pricing has been defined in many ways. One of the more robust views of pricing comes from T. Nagle, who says that it is "the harvest of profit potential." And while most would agree with his prophecy, effective pricing policy remains one of the most challenging as well as rewarding aspects of contemporary business strategy.   As a wag once said, "the value of a thing is the price it will bring."

Micro Marketing and the Firm

Historical observers of applied economics believed that micro economics were "the economics of the firm." Certainly in an uncontrolled economy, pricing was a micro economic function and, therefore, a firm producing an economic good or service could price the product as it chose. The economic "playing field" of the 21st century has changed this perspective. Generally, only the market leader in each industry can set price proactively. For other firms, the price debacle becomes a strategic but reactive search for an optimal price point.

Reactive pricing is not altogether a bad thing. In fact, if the seller is willing to develop a series of applied pricing options as well as carefully evaluate the pricing environment, reactive strategies can yield high returns. Not unlike the "human condition," many organizations react to the market leader's pricing decision by being a follower and reducing price. Clearly, price reduction is the easiest decision and by far the most popular. The fact that many firms will use this follower strategy provides a competitive advantage to the business that is willing to work hard to develop an alternative approach. Remember, the great likelihood is that when price is reduced, so are profits—many firms have reduced price and increased market share all the way into bankruptcy proceedings.

Assumptions about Price Changes

All pricing decisions should be made only after making a few fundamental assumptions about the constraints outside the firm's control. Among the most significant assumptions are those relative to (1) competition, (2) customers, and (3) profit.

Competition

Competitive intelligence must provide information to help determine such information as how financially sound a competitor is, forecasts of their cost of raw materials, capital goods, and labor. All of this information will assist in determining how capable these competitors are to maintain their price or lower it. Remember that producing industries can be seen as being at "equilibrium" or, in other words, selling on a "level playing field." However, when one organization decides to change its price (even your own firm), that change disturbs the playing field and will cause every other firm to reconsider its pricing policy. The more that can be known about the competitors' abilities or constraints, the more likely that correct assumptions can be forecasted regarding each firm's behavior.

For example, if you are considering a price reduction in order to attempt to increase market share and, in turn, increase overall revenue and profit, you must be able to safely assume that a competitor will not also lower his price; otherwise, the net effect is that both of you will have done nothing more than lower revenue and profit, while market shares remain the same. Your price-reduction decision benefits you only if the competitor cannot lower his price while you are able to reduce yours and attract some of his customer base that are price sensitive. Think back to basic micro economics, and you will recall that this marketing example will sound a lot like the beginning of a downward price spiral.

Consumers

Assumptions regarding consumers cannot be overlooked in price decisions. First, what is their need or want for the particular product or service? How great is the demand and desire? Second, do they have sufficient capital or discretionary income to purchase the product, even if you can get their attention, attract their interest, and create a desire? Do they have the resources to take the action (AIDA) and buy? Third, what about the customers' loyalties to your organization or to other manufacturers/sellers?

Just because a price is lowered does not necessarily mean that new customers will be attracted. For example, if your intent is to lower price and attract customers from your competitor and the competitor has earned a high level of customer and brand loyalty, the customer may well remain with your competitor even though the customer must pay a higher price to do so. Vonnage, Sprint, Verizon, and others have attempted to lure AT&T into joining their level of pricing. AT&T remains the industry leader and has continued to successfully maintain the highest prices for telecommunication services in that industry as well as the largest market share. AIDA must ultimately result in customer satisfaction if the sale is to be successful. (See Appendix D.)

Profit

There has always seemed to be a rush to judgment that "more is better" when it comes to market share. This belief must be accompanied by a very strong assumption that "market share pricing" will also increase profits. Increasing market share while at the same time maintaining profit margin is indeed an excellent objective. But, regrettably, market share strategy is usually explained something like this: "We will reduce price, and this will result in more sales, which will result in more revenue than we had before the price reduction."

That part may, in fact, be true, but unless the increase in profit is substantially higher from these increased sales, the new income may not even cover the loss of income from the price reduction, let alone provide any additional profits. Also, there are usually a series of additional costs incurred with a market share approach (new location, capital goods, additional labor, inventory carrying costs, etc.) that also will reduce profit.

There will always be ill-fated pricing arguments of "increasing market share," "establishing a market presence," or "winning the price war," etc., but the sound reason for any pricing or change in pricing strategy should be profit maximization— market share alone does not lead to profitability.

Pricing Strategies

Cost-Oriented

Cost-oriented pricing is basing the market price on the costs to manufacture and bring the product or service to the end user. Under these circumstances, the manufacturer evaluates all of the variable costs (*e.g.,* raw materials, labor, shipping, etc.) and fixed costs (*e.g.,* administration, rent, insurance, capital goods, etc.) and establishes a customer price for the product based on the aggregate cost to provide the product. While this may seem like a very logical approach, it has a fundamental flaw in application—will the customer pay that amount for the product? A second drawback to the cost-oriented approach is that it may, in fact, keep the manufacturer from realizing the full profit potential of the product. In other words, the strategy may provide only a "mini-min" or, at best, a "maxi-min" profit contribution.

Take, for example, the pricing policy of the Cabbage Patch doll. If this product had been priced based on cost (@ cloth $1.00, polymer and molding $2.50, stuffing, $.25, labor $2.00, packaging $1.50, overhead and shipping $1.25), the market price would have been slightly above $8.50—let's say $10.00 for each doll at retail. Yet at a price point of $65.00 each, the manufacturer could not maintain supply. In fact, retailers were able to "scalp" these particular dolls for as much as $125.00 each at the height of their popularity.

It is also fair to say, however, that if you are a diamond retailer/designer, the costs of raw material, quality, and availability are tightly controlled by DeBeers and the diamond-mining cartel. Under these circumstances, a cost orientation to pricing is an industry standard practice, nearly being required to compete in that business.

Mark-up

Mark-up pricing is similar to cost-oriented pricing in that it is based on cost. The main difference is that the manufacturer/seller predetermines a percentage of profitability and calculates the price by formula.

$$\text{Price} = \frac{\text{Product Cost}}{(100 - \text{Markup \%}) / 100}$$

For example, if Bloomingdales sold a pair of Evan Picone shoes costing $225.00, and "Bloomies" wanted a 30% profit, $225.00 would be divided by .7 to establish the price point of $321.42 for each pair of shoes to be sold at the store. Mark-up pricing is quite popular in the retail industry, evidenced by the shoe example. Where the chain of channel members includes several middlemen, each can determine easily a specific level of return for his or her value added to the selling process.

Demand-Oriented

Demand-based pricing assumes an elastic marketplace and perhaps even substitute products. A manufacturer uses market research to evaluate the level of propensity that customers have toward their product, and they then price the product accordingly. This strategy attempts to establish the highest price point possible before a customer will decide not to purchase the product at all or will instead buy a less desirable but acceptable substitute.

Suppose, for example, that you are an agricultural supplier from the Imperial Valley of California. You might very well price your Iceberg lettuce based on demand. Since you know that Californians enjoy salad and that their propensity is for Iceberg lettuce in that salad, it would make sense to charge a substantial price for each head of your lettuce. However, if the price point selected is above about $1.40 per head, you will find that Californians continue to eat salad but with leaves of spinach, romaine, or butter lettuce instead of your crop.

Skimming

Skimming is a price procedure that yields exceptionally high returns of profit if the manufacturer has the ability to not only charge extreme prices but is also assured that customers will pay the price they ask. This is likely to be the case if the product is unique, is at the leading edge of design, is based on new technology, requires high barriers to competitive entry, or consumers are price insensitive. Today the digital watch is taken for granted. In fact, it can be purchased for less than $4.00. However, when Hewlett-Packard brought out the first digital wristwatch in the early 1970's, its version was priced at

$400.00. Not only did that price skim the market of consumers, but as soon as competition entered the market and skim level strategy no longer provided exceptional returns, HP discontinued the product offering.

Penetration

Penetration pricing positions price at a low level in order to capture a large market share. It must be realized, however, that this low level of price per item provides a very low level of incremental profit as well. This strategy does tend to deter competitors from the market because they fear low profitability. The hope is that enough product can be sold to benefit from economies of scale in production and distribution. The consumer in these markets must also be very price sensitive.

An example of this type of strategy may be seen in the "burger wars." When McDonald's, Burger King, Jack-in-the-Box, and Wendy's first decided to attempt to penetrate by price, the competition was fierce and menu-wide. However, when penetration pricing is attempted by large, formidable competitors, one among them, usually the one with the deepest pockets, is predatory (offers products below cost) and drives the others from the marketplace.

In this particular application of penetration pricing, we can see that if several large companies are seeking to establish principal market share at the same time, it is possible that none of them "win." Rather, each finds that it is making less and less profit. When this happened in the case of the burger wars, each of these organizations then aimed for profitability by offering one or two loss leaders on their menus, "value meals" or "dollar menu" and substantially raised the prices on the rest of their offerings in order to increase profits.

Price Tactics

It is important, for this discussion of price tactics, to realize that each of the following alternatives to price reduction is just that. Each tactic is not universally applicable in each industry and in every situation, but, when considered, one or more may be effective while facing the price reduction of a competitor. The fundamental principle to effective pricing policy is to find a strategy, tactic, or practice that will permit you to maintain your price and profit margin while a competitor is reducing price.

It is also important to consider that customers are fickle even when it comes to selecting a product by price—each consumer segment will have its own agenda of unique selection criteria.

Cheaper Goods

The cheaper goods tactic is sometimes misunderstood. For that reason, let's begin with what it is <u>not</u>. A cheaper-goods tactic does <u>not</u> attempt to create "knock-off" goods or develop counterfeit products to compete with existing legitimate offerings. A cheaper-goods strategy <u>does</u> provide the customer with a legitimate but inferior choice or substitute in a particular market. Here the manufacturer is open about the low quality, inferior production, and inferior materials of its product but also offers the product at a very low price by comparison.

For example, some of us may have purchased one of the "cheaper goods" offerings that provides low-quality, low-price (@$15.00 for 3 ozs.) substitutes in the perfume industry. These substitute products attempt to show a similarity to Giorgio, Poison, Joy, and Shalimar, etc. which sell for $100.00 per 1/4 oz. and up. Cheaper goods manufacturers are careful to create a package that looks similar to the real version but is not an exact copy. They also advertise differently, and they must price radically differently in order to be legal.

Superior Services

There are those companies such as IBM in the computer industry, Ford in the automobile industry, and Nordstrom in the fashion industry that have attempted to go beyond what is expected in their respective industries in terms of customer service. These services may take the form of warranties, guarantees, repairs, installations, exchanges, personal attention, etc. in order to position themselves and their products as being a better value (even at a higher price) than the goods or services that competitors offer.

Prestige Goods

In markets where price insensitivity exists, high price can be maintained based on the high price itself. The concept of the "top-of-the-line" product or simply the most expensive product offered provides the incentive to purchase for many affluent customers. This type of price positioning counts on the fact that the group of customers willing to pay for prestige has a greater want, and that "want" is to belong to a segment that others, though they may desire, simply cannot afford to join.

The power of the prestige tactic can be vividly seen in a recent example of the luxury automobile market. Mercedes Benz was challenged for market share in the late-1980s by such automakers as Lexus and Infiniti. At the time, the MBZ SE and SD luxury sedans were priced at about $60,000. This new competition attempted to price just slightly under the $60,000 figure. Mercedes' reaction was not to compete at all. They instead raised the price of their luxury sedan to $80,000 and brought out a "more affordable" MBZ "C" class offering, starting at around $40,000 to compete with the Lexus and Infiniti products. The same example was seen in MBZ's SLK, available for about $40,000. The 500 SL continued in production at above $100,000. Today the "C" class continues an entry level with an MSRP of $35,000, the SLK at $48,000, and the SL at $100,000.   The flagship S class remains available for $85,000.

Intensive Advertising

While it is true that advertising is expensive, it is also true that the costs of advertising are write-offs against corporate taxes, affecting the annual report and financial statements. Advertising certainly helps to establish the first "A" in the AIDA model. It is, however, questionable and difficult to measure how much further advertising can effectively go to provide sales. This tactic can be a dangerous one due to the very high costs of media, particularly if there is another firm willing to advertise at the same intense level. However, intensive advertising has permitted some companies to maintain high prices even when their products are relatively inexpensive to produce.

Perhaps the best example here would be the cola drink manufacturers. It should be clear that the cost of manufacturing these products is very low. Anyone who has produced homemade soft drinks can tell you that the main ingredient is water, then sugar, seasonings, and bottling (altogether @ $.50 per six-pack). Yet, through intensive advertising, both Coca-Cola and Pepsi-Cola have been able to maintain very high levels of sales, market share, and profitability while continuing to charge @ $2.50 per six-pack of product. If you prefer a spirit example, Miller and Anheuser-Busch Brewing companies provide a similar application of this same strategy with similar costs.

Product Proliferation

This approach calls for launching many product offerings in a particular category to compete with other companies' brands. In other words, rather than to reduce price when a competitor reduces price, one alternative is to introduce yet another new product with little if any variation. This is a dangerous strategy because it is possible that your new product entry not only competes with the competitors' product but may also take market share away from your own existing product. The objective is to keep the customer from buying the competing brand, even if it means competing with yourself.

Probably the best successful example of this tactic is Procter and Gamble, which has regularly produced several similar products in the same markets at the same time (*e.g.,* Tide, Bold, Cheer, Gain, and Dash in the laundry detergent market and Joy, Dawn, and Ivory in the liquid dishwashing market).

Distribution Innovation

Some companies have been able to maintain high prices in competitive markets by providing superior delivery systems. Certain customer segments place a very high premium on delivery and are willing to pay higher prices in order to benefit from them. In the face of strong competition from DHL, Express Mail, UPS, and others in the overnight freight business, Federal Express unveiled its COGNOS computer delivery system. This system provided delivery, inventory, and parcel tracking enhancements that none of its competition could offer—Fed Ex was able to maintain its market leadership and price advantage.

Product Innovation

Technology, design, and research and development advantages permit some organizations to maintain price in competitive environments. Bell Laboratory, Microsoft, Intel, and Tandem (now a wholly-owned subsidiary of Hewlett-Packard) have earned positioning with customers, based on being consistently at the "edge of the envelope" when it comes to innovation in the voice/data communications industry. Certain customer segments respect a technological advantage and willingly pay for products and applications from these higher-priced manufacturers.

Manufacturing Cost Reduction

Whenever a company can reduce its costs to manufacture and provide a product, there is the potential to maintain profit even if there is pressure in the industry to reduce price. Chrysler Corporation made significant cost reductions in the robotic retooling of its assembly plants during the late 1980's. Some analysts argue that not only did that change make the Corporation more competitive, but it may have saved the organization from impending bankruptcy. Just-in-time (JIT) manufacturing and inventory control systems are now a familiar topic of discussion among contemporary manufacturing ventures that can afford to implement them. Other means of cost reduction can come from more efficient purchase of raw materials and negotiating lower labor costs.

Price Reduction

Price reduction as a tactic has been left for last in the discussion because it should be considered last, after all other possible alternatives have been considered. There does come a time when it is possible in the life cycle of a product offering that reducing a product's price might continue its profit stream. However, don't be among those who choose this alternative for its obvious and popular appeal—as my students say the "E" word "easy,"—because it's easy.

Pricing Incentives

Discounts

Discounting is a practice that enables channel members or customers to benefit in price by doing certain things. For example, purchasing in large quantities or "bulk" may provide an economy of scale that the seller is willing to reward by lowering the price per unit. A second example might be a discount for paying with cash. Closely related is the practice of offering a discount for paying an invoice early (*i.e.,* "2/10 net 30" would reduce the customer's account payable by 2% if he or she paid the bill within the first ten days after receiving the invoice).

Another typical discount is called "seasonal." This type of discount is given when a channel member or customer is willing to purchase products "off-season," that is, without regard to the traditional selling period (suntan lotion in December or snow skis in July). Allowances for freight are possible under the Robinson-Patman Act, as long as the discount is proportionately available to all purchasers equally. (A manufacturer may provide FOB shipping—free on board freight—to the customer's location.)

Special discounts may also be available to dealers who resell the product. A common example here is when Ford Motor Company issues a manufacturer's suggested retail price, but, clearly, the dealer pays significantly less than this total amount listed on the window sticker.

Rebates

Rebate practices have become quite common. Rebates are amounts of the purchase price that are returned to the customer after the total purchase price has been paid. These allowances have an obvious value to the customer but also have value to the manufacturer and seller. The best example here comes again from the automobile industry. If a customer purchases an automobile for $20,000 and receives a 10% rebate, it is true that the actual price of the auto is $18,000.

But if the car was purchased on a contract for credit, the buyer qualifies for the $20,000 figure. It may be that the customer has done little more than make himself or herself a $2,000 loan for cash. At best, even if the loan balance remains at $18,000, the seller benefits from security of the qualified credit at the higher amount and will also benefit from the "float" of the rebate money until it actually is returned to the customer.

Probably the best feature of this practice is that the purchase price remains the same—price has <u>not</u> been reduced; therefore, the rebate can be changed or discontinued at any time without the problem of trying to increase a price once it has been lowered. (All will agree that the latter is almost impossible.)

Loss Leaders

Loss leaders are products that are offered for sale at prices below their cost to produce. The reasoning here is that these particular items will draw customers who will purchase additional products from the firm. There are problems with this practice. The most obvious is the "bait-and-switch" technique that may be used once the customer attempts to buy the loss leader. At this point, some organizations will attempt to move the customer from the loss leader item to another item of greater price. Domestically, many states have enacted laws to oversee minimum price practices. So far, the discussion has been one that has attracted sales, but the practice can be used to attack other competing organizations or even industries.

This type of loss-leader approach is referred to as predatory pricing. The object here is to price so low that smaller companies would be unable to compete and would then be eliminated. The United States' Sherman and Clayton Acts prohibit loss leaders with this objective. This practice has been a serious problem in international markets that have been unregulated, particularly in the computer industry. The General Agreement on Trade and Tariffs (GATT) attempted to make this approach more difficult.

Push vs. Pull

Price incentives (increased commissions or "spiffs") may be used among channel members to create a reason for them to particularly favor the sale of your product. By doing so, these channel members will encourage potential customers to select your offering instead of one from a competitor, thus "pushing" the product through the channel to the customer. In the opposite case, incentives (*e.g.,* coupons or promotions) may be offered directly to the potential consumer. These incentives will, in turn, encourage the consumer to seek out your particular product from their choice of retailers, thus "pulling" the product through the channel to the consumer.[68]

Bundling

The practice of bundling, in effect, reduces the price to the consumer by offering several related products or services at a single retail price that would be less than adding up the individual retail prices. This practice can be very effective in certain markets because the manufacturer's sales volume and the value to the customer can be quite high. A common example in the computer industry might be to offer a $1,000 personal computer, a $200 printer, and a $150 operating system software program as a bundle for a single retail price of $1100, if all three products are purchased at the same time.

Summary

Although pricing may seem more like an art than a science, well-thought-out strategies, tactics, and practices will inevitably lead to two things: hard work and a superior profit position.

It is clear that one additional characteristic must be made part of the pricing decision. Price decisions must be consistent, not erratic. What is at stake is customer loyalty, which is extremely difficult to develop and very easy to destroy. Customers seem willing to pay different prices for different segmented reasons but not willing to have companies send them mixed pricing messages in the same industries and/or among competing products.

For sample study questions, see Appendix J.

The foundations of this presentation were first delivered as a professional development seminar to the Genesis Electronics Corporation and was entitled "Segmentation: From Boomers to Busters to the "X" Generation and Beyond."

Segmentation

Contemporary marketing managers are faced with the reality that the days of mass markets are gone—the familiarity of dealing with the needs and wants of the largest domestic population post war glut (boomers) is now met with retirement; the emerging workforce (busters) are not politically nor control driven; and high school and college-age students (X's) no longer find goals and achievements their driving forces, and Generation Next (Millennials) expectations remain to be seen. Without attempting to ferret out each individual characteristic of these changing/emerging groups, it is possible to consider a few basic tenets of applied segmentation which help the practitioner to go beyond nominal definition of the term and to focus on the value of a particular group as a potential profit center.

Later in this discussion, specific "tests" for the implementation of a segment will be presented, but it is appropriate here to agree on a fundamental definition of the concept. "Segmentation" is, then, (1) isolating, discovering, and observing a unique sub-group of a larger market, (2) based on homogeneous characteristics that the members have in common, and (3) that are measurably correlated to the propensity to purchase a particular product or service.

Principal Market Segments

Many terms, sub-terms, and coined semantics abound with regard to segmentation. However, the central themes in segmentation fall into five basic categories: demographic, geographic, psychographic, behavioral, and hybrid.

Demographic

Demographic segmentation is the most familiar and among the simplest to identify. Observing a potential customer's age, sex, income, etc. is comparatively easy using descriptive statistics to collect, order, classify, and present these data. The fundamental problem with descriptive data is that while it is easy to accumulate, it becomes difficult to establish and measure any valid relationship with customer propensity. Remember, the last "A" in the AIDA model is action—if the marketer cannot establish/predict this relationship, s/he has a nominal segment but not a practical profit center.   The operative word here is "easy." While it is true that there is much available (secondary) demographic data, these may not be the best way to characterize a market segment.

Geographic

Segmenting by location is effective if the product or service is solely related to a geographic cluster. Again, this is a simplistic approach and one that is suspect for most products and services, particularly in the markets mentioned above, where other characteristics as well as location affect buyer behavior. This type of segmentation may be more effective for product/service applications that are generic, such as snow shovels in Detroit or sun block in Phoenix, but not as effective as the offering moves away from basic lower-order needs (Maslow) and on to the "me/we" products at the higher levels of desire.

Psychographic

Unlike the "who" characteristics of demography, psychographics are distinguishing elements that describe why potential customers manifest certain buying behaviors. Remember that the fundamental application of this type of segmentation requires that the practitioner investigate customer beliefs which should lead to their attitude, which should lead to their behavioral intent, which, in turn, should lead to their propensity, then to action—the sale. It sounds complicated—it is! The calculation of psychographic correlation to propensity is discussed in "Multiple Regression and Factor Analysis in Psychographic Research." But, pragmatically, psychographic segmentation is the attempt to observe lifestyle characteristics which explain why customers of similar demographic and geographic backgrounds make very different purchase decisions.

Behavioral

Behavioral segments are particularly important in the event that technological applications or products are being marketed but may also prevail in other markets as well. A behavioral segment is made up of individuals who have *a priori* knowledge concerning a product or service to be offered. These are not quite the same as the more traditional early adopter segment (Rogers) who investigate a product before purchasing. Behavioral customers already have unique and fairly complete knowledge concerning the offered product or service.

This segment must be treated very differently (develop a unique respect and a unique preparation) than the more traditional segments so as not to alienate them. While this segment may seem fairly obscure, some specific markets are well represented by potential customers with this buying characteristic.

Hybrids

Again, there are several coined terms for unique combinations or aberrations in "benefit" [69] segmentation, such as geodemographic, economic, key-element, multi-variable, and others. These names are not significant. What is significant is to realize that today's changing social/industrial cultures create the almost certainty that more than one factor will contribute to a successful explanation of buyer propensity and the resulting matrix solution will be the most effective one.

This observation can be good news for the capable marketer who is distinguished by having strategic market management savvy as well as the capability to apply significant quantitative "engines" (regression analysis, conjoint analysis, factor analysis, etc.) required to help make sense of the heterogeneous attitude/lifestyle markets.

Conceptual Segmentation

In order to consider the complex attitude/lifestyle and heterogeneous segments of the 2000's, it may be useful to think about basic configurations among segments in models which are familiar. Think about the grouping of individuals by Abraham Maslow.[70] Maslow postulated that human beings seek to meet these five needs (as shown in the diagram below) in a sequential order, beginning at the bottom with physiological needs. But he also postulated that people are not concerned about safety needs until their basic physiological needs are met; they are not concerned about a need for belonging until their safety needs are met, etc. Each grouping was based on specific attitudes and behaviors.

These groupings were not based specifically on demographic or geographic issues. Keenly, one can speculate on the kinds of products and services which might be successfully sold to physiological, safety, social, esteem, or even self-actualizing segments. A marketer might even further speculate that product offerings would be more likely at the lower levels (*i.e.,* levels 1 and 2) of the model, while later segments would gradually migrate toward service consumption to meet more advanced needs *(i.e.,* levels 4 and 5). Here time advances vertically as consumers migrate from lower-order needs (1) to higher-order needs (5).

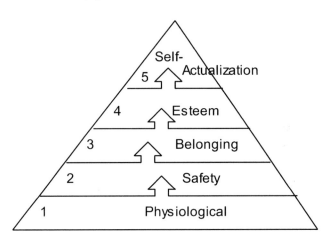

Consider another familiar group model, again based on attitude and behavior, not on geography or demographics—the "diffusion of innovation" (E. Rogers) demand model. Here an "average" market is segmented into five groups of individuals whose relative propensity, again like Maslow's, differs over time. While it is true that Rogers' distribution of individual consumers may change depending on the particular product or service, it remains a valuable visual aid in configuring segment strategy. Diffusion is the process by which the adoption of new products or services spreads.[71]

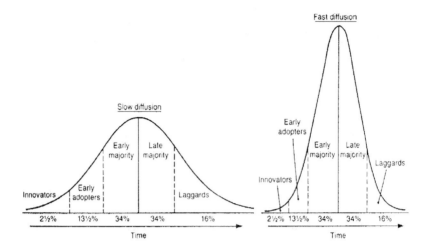

The diagram above assumes a segmented market. If the aggregate market were considered, there would almost always be a sixth category of refusers. Also, not only the relative standard deviation of the curve may change, but its degree of skew may shift, depending on demand diffusion. For example, a fad product or service would skew the curve to the left, and a staple product or service would skew the curve more to the right. Notice that the product life cycle (PLC) curve emulates the diffusion of innovation demand curve for a particular product or service offering.

Tests for Applied Segmentation

No matter what configuration is considered for the deployment of segmentation strategy, a group remains just that—a group—unless it meets three tests of applied segmentation practice: (1) identifiability, (2) accessibility, and (3) substantiability. These are questions that must always be answered before any group—even a differentiated group—can truly be defined and operationalized as a market segment.

Identifiability

A potential segment of consumers must be able to be specifically identified. This test requires more than a proportion or percentage of a target or general market. Identifiability requires in this context enumeration of specific customers by quantity as well as individually for contact. This is not to say that each will be evaluated/questioned; however, there must be a unique collection among the segment that could be identified in a representative sampling frame or routine. Unique collection includes the requirement that all members of the potential segment be associated with a specific identity such as a social security number, water billing number, telephone number, etc. in order to confirm each person's identity with the group and to assure a valid means of access to them.

Accessibility

Even though it may be possible to specifically identify a potential market segment as well as enumerate individual prospective consumers, it may not be possible or practical to reach them to complete a sale. Remember the basic requirements for a market transaction? Among these is communication, and international markets may pose a substantial barrier to entry in this way as well as tariff restrictions (*i.e.,* the North American Free Trade Agreement). Cultural, moral, and religious complications can also negate the fulfillment of an operationalized segment.

Domestically, other obstacles may include legal restrictions, inter/intra-state trade agreements, OSHA regulations, etc. Another complication in reaching market segments is where the prospective customers/clients are located, from a logistics point of view. For example, 100 customers may well be worth selling to as a group if they are centralized geographically, but what if that same 100 are domiciled in ten different states or ten different countries? Realize that in each test for applied segmentation, there may well be an identified group "ready, willing, and able" to complete a transaction; however, if for one of these or other reasons the firm cannot reach them, they, by definition, are not an applied segment.

Substantiability

The test for substantiability includes two concepts: first, a consideration of the return on investment for each of the product/services sold, and, second, a penetration requirement in the potential target market. If the sales manager for Dixie Cups is to measure substantiability, s/he has to recognize that the ROI on each cup is extremely low; therefore, a "trillion" individual cups may have to be sold in order to provide a profit center that is substantial. On the other hand, if the sales manager is employed by Cray Computer, annual sales of 30 units would probably be seen as an exceptional revenue stream.

Limitations of Segmentation

1.   Unless all applied tests for segmentation are met, there can be little practical application of a segment.

2.   Unless valid demographic, geodemographic, psychographic, and behavioral data are collected from among the specific group members that provide correlation between segment characteristics and propensity, the segment is difficult to justify.

3.   Due to complex heterogeneous markets, it may be that no significantly contributing segmentation characteristics can be identified. Rather, propensity may be explained by fairly insignificant contribution of a high number of different and relatively unmeasurable factors.

4.   After successful identification of a segment, a positioning of the result in the larger market may show the niche already filled

by a competitor or that required dimensions of price, quality, guarantee, etc. cannot be met efficiently <u>or</u> met at all.

5.   The constant change of customer beliefs and values (purchase behavior) as well as economic conditions and emerging technology add uncertainty to any defined segment.

6.   The most efficient time to segment is usually restricted to the rapid growth/competitive turbulence periods of the product/service life cycle, because, after this period, established competitive niches reduce available positions and attacking existing ones present high barriers to entry.

For sample study questions, see Appendix J.

These remarks were presented as part of a lecture series at Apple Computer and was entitled, "Communicating Marketing Fundamentals."

Marketing Mix: The Fundamentals

Decades ago, when Dr. Jerome McCarthy conjured up his "Four P Approach" (price, product, place, promotion), most observers saw it as a clever way to identify these four anchor issues in Market Strategy. Then, some realized that by categorizing the detail in each, a matrix of sub-action elements began to emerge that fleshed out a much more complete understanding of what is now more commonly referred to as "the Marketing mix." Virtually all activities related to Marketing can be placed into one of the 4 P's categories.[72]

Even more profound is the realization that the model is not simply a static diagram and list of sub elements, but, rather, a dynamic allocation model when properly applied, together with a focus on the Market Concept, positioning, market share, and market ethics. Each of these categories and concepts will be explained in the paragraphs to follow.[73]

Marketing Mix

All businesses in the private sector must have either a product or service to sell. Their goal is to sell their product or products to the retail consumer (private) or business to business (B2B) and to make the most profit in the exchange. To meet this goal of providing consumers (the market) with a product for a profit, all businesses must make decisions regarding (1) product, (2) place (distribution), (3) price, and (4) promotion. These four elements comprise what the field of marketing calls "the marketing mix."

<u>Product.</u>   Marketers need to decide what product/s to sell, what level of quality to put into their products, and what features to include with their products (such as options and warranties). They also must develop appropriate marketing programs to effectively sell these products, maintain successful products as long as possible, make plans for products in trouble or nearing the end of their life, and assess new market opportunities.

Product planning begins with developing products or services that are consistent with the segment of consumers that the firm hopes to attract, the existing or available human asset (employees and management), available technology, the fit with existing products, and established mission of the firm. With these characteristics in mind, the following decisions must be made with regard to product: quality, number and types of products offered), features and styling, warranties and guarantees, installation, service, branding, labeling and packaging. (For a detailed product discussion, see Text, Part 3, "New Product Development.")

<u>Place.</u> Firms must decide how to get their products to the consumer, or market—the "place" where the sale will occur. They must decide whether to sell their products directly to the consumer or to use intermediaries. If they plan to use intermediaries or "channels," how many should they use before their product reaches the consumer? They must also decide whether to cooperate with other channel members, what purchasing terms to negotiate, which stores they want to supply their product, how to package their product, and so on.

Taking the example of Kodak again, Kodak decided to make its products available to the entire domestic market through retailers rather than selling the product directly itself. Therefore, Kodak has to pay its retailers a portion of the sales revenue for the help they receive in selling the product.

Place includes both channels (people) and physical distribution (equipment). When combined, these applications are the basis for a logistical system responsible to provide the right product at the right place at the right time, fulfilling the "price, place, time, form, and utility."

The market manager must also be concerned with not only having the product priced correctly, but he or she must also offer it at the right place, at the right time, and in the proper form. When price is added, these four principles are referred to as "the market utilities." J.L. Heskett, N. A. Glaskowsky, and R. M. Ivie put it this way:

> When is a refrigerator not
> a refrigerator? When it is
> in Pittsburgh at the time it
> is desired in Houston.

Again, they might have added, "...and it is the wrong model" (form). There are many examples of fine products that have failed due to problems with price (too high or too low), place (low/no inventory or location), time (too early or late a market entry), and/or form (good application but unproved technology). Kaiser in the 1940s (time), Edsel in the 1950s (price), Delorean in the 1980s (place) are each auto industry examples of problems with market utility, and Toyota in 2010 (form) with recall after recall due to safety issues.

Transportation, storage, and materials handling require channel intermediaries, including wholesalers, retailers, warehousers, and facilitating administrators. Physical distribution activities include inventory decisions, storage facilities, distribution centers, and transportation mediums. (For a detailed discussion of "Place," see Text, Part 3, "Channels and Physical Distribution.")

The Market Mix

Notice that the Market Mix is not symmetrical in practice. Different products and services will need to be positioned with greater or lesser emphasis on the four elements of the market mix.

Marketing Mix (4P's)

PRICE
- raw materials
- labor
- profit
- credit terms
- discounts
- trade-ins
- trade allowances
- transportation charges
- capital investment

PRODUCT
- quality
- production quantity

- features/styling
- branding
- warrantees/guarantees
- installation/service
- labeling
- packaging

PLACE
- transportation mediums
- materials handling
- intermediaries
- inventory
- storage facilities
- distribution centers
- freight decisions

PROMOTION
- advertising
- personal selling
- publicity
- sales promotion
- public relations
- merchandising

Price.   Companies must make decisions about what to charge for the product.   They must decide the overall level of prices— is it going to be high, medium, or low?   They must also determine the range of prices—lowest and highest. They must determine how they plan to react to competitors' prices. If competitors raise or lower prices, will they too? The business must also decide what billing terms to have when sending their product to the customer or store that sells the merchandise. Are they going to give substantial or small discounts to customers who pay for the merchandise in advance, within ten days or for example, those who wish to buy in very large quantities? In terms of pricing their cameras, Kodak has positioned itself in about the middle of the market. There are cameras much more expensive than Kodak's, but some that are less expensive as well. The same is true of their film products.

Price includes determining the cost to produce or provide a product or service for sale. Do not confuse cost with price. Price is the amount of money given in exchange for a product or service. Cost is the amount of resource that a business must invest to produce the item for sale. Profit is the difference between cost and price. Price is subject to change, and a part of the strategic economics of the firm. Generally speaking, however, too high a price reduces market share, and too low a price reduces profit. Effective pricing recognizes that the exchange process and sales price incorporates raw materials, credit terms, discounts, trade-ins, allowances, and application of transportation charges. (For a detailed price discussion, see text, "Pricing Strategies.")

Promotion. With competition and the vast array of products on the market today, most companies find that they must "promote" or call attention to their product if they hope to sell much of it. Thus, companies must make decisions about how they will promote their products—what mix of advertising, publicity, personal selling, etc. to use. They must decide the image to project, and the choice and format of media advertising. In the 1980s and 1990s, since Kodak wanted to sell its product to adults domestically, it chose as its spokesperson a very familiar face—the star of the number one situation comedy, Bill Cosby, to closely identify with the average adult American. But most recently, the aging Cosby has been replaced by Paige Davis to continue to identify with the 40- to 50- year-old demographic.

Promotion is the communication component of the market mix. Its objective is to inform and educate through advertising, as well as sell product by persuading customers to purchase. Promotion provides information that encourages customers to respond. The "promotional mix" is a combination of advertising, personal selling, publicity, sales promotion, public relations, and merchandising. (For a detailed discussion of promotion, see Text, "Advertising, Promotion, and Publicity.")

Market Concept

The market concept is the cornerstone or anchor of any effective market planning or action. It is comprised of three fundamental strategies:

1. To have a customer orientation regarding each marketing decision made.

2. To focus on company profitability both in the short and long term, assuring the longevity of the company.

3. To assure an integrated company effort in the development of products and services, sales, delivery, and warranties.

A "consumer orientation" or "customer orientation" means that the firm focuses on customer needs when it determines what to produce. It does not focus on what it would like to produce then force the customer to accept it. In other words, product choices are customer-driven, not company-driven. Market entities have been successful, however, to create wants and then fill them. (Needs cannot be created.) While this approach may not meet the test of the market concept, it is viable in certain markets.

Having a "profit orientation" means that firms must make all decisions based on the possibility of furthering company goals. A firm can make a decision to increase sales, but if costs rise proportionally more in the process, the firm will be worse off. Attempting to increase sales in this case would not further company goals (which is, obviously, to increase profit).

"Integrated efforts" means that all business activities related to the production of goods or services (finance, production, marketing, research and development, etc.) are coordinated to better realize the company's goal of maximizing profit.

The customer has ultimate purchase power and decision-making, considering whether or not to purchase a good or service. Determining their needs and wants and filling them will be at the heart of any successful market strategy. (Hint: again, the marketer can create wants, but needs cannot be created—only filled.)

The customer controls the close of the sale or transaction. Therefore, they are the central point around which market decisions must pivot. This is not to say that the business organization or "means of capital" is hostage to them in terms of decision-making. But it is clear the customers are an equally important element of the market concept trilogy.

The casual observer of business would assume that all departments, divisions, management, and employees would work in harmony toward the company's goal of offering and selling products and services to the customer. After all, each of them receives their paycheck based on the overall success of their business unit and the company as a whole. However, the corporate culture, just like the employees in it in many cases have differing and competing goals.

Each may look differently at a decision based on how it affects their division of the company, their bonus, their promotion, or personal bias about a given business decision (age, gender, education, ethics, income, politics, etc.). The challenge in applying this aspect of the market concept is to reduce the incongruence among the competing goals to the best of one's ability.

A profit orientation is in the best interests of the business and the consumer. Of course the company wants as much return on investment as possible, while at the same time the consumer wants to pay the lowest possible price. But if price is set too high, market share will be lost as sales go down, and if price is set too low, although market share and sales will go up, company profit may go down.   Planning for sustainable profit is the only way to assure company longevity and sustained availability of goods and services to the consumer. Both customers and marketers must realize the symbiotic relationship goals—uninterrupted arrays of products at fair prices.

The 4 P's and Market Concept Applied

Open any basic marketing textbook, and look under the heading of the marketing mix, and you will find the same symmetrical model (usually a circle) displaying a quadrant displaying product, price, place, and promotion, all of equal size, suggesting that each is an equal "player" in the matrix of influence on market decisions. If this were really true in application, we would be dealing with an average product, average consumer, average quality, average value, average communication, average distribution, and so on, when we know that this is not the case.

The center of the market mix model or origin of the circle are the elements of the market concept with the earlier discussed focus on customer, integration, and profitability.   Using market research to refine customer wants and needs as they apply to company goals and return on investment, the 4P model should change in shape, becoming asymmetrical based on appropriate resource allocation among the four categories. For example, a large, heavy generic product like a washing machine would require a much larger resource allocation in the areas of promotion and distribution than product and pricing.

We can see that in application, the market mix proportions will be different from industry to industry and product to product. But the most significant changes in resource allocation should be based on the market and consumer research measuring the consumer's views concerning the market mix elements. That data collection should guide the mix allocation to persuade customers, fill their wants and needs, and create the greatest customer propensity for the company's products and services.

Positioning

When allocation resource decisions about product, place, price, and promotion are made in order to place the product/service specifically in the minds of consumers/buyers, businesses are "positioning" the product. Depending upon its positioning, a product or service will be compared (by consumers/buyers) in the market relative to competing products and will generate a specific demand from those who are interested in acquiring it.

The effective and consistent application of position can lead to a unique image, brand preference, or niche market for the manufacturer, seller, and/or provider of the good or service.

The 4P contribution made by Jerome McCarthy is significant, and when put in context with the market concept and asymmetric allocation, the model has profound application to the offering of a good or service. Not last here, these remarks have focused on consumer products and services, but may be applied in business to business marketing and "clients" as well as consumers.

Market Share

The product or service once effectively positioned in the consumer's mind should promulgate demand. The question is, how much demand and how to evaluate demand. First, the product or service may be a new product and have no competition, or it may be entering an already proliferated market. In any event, it is unlikely that the product or service will enjoy 100% of the market; rather, it will capture a portion of the whole market, and we refer to these cumulative sales as its "market share." The attempt to increase a firm's sales in a particular market is called "penetration." So the greater our effectiveness to penetrate any market is measured by the resulting market share gained.

Marketing Ethics

"Marketing ethics" refers to behaviors (by both a person or a company) that are considered socially and professionally honest and proper, based on a code of ethics developed by the AMA (American Marketing Association). Behavior described in the code relate to many areas, including satisfying all relevant publics, being honest in serving customers, providing products that function safely and as advertised, honest advertising, fair distribution of products, fair pricing, maintaining research integrity, and refraining from coercing others to be unethical.

Ethical issues can be divided into two areas: (1) process-related issues and (2) product-related issues. "Process-related" ethical issues involve the unethical use of marketing strategies or tactics. Examples of this include "bait and switch" tactics sometimes employed by salespeople, price fixing, and selling products outside the United States when they have been banned in the United States. "Product-related" ethical issues involve the production and marketing of products known to be harmful to the public, such as tobacco, alcohol, tanning beds, etc. The more difficult issue is for each of us to consider what our personal moral absolutes are (absolute rights and absolute wrongs).

When our moral absolutes are congruent with the ethics in our workplace, we feel no conflict; however, when our job requires behavior that violates our personal moral absolutes, then our own personal values are tested. If we're faced with a moral dilemma, we need to ask ourselves what our moral rules or limits are.   Be careful!   The answer to this question reveals and defines the quality of our own character.

Altruism	Social Responsibility	The Law	Illegal

≡ = Personal Morals
▦ = Business Ethics
▨ = Inappropriate for business environment

The graphic above shows, from left to right, the range of moral behavior—from altruism through illegality.

Within this framework are shown possibilities for personal behavior (or "personal morals") and possibilities for a business's behavior ("business ethics"). As you can see from the graph, a person's individual moral position might involve anything from altruism through illegality. But notice that a business's moral behavior, or business ethics, spans a much smaller area than personal morality. Successful companies must avoid behavior on either end of the morals spectrum; they cannot afford to be altruistic nor can they afford to break the law. They find an ethical standard and operate between the two.

Altruistic gestures made by a company might be seen as praiseworthy; however, such behavior is beyond the scope of a business environment because businesses (at least "for profit" businesses) must put profit first, and altruistic gestures would always have a cost, and possibly a high one.   On the other end, illegalities are clearly inappropriate in a business environment and oftentimes punishable, thus hurting the "bottom line" as well.

Conclusion

The market manager must develop and communicate effective market mix, positioning, market utility strategies, and market ethics. The description of each presented here has enumerated the fundamental concepts. The serious observer must now search out the customer-specific research and allocate necessary resources to position the product or service in the mind of its market segment. The result will be customer propensity and market share. If market "utilities" are maintained as priorities and implemented ethically, profit will follow.

For sample study questions, see Appendix J.

This article was first published in the OPASTCO Roundtable *and was entitled, "Telemarketing—It's More than Telephone Sales."*

Web (www) Sales and Telemarketing

What is telemarketing? Telemarketing is not merely telephone sales. A true telemarketing campaign involves identifying an appropriate product or service and target market; selecting first-rate staff; developing effective scripts; training employees; promotion/advertising; constructing database and market research capabilities; and developing backup and order fulfillment support.

Telemarketing and Telephone Sales

By 2006, telephone marketing accounted for 22% of all direct marketing sales. [74] It is estimated that over 30,000 telemarketing centers are operational in the United States today, with phone sales (land line, cellular, and PDA's) producing an average of over $800 per industrial order and $50 per consumer order. While some argue that the effectiveness of telemarketing has dropped due to caller ID and voice message systems, [75] aggregate sales numbers support the notion of substantial sales. Some of the most successful TM applications have been found in small- to medium-sized companies due to relatively low startup expenses. Also, telemarketing success depends not on the size of the center, but, rather, on the dollar amount of sales EACH employee generates. Given the high cost of field selling today, TM sales "calls" can "reach" more customers more often at a far lower cost to the company, resulting in a much higher return on investment per sale.

TM can also reach customers outside a company's normal service area. This additional "reach" becomes even more important as the companies attempt to attract customer segments which have been geographically unavailable to them. Valuable customer data can easily be developed with every sales call and sales close—the principal decision maker, his or her name, address, buying behavior, and any other pertinent data can be stored. From this database, market research can effectively be done, saving companies the expensive costs of full-scale market research. TM market research is an ideal solution for small- to medium-sized organizations that cannot afford larger research designs.

How to Get a Telemarketing Program Started

Phase One: Planning

First, get commitment from top management on down. TM cannot reach its potential without the support of marketing and executive management. Second, decide how the TM operation will fit into the current operating structure and consider getting professional help to develop an effective program and campaign. If your company has an existing traditional marketing program, the telemarketing program should be integrated into it. However, if no formal marketing program exists, TM can do very well as a stand-alone marketing effort.

Third, develop a marketing plan: Analyze your company's current marketing **capability** and product/service offerings (assess skill and the will of both management and staff and products targeted for TM).

Develop **goals** and sales objectives for your TM program. (Evaluate specific time lines for implementation and realistic, achievable sales levels.) Are there reasons beyond sales volume such as reach, positioning, add-on sales, inventory reduction, product or service trials, or customer research that make a TM program worthwhile?

Consider both internal and external "**threats and opportunities**." (Consider political opposition, competitive product offerings, existing and new markets.) Are you trying to provide a TM sales venue to remain competitive, or is this a proactive offering?

Determine the **tactics** which will be most effective in meeting program goals. (Develop market segments, product-specific prospect lists, telephone scripts, and training). Is Telemarketing a unique opportunity for experimenting with new product or service "rollouts"?

Determine a pro-forma **budget** for the "start-up" and initial follow-on stages of the program. (Forecast any capital investment, additional or allocated salary, overhead, variable and fixed costs.) How much capital is available as a sunk cost to initiate TM? What is the cost of that capital and where will it come from?

Develop the **standards** and expectations by which the program will be evaluated (*i.e.*, sales revenue, market share, number of services or products ordered per hour, etc.). Are basic product and service sales, for instance, the test of success, or are additional revenues expected through add-on sales? Specific standards developed in advance must prescribe a threshold for success.

Should you get professional help to start your telemarketing operation or should you "go it alone"? A fairly common approach is to get consulting help in the beginning to develop the basics of the procedure and to train existing personnel. The company can then take over and manage, expand, and develop the growth of the campaign on its own. However, many companies plan and implement a successful telemarketing program with no outside consulting help.

Phase Two: Implementation

Select a product or service that can readily be sold over the telephone. In the early stages of program development, it is wise to start by selling products or services which are easily explained (not new products) and ones which have quite obvious generic applications (not technical).

Identify a target market. This could be a market segment that is not well represented by news print or television, those customers who do not think of your company when purchasing products, or those customers you don't interact with regularly.

Generate a list of potential telemarketing customers from your database of current customers. In the early stages of your program, stick to in-house lists of current clients. These customers are already "qualified buyers" and already have confidence in you and your products/services. Since costs of telemarketing sales calls can range from $4.00 for a consumer call to $10.00 for a business call, save "cold" canvassing until your program and staff have had success and have matured in their TM experience and skill.

Dedicate a staff of well-qualified sales representatives and compensate them appropriately. Many a telemarketing program has failed because poorly paid, ill capable, and uninterested individuals were making the calls. The most important criteria are a sincere voice, stick-to-itiveness, listening ability, clarity of voice and diction, courtesy, and a customer service orientation. Most TM staff are paid a base salary plus commission for dollar amount of sales generated. Whatever incentive plan you use, be sure that the rewards are quick to return to the staff and that the process for allocating incentives is easy for the staff to understand.

Consider whether you want to **develop a script** for telephone personnel to specifically follow or whether you want to use a more "free-wheeling" approach. Most effective TM programs do use fairly rigid scripts. There are three reasons for their use: (1) most calls are fairly standard in nature; (2) with a script, staff can be more prepared for each call; (3) such standardization of calls and a prepared staff result in a more efficient utilization of labor per sales call.

Develop a training program for the telephone staff. Staff need to learn how to read a script so that it sounds natural, cope with a 50% non-response rate, deal with many no-close calls, become very familiar with products and services sold, and quickly find the appropriately scripted answer to potential customer questions. These are but a few of the challenges that need to be addressed in TM training.

Advertise and promote the new TM Program among customers. Typical types of inexpensive advertising include a mailing to prospective telemarketing customers and newspaper announcements. Promotions might include a bill "stuffer" announcing the TM campaign and offering a discounted price for customers who will in-bound a call for service. Larger groups can be reached simultaneously through local radio and television spots. This media advertising expense may be warranted, depending on the potential of the specific market.

Get management support to complete order fulfillment. There will be initial and on-going support requirements. Be prepared that sales closes must be audited for accuracy, timely fulfillment, service, and courtesy. With careful monitoring of sales calls, the "good will" generated between your company and the customer can extend the telemarketing program by word-of-mouth to the next customer.

Don't expect too much too soon. When AT&T began their telemarketing campaign "Phone Power" to sell call forwarding, call waiting, three-way calling, and speed dialing, the program did not show impressive returns in its early stages: in its first few months, only 4% of customers contacted placed orders on the initial call. However, half of these customers did order the full package of features. After one full year in operation, results were much more impressive: of 20,000 features sold by AT&T in one year, 80% were sold through outbound telemarketing.

Telemarketing **is** much more than telephone sales. With thoughtful planning and implementation, small- and medium-sized companies can realize substantial additional revenues.

Web Marketing and Internet Sales

What are Internet sales? Much like the development of fax technology, the timing of Marketing over the Internet was dependent on developing technology. The concept of completing a market transaction[76] using software is a relatively new possibility. Transmitting a message from a single terminal to another single terminal was possible before the advent of computers (*e.g.,* telegraph, telex, fax, etc.). But much like the "compression technology" required in telephony to send a fax, there was no hardware or software solution allowing Internet communication among multiple remote terminals and a central processing unit (CPU). Again, like fax, until the technology permitted fax to communicate between and among individual homes over "compressed" 56 kb telephone lines, there would be no demand or availability of the product or its service.

Internet availability depended on research and development efforts of the 1970s, 1980s, and 1990s by several entities— universities (UCLA, Stanford, MIT, among others), corporations (Rand and Bell Laboratories among others), and government (Department of Defense, NASA, Department of Energy, among others). The mid 1990s brought about the hosting of search engines for information retrieval or "browsers" on the Internet. Only after the *concept* of email in 1965[77] led decades later to the actual transmission of messages and then to data searches did the public begin to "surf the web" regularly for information. Demand grew exponentially. North America will remain the heaviest user of the Internet (over 75% of its population) by 2011, at the same time 22% of the world's entire population will surf the Internet regularly. Currently, 1.1 billion people have web access in one form or another.[78]

What does this mean for business? By the end of 2009, the top 50 Internet advertisers were spending over $350 million on web ads. Among them are many major corporations including AT&T, General Motors, Bank of America, Walmart, McDonald's, Ford, and Neiman-Marcus. [79] The significance? These corporations represent the industries of communications, transportation, finance, department stores, and restaurants—a quite eclectic and diverse population of major industry participants.

How to Get a Web Marketing Program Started

Phase One: Planning

First, get commitment from top management on down. WM cannot reach its potential without the support of marketing and executive management. Second, decide how the WM operation will fit into the current operating structure. If your company has an existing traditional marketing program, the telemarketing program should be integrated into it. However, if no formal marketing program exists, WM can do very well as a stand-alone marketing effort. Third, develop a marketing plan. (See the Telemarketing "Phase One" section presented earlier in this article, delineating the market plan fundamentals, which should also be used here as a startup WM template.)

The follow-on step is to recognize both the advantages and the risks associated with Web marketing. Advantages[80] include the **flexibility** to make ad copy or graphics changes due to errors, shifts in business planning, or changes in competitive intelligence due to monitoring and tracking of initial customer response. Real-time **tracking** allows you to monitor online advertising campaign performance "in the moment." Immediate customer reaction measured by online analytics can enumerate and "daylight" opportunities as well as measure current financial returns of this portion of the market plan.

A company can **target** specific demographic and psychographic customer profiling on its advertising data base. Data collections of gender, age, location, income, education, and occupation, as well as lifestyle, attitude, and behavior information is more quickly and readily available to help specifically target markets and segments. Also, a **variety** of different contact mediums can be used to quickly, efficiently, and inexpensively reach customers. Email, video and audio streaming, blogs, social media (Facebook, MySpace, YouTube, Scribd, and Groupon), [81] Twitter, Bing, and electronic newsletters can all be utilized without hiring a public relations firm or paying a single media outlet.

Entire company sales catalogues and large sales brochures can be put on a company website, encouraging customers to "shop" from their electronic format, thus saving the company the cost of printings and mailings as well as dissemination of expensive company sales brochures. Don't ever underestimate the viability of these platforms. At the end of 2009, CNBC predicted that Twitter would fail in 2010. In fact, by the end of 2010, Twitter had nearly tripled in size and raised its company value to $3.7 billion.[82] And at this writing, "Facebook has become a company with more than 500 million users."[83]

Instant customer **conversion** or "closing the sale" is much easier in a web format than traditional advertising. Taking advantage of impulse buying as well as a reduction of pre-purchase dissonance is much easier when all it takes is an immediate mouse click, key stroke, or touch of a screen to close the sale. Traditional radio, television, and print media require far longer times for the customer to process, longer times to order, more time to change their mind, and a larger marketing support staff to capture the transaction.

Disadvantage of Internet marketing are many.[84]Despite **rumors** of all the easy Internet riches that await the entrepreneur, instant millionaires and DOT-COM legends, there is also a genuine ugliness to the Web. Unknown to newcomers, the Internet is not safe, and to the unprepared, it can be outright dangerous.[85]

Blogs, chat rooms, and other social media are dangerous web marketing alternatives. Examples of these customer-controlled dialogues have had **consequences** for firms such as State Farm (insurance), PepsiCo, and Georgia Pacific, which had to pull ads from these venues in the past[86]due to inappropriate interactive contributions made by the public and consumers. While filtering technology continues to improve monitoring oversight, the lasting damage to a product, brand, and general reputation can be catastrophic.

Necessary second- and third-party tiered vendor **contract obligations** are vital to developing an effective Internet marketing campaign but can also mean peril for the principal company that is a novice, uninformed, or unprotected from PPC (pay per click) search engine companies. The terms and conditions of these agreements are legally binding and can cause you to risk more than you can afford.

Contracts with even the most reputable search engine and browser providers are at best legally complicated and at worst tricky or misleading in language embedded in the document. Focus on search engine optimization (SEO). Insist on a short-term obligation. If all goes well, the PPC will be eager to extend. If things don't work out for you, make certain you are not bound long-term.

Following the same logic, begin with a small, less ambitious campaign in the beginning. The program can be easily expanded in the future. If your company is small, one way to afford a web campaign launch may be to find an ally—a similar-sized retailer with a compatible service or product offering to your own and share the initial financial obligation required to get started. Unfortunately, **online fraud** is a major risk. Check lead validations such as IP (Internet Protocol) addresses and credit card validity. Instruct your web master to block any fraudulent leads to preclude redundancy. Internet sales can dwindle just as rapidly as they evolved. Make certain that you **qualify multiple vendors** and have more than one stream of leads. Even a successful vendor or campaign may fatigue and stop generating convertible leads and sales, or a competitor can "suck up the oxygen" of a previously potent market position. Be prepared to quickly replace one or both, depending on what your tracking research tells you.

Phase Two: Implementation

Unlike a telemarketing offering, web marketing is more complicated and inherently more risky. In the case of WM, "going it alone" is not a good idea. Get early-on advice and consulting regarding website development, PPC contracting, WM campaign design, and legal issues.

Select a product or service compatible with web sales and electronic distribution (*i.e.,* movies, e-books, software) or products that customers will be willing to wait to be delivered by ground transportation (*i.e.,* DVD, CD, hard copy). Certain products or services will intuitively lend themselves more toward "brick and mortar" physical locations than web sales.

Identify a target market of consumers for your product or service offering. Research their usage patterns. Is your prospective segment watching television, listening to radio, reading certain news or entertainment publications? Are they spending time on web browsers or social media? If so, concentrate your effort toward a specific profile of interest.

SEO development is essential. Browser selection and development must be coordinated with the existing company website as well as be compatible with the emergence of the

Internet sales campaign. Among major search and related companies are AOL, Amazon, ASK, E-BAY, Google, MSN, and Yahoo, *et.al.*[87] Again, **management commitment** is essential for effective web sales. Managerial, administrative, and financial commitment are required to develop a successful market plan, replete with time lines, deliverables, and bench marks, leading to long-term Internet sales. Capable Internet sales are developed and sustained by recognizing the program as a concomitant partner to already-existing marketing platforms of catalog, in-store, and telemarketing. While each platform can be stand-alone, if they are not, management must see them as equally important, not one as the "step-child" of another.

Advertising and **web marketing promotion** are essential to a stable stream of WM revenue. Advice from a public relations firm is helpful here. While the target market and product array to be offered and positioning have been established, the decisions of media mix (video, television, radio, print, electronic, etc.), budget allocation, and specific media venues to reach prospective customers remains complex. Benefiting from PR's experience and their established media relationships can be invaluable here.

Broadband in households and on PDA's are making banners, pop-ups, display ads, music, and videos much more interesting, capable and offering the greater possibility of "going viral." Add to this embedding advertising in Internet games, "friend" registrations by customers, and global positioning system (GPS) promotion opportunities, one can see the current and potential future applications. Well over $20 billion are being spent annually on Internet advertising to try to tap these markets.[88]

These remarks made about the nontraditional sales approaches of telemarketing and web marketing are meant to be basic and general in nature. The enumeration, particularly with regard to implementation, should be augmented with a detailed market plan and much **deeper research** of the potential features and failures inherent to these two applications.

For sample study questions, see Appendix J.

This article was first published in Proceedings of the American Business Communication Association Conference *and was entitled, "The Retail Lease vs. Purchase Decision: A High-Technology Perspective."*

The Retail Lease vs. Purchase Decision

Marketing managers have a significant opportunity cost decision to consider with respect to the kind of sophisticated, ever-changing equipment that can help them remain competitive. Physical distribution, inventory, and billing are just a few of the myriad of necessary applications which require attention in today's marketplace. The decision requires an investigation of available technology, its limitations and its potential.

In addition, marketers must consider whether their organizations can afford or can afford not to generate necessary funds to obtain this equipment. These issues have become manager-specific and must be considered strategic marketing decisions. They can no longer simply be reduced to financial analysis without first making certain that all salient acquisition variables have been enumerated.

Introduction

Early records of lease transactions occurred as far back in history as 2000 B.C. Agriculture, maritime, and land agreements were most prominent through the 1400 B.C. period.[89] Leasing developed into an industry during the post World War II period. Among variables which made leasing attractive were a lack of liquidity and a need for additional means of production.

Through the 1950s, the principal lessors were American Telephone and Telegraph Company and International Business Machines Corporation.[90] Exponentially increasing demands for gathering, managing, analyzing, receiving, and sending information require today's retailer to select and efficiently use high-technology business solutions if he or she wants to remain competitive. The decisions require a more complete investigation than return-on-investment calculations or a determination as to where the investment capital will come from.

Whereas both leasing and purchasing have strengths and weaknesses, the decision maker must consider a "best fit" solution of the matrix of possible contributing factors before his or her evaluation can be considered adequate. Should an organization choose a financial lease, operating lease, leveraged lease, or purchase configuration?

The objective of this paper is to assemble essential characteristics relevant to the lease-purchase choice in the high-technology and supercession or obsolescence environment of today's retail decision maker. Further, by integrating qualitative and quantitative aspects, the paper assembles important variables to be considered by each evaluator before he or she chooses an appropriate application for the specific organization.

The need to discuss an eclectic approach is demonstrated by the fact that a retailer can be active in each of four areas simultaneously: operating lease, financial lease, leveraged lease, and purchase. With leases accumulating to $1.3 trillion[91] nationwide and the ability to purchase technology that was previously prohibitive, one must consider more than whether the decision is division- or corporate-oriented, balance-sheet or income-statement motivated, or whether it is a numerical hurdle-rate calculation. There are characteristics which are unique to each decision and also areas which are common to all. Some depend on another's occurrence and others do not.

Page 168

Lease Configurations

Leases fall primarily into three main categories: operating lease, financial lease, and leveraged lease. An operating lease provides that the lessor retains title, rights, and benefits to the equipment as well as assumes the responsibilities associated with ownership. A financial lease provides that the lessor may transfer all rights and responsibilities to the lessee for a period less than the economic life of the asset and provides for purchase options. The leveraged lease is an operating/financial lease hybrid which provides for several parties' participation.[92]

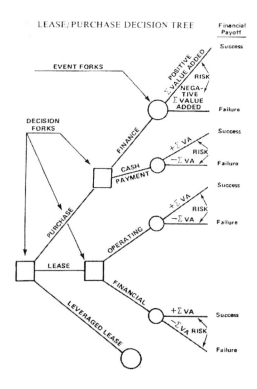

LEASE/PURCHASE DECISION TREE

Among proposed advantages of leasing high-technology equipment are (1) financing alternatives and capital formation, (2) lower payments by possible "pass-through" provisions of investment credits and cost recovery deductions, (3) pre-tax lease payments, (4) 100% financing including installation and "bringing up" the system, (5) off-balance-sheet financing, (6) hedging inflation, and (7) circumventing loan covenants. However, each of these areas has a specific meaning only when placed in the financial context of the individual firm and in conjunction with the implications of the Statement of Financial Accounting Standards No. 13, the Economic Recovery Tax Act, the Tax Equity and Fiscal Responsibility Act[93]and the Tax Reform Act of the 1980s[94], together with a series of 1990s and 2000s legislation.

As of 2009, the Tax Reform Act of 1986 remained the most significant major change to law. The American Recovery and Reinvestment Act of 2009 (ARRA), commonly referred to as "the stimulus," and, most currently, President Obama's 2010 Investment Tax Credit and Cost Recovery proposals provide the latest decision variables.[95]

SFAS Number 13

The effect of the SFAS No. 13 provisions, which require disclosure of lease agreements in financial statements, is an important one. Early on, off-balance-sheet accounting was considered to be a strong defense for lease decisions. Although disclosure is required only in footnote form, it has brought the "pre-tax" lease payments into a "post-tax" serial debt reality.

ERTA and TEFRA

Tax provisions of the ERTA established the Accelerated Cost Recovery System (ACRS), the Investment Tax Credit (ITC), and Rules Governing Safe-Harbor Leasing. This act created business incentives for equipment investment and promulgated leasing configurations. The TEFRA curtailed, repealed, and amended earlier guidelines. It curtailed the "pass- through" provision; it repealed the safe-harbor rules; and it amended the ACRS and ITC rules. Further, TEFRA established a new lease category, the finance lease.

The order of the financial decision maker's evaluation is changed by the relationships among SFAS No. 13, ERTA, and TEFRA. Based on the implications of the Internal Revenue Service defining certain leases as purchase agreements and disallowing payments as "rent," one must first consider IRS provisions and then SFAS. The freedom of the lease analyst is sharply restricted by each of these characteristics. Every detail must be fully ordered, evaluated, and placed in the firm's financial perspective. Both short-run and long-run scenarios must be considered, including variables other than "sharp-pencil" calculations.

"BUY IT, LEASE IT, FORGET IT"

TRA

By passing the Tax Recovery Act, the 99th Congress decreased individual tax obligations. The net effect was chilling to business, as it increased small and corporate income tax liability by drastically reducing the number of deductions and undermining the 10% investment tax credit of the 1980s ERTA and TEFRA eras of now 25 years ago. Specific effects of the TRA are dealt with in a later section of this article.

Purchase Configurations

Purchase configurations also provide several advantages to be considered by the analyst: (1) preferred interest rates, (2) direct benefit of any available investment tax credit, (3) direct benefit of the Accelerated Cost Recovery System, (4) control over vendors, and others. Large organizations which are well capitalized have greater purchase flexibility; however, smaller, less affluent firms should also consider purchase opportunities. Any firm that has liquidity and the ability to benefit from tax concessions should investigate buying. Further, certain acquisitions of low technology/low cost should not be leased.[96]

While the amount of equipment leased is growing, purchase of equipment is still the major means of acquisition, depending, in some cases, on the level of technology and cost of capital. The principal obstacle in purchase is a source of funds. Today many options are available to most firms. Funds to accommodate investment proposals may be procured in many ways. The firm may choose short-term options of trade credit, bank credit, commercial paper, equipment financing, conditional sales contract, chattel mortgage, bank float, receivables factor, ordinary term loans, revolving credit, insurance company loans, small business administration loans, equipment financing, or conditional sales contract.

Choosing a high-technology equipment system, whether communication voice/data, manufacturing, computer, or other, is a major decision in any organization. Each available option must be evaluated. The difficulty stems from the fact that included in some vendors' costs are important services that may never appear in a hardware (sale) proposal. To assume that these services are unimportant or automatically provided by all vendors equally is both dangerous and fallacious. The task of the competent analyst is to enumerate these services and apply a cost or value to each of them. This is an arduous task. Placing a dollar value on services and risk is clearly a stochastic process as well as a practical one. Acquisition decisions should be based on price, value, and cost.

Decision Variables

The following are variables which must be quantified and expressly evaluated in the common factor lease versus purchase decision in order to determine a true value-added comparison: (1) rate stabilization; (2) installation, moves, and changes; (3) product mix and "growing"; (4) consulting/studies; (5) maintenance; (6) inflation; (7) casualty losses; (8) end-to-end responsibility; (9) longevity; (10) training; (11) financing.

When either leasing or purchasing is suspected of having an economic advantage, an evaluation should be made to measure the advantage. When one or the other is chosen regardless of the economics (for example, convenience or other human factors), an analysis is still useful because it measures the effect on the company of selecting a more costly alternative.[97] Below is the lease vs. purchase decision presented in a double-approach-avoidance model.

NEED FOR EQUIPMENT ACQUISITION

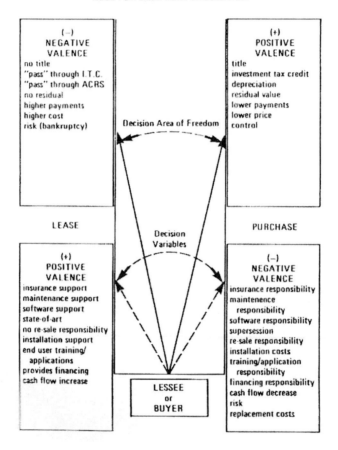

Chief Executive Officers' Objective Criteria

Chief Executive Officers' objective criteria also have substantial effects on decision-making environments within the firm. Capital investment policies and philosophy of CEOs generally fall into the following categories:

1. The CEO's position may be routine, well understood, and documented in all of its aspects, or it may require human

involvement and judgment at one or more stages in the process.

2. It may involve well-defined quantitative parameters, or it may refer to matters for which numerical values of outcomes are difficult to define.

3. It may be undertaken against a background of certainty in terms of the outcome of any course of action chosen or in the face of uncertainty with regard to future events or the actions of others.

4. It may require that well-developed mathematical techniques be applied if such a well-defined structure has yet to be developed.

5. It may require a solution at one point in time, or it may consist of a sequence of interrelated decisions.

6. It may involve a question which can be resolved by an individual alone, or it may involve the responsibility of a group of individuals who may not have identical views or approaches with regard to the problem.

Whether the CEO is predisposed toward specific decision criteria based on centralization and decentralization, discounted cash flow, return on investment, uncertainty and risk, stockholders/equity, return on equity, pre-tax cash out, or others, the most important concern is that no criterion stands alone. Alone, each prejudices a truly competent analysis of leasing or purchasing high-technology equipment. Each must be augmented, refined, and purged by the decision variables and human factors.

Clearly, there are successful retail organizations which are retrenched in a particular criterion—the question is to what extent their profitability could be increased through a more global analysis. The synergy is evidenced not by a change in philosophy but by incorporating heretofore unrealized or ignored characteristics in the evaluation process.

Implications

The retail lease versus purchase decision cast on the high-technology milieu, when further complicated by the Financial Accounting Standards Board SFAS No. 13, Economic Recovery Tax, and the Tax Equity and Fiscal Responsibility Act the Tax Reform Act is a catalyst for a complicated matrix decision. The matrix must be further expanded to include qualitative value-added variables and the chief executive officer's objective criteria.

When the implications of federal tax changes are objectively considered, the monetary outcome (price) between leasing or purchasing is very similar. The greatest difference in cost will be based on the organization's ability to utilize tax advantages and its accurate (and inclusive) quantification of "soft" dollar value-added benefits provided for in the agreements among buyers, sellers, lessees, and lessors.[98]

The popular internal debates of centralized, decentralized, corporate, division, and off-balance-sheet accounting are non-issues in a tax environment which may disallow their outcome at fiscal year-end. A proposal that erroneously provides short-run evidence of least cost is not competent. It must (1) provide for, and quantify, all necessary support requirements to the acquisition, and (2) provide evidence of long-run fiscal savings in terms of both tax and efficiency. These criteria must be evaluated by accomplishing the following:

1. Determine the net federal tax (year-end) impact that the acquisition will have on the firm, not treating off-balance-sheet financing as rental payments only to have them ruled long-term serial debt under year-end federal or state tax provisions.

2. Clearly evaluate "pass-through" contract provisions. Are the benefits substantially reflected in lower payments in a lease arrangement? Some retailers have established standard financial procedures which prohibit consideration of a lease that does not fully forward the entire benefit.

3. Identify all necessary "hard" and "soft" support costs. These characteristics will be required and are rarely mentioned and almost never quantified by vendors. It is insufficient for vendors, lease or sale, to give "blanket" confidence such as, "We provide for . . . and if you are going to bet on the future, bet on us." Ask them to quantify their value added in terms of cost, benefit, and revenue.[99]

4. Enumerate all sources of possible capital and their actual as well as opportunity costs. What typically appears to be a favorable cost of capital may well turn out to be hidden in higher acquisition costs or absence of required services, software, etc.

5. Identify the chief executive officer's philosophy. Treat it as a synergy to the myriad of other decision variables, not as a prejudice. The CEO objective criteria are based on many years of valuable experience. (These criteria are almost impossible to overcome, so include them.)

6. Be certain to evaluate the difference between obsolescence and supersedence in the high-technology decision. Lack of technological understanding is not sufficient reason to purchase equipment or to be manipulated by a vendor.

Areas one and two are extremely important given recent tax changes; however, given these changes, item three, when clearly delineated, will provide the current competent financial difference between lease and purchase configurations.

Effect of the Tax Reform Act[100]

The sweeping changes in the Tax Code affected by the Tax Reform Act had a profound effect on the use of leasing as a financial tool. There were several significant changes:

1. Elimination of the Investment Tax Credit. This change had the effect of discouraging corporate purchasing of equipment in favor of leasing. The change effectively raised the purchase price of the equipment, since the tax credit had been eliminated while not affecting the leasing cost.[101, 102]

2. Changes in Depreciation Schedules. In some cases, depreciation schedules were lengthened. This eliminated the tax advantage of purchasing equipment over leasing, since depreciation write-offs were reduced. In addition, depreciation charges could no longer be used to offset net income, but could only be used for determining alternative minimum tax liabilities. This further reduced the usefulness of depreciation as a tax strategy.[103]

3. Mid-Quarter Convention. The most significant part of this rule is that equipment placed in service at the end of a company's tax year could lose most of its depreciation allowance for that year. If a company acquired more than 40% of its capital acquisitions in the last quarter, it is disallowed from using the mid-year convention for depreciation purposes and must depreciate beginning at the middle of the fourth quarter.[104] The practical effect is that the company loses 4½ months' worth of depreciation allowances. This change was intended to curb abuses by companies that had rushed a purchase decision and put the equipment into service late in the fiscal year in order to be able to write off depreciation for the entire year.[105]

4. Alternative Minimum Tax (AMT). This new alternative tax is based solely on net income. This forces companies to look hard for ways to reduce income. One way was to increase operating

expenses by leasing equipment instead of purchasing. Some companies are considering sale/leaseback agreements in order to increase operating expense and reduce their AMT liability on net income caused by equipment already in service.[106] Other companies who were saddled with heavy debt payments from takeovers and acquisitions were restricted from taking depreciation deductions by being subject to alternative minimum tax.[107] In general, ownership is now being considered a potential tax liability because of the provisions of the AMT.

5. Reduction of the Corporate Tax Rate. The reduction in tax rate also translates to the reduction in value of tax write-offs. This tips the balance away from tax-reduction-driven financing strategies to make them less competitive with reduction of net income through operational expenses. Multinational companies are considering shifting taxable income back to the U.S. because of the lower tax rate; equipment leasing is a flexible way to do this. These companies would also be able to deduct lease payments from operating income to further reduce their tax liability.[108]

6. Allocation of Interest Expense for Multinational Corporations. The allowable allocation of this expense was changed so that it was allocated to the entire company as a whole instead of to particular operations. Historically, multinational companies would allocate most or all of their interest expense to U.S. operations in order to drive foreign-based income up. This allowed them to maximize use of foreign-tax credits and reduce overall tax liability. Since this activity has been curtailed, these companies are now trying to use leasing to selectively allocate operating expenses and accomplish the same strategy of maximizing foreign-tax credits.[109]

The tax effect of a lease decision is often a critical deciding factor. The IRS is aware of this and has disallowed deductions for what they term as "sham transactions." Tax Court decisions involved sale-leaseback transactions of computers. In general, they have used a two-part test. The first part requires determining whether there was a business purpose for engaging in the transaction other than tax avoidance. The second part of the test requires establishing whether the transaction had any economic substance other than the creation of tax benefits.[110]

Additional Lease Types and Examples

True Lease

This is the tax definition of an operating lease. The IRS has set very definite guidelines defining the conditions under which a lease is considered a true lease. Most of these conditions involve whether the lessor grants any equity position either through lease payments or an option to purchase for a nominal value at the end of the lease. Other conditions involve payments recognized as interest or excessive payments which may be recognized as extraordinary compensation for use of the equipment. Any of these conditions may invalidate a true lease for purposes of tax reporting, and full deduction of lease payments may be disallowed.[111]

Conditional Sales Lease

This is the tax definition of a capital lease. A conditional sales lease is essentially 100% financing of equipment. The lessee technically owns the equipment and can deduct for depreciation and the interest portion of the lease. The entire lease payment is not deductible. The lessee also gets the benefit of any residual value of the equipment as specified in the lease agreement. Conditional leases are considered not to be true leases for the purposes of tax reporting, and full deductions for lease payments may be disallowed.[112]

Vendor Leasing

Typically, the vendor can choose to finance the lease themselves or arrange the lease through a third party. Third-party leasing is becoming more popular since the vendor receives immediate cash payment for the sale. The vendor also escapes the risk of being stuck with a low residual value asset after the lease expires. These leasing arrangements are also good for distributors, since they are not required to buy and hold inventory because ownership has been transferred to the third-party lessor. The vendor also reduces the exposure to AMT obligations which may be caused by income from leasing receipts.[113]

Short-Term Operating Leases

Many companies are increasingly becoming concerned with flexibility in asset management. These companies are requesting operating leases for terms shorter than the economic life of the equipment, with options to renew. They also ask for special terms in the form of cancellation rights and equipment upgrades. All of these items are requested as ways to increase flexibility in equipment procurement.[114]

Full-Service Leasing

This type of lease has been common in the trucking industry, but similar arrangement can be applied to other types of capital equipment. In this type of lease, the lessor provides a fleet of trucks and trailers designed and built to customer specifications, including color and company logo. The lessor also supplies all maintenance, fuel, oil, tires, washing, storage, and surplus vehicles when needed. They may also arrange for permits and licensing as well as pay fuel tax. The lessee pays one fixed charge plus a mile charge per truck. This setup consolidates a large portion of the trucking company's operating expenses and eliminates a considerable amount of administrative and operating overhead. A full-maintenance lease is a similar lower-cost version but offers fewer services compared to the full-service lease.[115]

Contract Maintenance

This type of lease allows the lessee to maintain ownership of the capital equipment while obtaining the same services as in a full-service or full-maintenance lease. The leasing company also provides extra equipment during peak periods or when company-owned equipment is down for repair or maintenance. In some cases, leasing companies have taken over on-site facilities to provide repair and maintenance and spare parts inventories.[116] However, sub-contracting service can lead sometimes to confusion as to who is responsible for certain items if the contract is not written carefully.[117]

Upgrade Options

Lessors are often willing to upgrade equipment in the middle of a lease agreement without a cancellation penalty. This is called a "rollover" option. It allows the lessee to acquire more useful equipment when the need arises. The lessor rolls the previous lease balance into a new lease payment and is able to continue their cash flower for a longer term.[118] However, the lessee must be very careful when evaluating this part of the lease because the costs of upgrading may be extremely high. An acceptable upgrade clause should be included in a lease contract, particularly with items which are sensitive to obsolescence such as computer equipment. If there is not such a clause, the risk of obsolescence is being passed on to the lessee.[119]

Sale-Leaseback

Some companies in need of raising capital are now able to sell all of their office equipment, computers, and furniture to a finance corporation and then lease them back. This approach generates working capital from the fixed assets of a company.

G. E. Capital, which deals with contracts of $1 million or more, specializes in this method.[120]

Wraparound Lease

This is a complicated version of a leveraged lease with several players. A leasing company purchases equipment from a manufacturer with money borrowed from a bank and leases it to a user. The leasing company then sells the equipment along with the leasing contract to a third-party broker, referred to as the "middle company," for a cash down payment and a debt obligation. The middle company then turns around and sells the equipment and lease contract to investors on essentially the same terms. In the last step, the investors lease the equipment back to the original leasing company.

The net effect of all of this is that the tax benefits of interest and depreciation deductions are essentially sold to the investment group with everybody taking a cut on the way around. This typically has no effect on the lessee who may never be aware that any of this has taken place, since their only interaction was with the leasing company. The downside for investors is that the determination of who, for tax purposes, technically owns the equipment may be in question.

Recent tax decisions have taken the position that the party who is financially "at risk" if lease payments are not made is technically the owner and should be the recipient of any tax benefits. The Tax Court also uses the test of whether the transactions involved in a wraparound lease had any other significant financial benefit other than tax avoidance. In some cases, the Tax Court disallowed deductions made by investors who were involved in wraparound lease transactions.[121]

Income Funds and Limited Partnerships

Because the demand for equipment leasing has increased, a secondary market has developed of pooled investor funds to service this demand. The core concept is that these funds can produce passive income for investors which can be used at tax time to offset passive losses. The growth of these funds has provided another source of off-balance-sheet financing for growing companies. However, the Tax Reform Act reduced the tax deduction benefits of these funds by limiting passive loss deductions and reducing the individual tax rate.[122]

Second Stimulus?

The current political climate suggests that President Obama's 2010 proposal to allow businesses to deduct new investment expenses over a shorter term and reinstating some form of investment tax credit may be forthcoming. Currently only a few technologies such as energy, biomedical, and infrastructure (road, rail, and public works) applications were promulgated as exceptions to ITC and ACRS rules under the first stimulus ARRA (2009).[123] At this writing, Capitol Hill appears poised to reinstate some broader type of accelerated cost recovery and investment tax credit, as well as extend the more general "Bush tax cuts," thus promoting capital investment in plant and equipment.[124]

As of 2011, the FASB (Financial Accounting Standards Board) and the IASB (International Accounting Standards Board) are working jointly to develop new lease accounting standards with the objective to capitalize all material leases. The approach would record present value as an asset or liability and then depreciate the asset on a straight-line basis, thus "front ending" the lessee's expense.[125]

Conclusion

Market managers should not be expected to develop the financial analysis associated with high-technology acquisition. Neither should they ignore the characteristics which must be considered in a competent analysis process. Technology and its application are elements of effective strategic market management. Therefore, an efficient firm must consider the use of up-to-date equipment that can ensure cost reduction and improved productivity without the loss of quality standards. Remaining competitive in this high-technology environment is complicated by both design and capability improvements which render yesterday's state-of-the-art equipment obsolete.

The responsibility of the prudent marketing manager should not be to attempt to provide an optimal financial equation or decision hurdle, but rather to make certain that all appropriate variables are examined in order to establish an unbiased basis for the lease/buy decision. The responsibility of the marketing manager, then, is to assemble the implications of the broad issues which should complement the competent financial analysis and make certain each is included in the decision.

Other Works to Consult

Babber, John E. "Improving Capital Budgeting Decisions: Seeking a More Constant Hurdle Rate." *Financial Executive*, 50 (8), 37.

Bierman, Harold Jr., & Seymour Smidt. *The Capital Budgeting Decision: Economic Analysis of Investment Projects.* New York: Macmillan.

Bigelow, Robert P. "Legal Info." *Infosystems*, 28 (5), 128-129

Donaldson, Gordon. "Financial Goals: Management Versus Stockholders." *Harvard Business Review*, 41 (3), 116.

Gitman, Lawrence J. *Principles of Managerial Finance*. New York: Harper and Row.

Lerner, Eugene M., & Alfred Rappaport. (1975). "Limit DCF in Capital Budgeting." *Information for Decision Making: Quantitative and Behavioral Dimensions*. Englewood Cliffs, NJ: Prentice Hall.

Liao, Shu S. "Shareholder-Oriented Managers Versus Entity-Oriented Managers." *Financial Analysts Journal*, 31 (6), 63.

Moore, Roger A. "Risk Factors in Accepted and Rejected New Industrial Products." *Industrial Marketing Management*, 11 (1), 9.

Radford, K. J. *Managerial Decision Making*. Reston, VA: Reston Publishing Company.

Schaifer, Robert. "Decisions, Decisions." *Harvard Business School Bulletin,* 58 (2), 137.

Van Horne, James C. *Financial Management and Policy*. Englewood Cliffs, NJ: Prentice Hall.

Whitehead, Alfred North. *Adventures of Ideas*. New York: Macmillan.

For sample study questions, see Appendix J.

This presentation was first delivered as a regional professional development seminar to Illinois Bell Telephone Company and was entitled, "New Product Development—Myth and Application."

New Product Development

Pre-Product Lifecycle (PPLC)

New Product Myth

What is a new product? My students complain that the answer to this question is ambiguous and frustrating. On one end of the spectrum, we have a product or service developed truly on "original thought." Yet philosophers tell us that there is relatively little original thought which takes place. (However, I believe that most observers of marketing would agree that a product originated in this way would meet any test for "NEW.")

Clearly, the position on the other extreme is that any product is new as long as that is what it is called, or that it is a "new" product as long as the company offering the product for sale has not done so in the past. Hardly anyone is fooled any longer by the many claims of "new" and "improved," but companies keep on using this worn-out prose. Perhaps these misguided organizations really believe that consumers are that gullible, or that if enough companies use this promotional ruse, customers will be confused.

I am reminded of a similar political analogy explained by the comedian Bob Hope. When faced with the proposition that both Republicans and Democrats argue against raising taxes and yet no matter which political party is in power taxes still go up, Hope concluded that the Republicans can't fool all the people all the time and the Democrats can't fool all the people all the time. That's why they need a two-party system—to fool all the people all the time!

Well, then, where is the truth of what a new product is? A new product is not new based on giving it a different nominal "moniker" (name).   In order to be considered new, it must be SUBSTANTIALLY different in terms of performance, application, and market. For example, touch-tone telephone and rotary dialing coexist on the same 56-kilobyte voice-grade telephone line. Both provided dial tone to the customer and basic in- and out-bound features. From the customer's point of view, these products are very similar other than the cosmetic difference in making or receiving a call (not a new product). But, the moment we offer a customer the capability of on-line computer access or fax with the basic service, only touch-tone can provide the necessary transmission and switching capability (a new product).

Application of a certain technology may also make the difference in observing a truly new product delivery. One can argue that the emergence of the digital wristwatch was not a new product. In fact, other than observing numbers instead of "hands," the devices provided the same output—time. However, when we look at the date stamp of calls on our personal, business, and cellular phone bills, we realize that the application of digital technology was necessary to develop this powerful, new application. (Hypothetically, analog measurement could have provided a similar application but not practically.)

Providing a certain existing service or product can qualify as new if it is being offered in a new venue or market for the first time. For example, when Italian pizza was introduced to the United States in the early 1900's, and again to the former Soviet Union in the late 1900's,—it was the same offering, nearly a century apart (a new product).

Whether practitioners and observers of the marketplace agree or not on the definition of "new" may not really be that important. (In each of the preceding cases, ultimately the consumer's perception will determine whether a product is new or not new.) What is important is that we understand how the consumer sees a particular product or service and then react correctly from a strategic and tactical standpoint in order to achieve a successful product entry.[126]

Idea Generation

The introductory study of new product development generally assumes that somehow there is an existing product to relate to—an obvious assumption, to be sure. But where, then, DO new products come from? Product/service ideas come to those organizations and marketers that maintain a vigil to look for them. There are the more obvious places such as research and development (the AT&T transistor or DuPont's Teflon); employee suggestions (Sears' pin release hand tool ratchet or 3M's post-it notes); and market research (7-up Bottling Company and diet 7-up or Pacific telephone and voice message services, VMS) or Apple and the iPhone. Following is a list of not so common places where new product idea generation may be evident: customers' suggestions, sales representatives, competition, byproducts, R&D "mistakes," and government "Star Wars'" type RFP's.

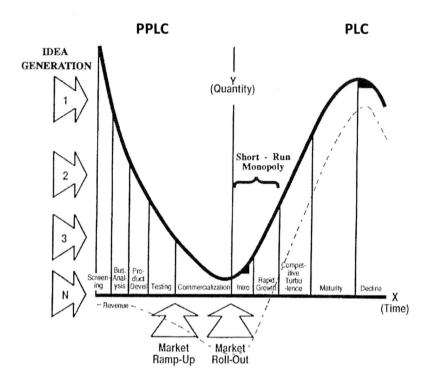

Note: When observing a company's individual new product revenue in the market demand analysis, do not confuse a revenue curve with a profit curve.

Screening

Business "types" sometimes have a difficult time maintaining focus on this stage of the process. We feel much more comfortable moving right on to business analysis and, in fact, confuse some parts of screening with our basic business instincts and skills. The best way to apply proper screening is to make no revenue, break-even or return on investment calculation here.

While it is prudent to consider the general viability (concept) of the product or service, the discussion should focus on an overview of the characteristics of demand, capital goods, human asset, distribution, and design capabilities of the offering. (Specific measurements and forecasts will be developed in the business analysis stage.) The critical elements of screening to consider are the congruence or compatibility of the product service offering to the mix of products currently being sold. Is the offering of this "new" product going to interfere with success of existing ones?

The outcome can go either way. For example, the original diet 7-up offering was not successful and, in fact, caused a decided market share decline in its healthy regular 7-up position. Yet the unusual union of Phillip Morris' purchasing Kraft has been reasonably successful. Again, the issue of most interest to the marketing manager should not be a definition or clinical set of operational procedures but, rather, an evaluation of potential customer reaction/perception. Some early consumer panels, trials, or SMSA (standard metropolitan statistical area) evaluations could be useful here.

Business Analysis

This phase of the PPLC (pre-product life cycle) examines, in detail, the fiscal calculations leading to the comparison of the product/service return on investment to the hurdle rate of the host organization. In other words, the basic two parts of the business analysis "boiler plate" are the specific project ROI and the individual organization's minimum fiscal risk profile (hurdle rate percentage).

The hurdle rate is, in fact, an *a priori* decision of return based on industry standards, organizational fiscal health, and relative aversion to risk. Once the rate is set by the firm, each new product idea must provide at least that level of return or be rejected as an unacceptable opportunity loss. In order to make an accurate forecast of ROI, we need first to determine the levels of a few basic variables in that equation: propensity, pricing, and promotional research—to determine the breadth of the potential segment (industry) and the possible depth of the segment (firm's penetration/market share).

Next, load the indirect and direct costs of production: raw materials (don't forget to consider economies of scale here), administration and overhead, human assets (production), capital goods, any unique costs of technologies, costs of capital, and opportunity loss of potential competing product offerings or other fiscal opportunities.

Based on these specific calculations and by adding the pricing data we collected in the propensity analysis of the consumer, we can multiply [price x units] to determine a forecast revenue, subtract total costs, compare the result to the capital investment required, and determine the approximate return on investment. And, by comparing it to our *a priori* hurdle rate, we determine whether or not this particular product "survives" the business analysis phase for new product development.

Product Development

So far, the entire analysis has been forecast, speculative, or *a priori* in nature. But now the specifications presented to the production engineers must be brought to actual fruition in the form of an operational prototype. Many times the engineers are faced with idea generation outcomes of lighter, faster, stronger, cheaper, etc., and any one of these value-added characteristics may prove impossible to produce in reality.

Product development is where the "rubber meets the road." Certainly, if a product fails here because of a raw material, plastic may have to be changed to aluminum in the specification. But, necessarily, this will cause changes in the business analysis evaluation—once again the product may not survive. Design flaws may not be so easy to correct. But, if engineering is capable to create the functioning prototype, it is now on to the quality control engineers for testing.

Product Testing

Product testing is not a requirement in many cases. But, there remain two basic reasons to consider testing before taking a product or service to market. First is a legal/ethical issue (*caveat venditor*). Examples might be Upjohn's development of the pharmaceutical Rogaine; or Morton-Thiokol's production of rocket booster components for a space vehicle launch. The second reason to test a product is to find out if there might be a potential loss of loyalty to the specific product or the firm's entire product mix, brand, or trademark. An organization cannot "flirt" with the possibility of damaging so fragile a relationship as the customers' positive perception of the firm's image.

Now two main reasons that some companies choose not to test: First, time is always an issue in an efficient product deployment, particularly if there is imminent competition. The "strategic window" is ever-moving, and the fear of missing the opportunity can be a strong deterrent to testing. The second persuasion to forego testing is the constant nemesis of budget constraints. Product testing can be a very expensive phase of product development.

Most organizations do decide to do some form of product testing. The question now becomes, "How extensive a testing program should be used?" There is no specific operating procedure here or even a basic "rule of thumb." I have been in a position to make an interesting observation of the divergent opinion, however. Being involved with many high-technology clients, I have been faced with the philosophy of "zero defect." In fact, this phrase may be seen plastered on posters covering walls in administrative offices, engineering laboratories, production floors, and physical distribution facilities of many well-known companies. For some, it is a slogan and no more than that. For others, it is a passion, almost an obsession.

For the organizations that make critical components or products such as heart pace-makers, the "slogan" must be a reality. But, if we are making automobiles zero defect for the entire product and its components is a promotional feature not a production reality. Why? A crusty (but very successful) national sales manager for a Fortune 100 company remarked to me that if a product does not have a reasonably substantial return or failure rate, then the organization is paying too much of its profit out for unnecessary quality control standards. While this may seem, at first, an irresponsible remark, if we plot a dependency relationship between dollar cost and zero defect, there is a very interesting result.

High levels of product failure are associated with relatively low costs of quality assurance. Even moderate levels of QA are not terribly expensive, although this relationship between cost and zero defect does produce a curve which increases at an increasing rate. But, as the company attempts to move those last percentage points toward zero defect, the cost curve becomes exponential. And, if as the sales manager suggests, the product or service does not warrant a perfect (or near perfect) level of assurance, then perhaps the company is paying too much for an unrealistically low level of returned product.

A classic example was American Telephone and Telegraph Company. The QC decision for telephone sets (both PBX and residential) was 100 years of service before failure was acceptable. While this level was extreme, it may have made some sense in the days when AT&T only leased their equipment. But, in the mid-1980's, the decision to sell equipment made the cost of this quality control unrealistic for profit maximization.

Who does the testing? There are several well-respected laboratories such as UL which test products and provide credible results. The firm can do its own testing, but, clearly, the results may be somewhat more suspect. (In the case of certain technology firms which are radically advanced to the edge of the "applied envelope," no one else is capable to test their products.) Occasionally, "beta" testing is useful in certain product deployments. But, be careful: (1) results can be spurious since the environment is not laboratory-controlled, and (2) this approach constitutes a partial rollout of the product—can we afford to expose the product offering? Several trade associations have established acceptable industry standards and do effective testing of certain types of products as well.

A last remark on testing. A great many authors and educators discuss testing of markets and market research at this juncture. I believe that most practitioners will agree with me that whether originated from a consumer need or created to fill a consumer want, the time for effective market research occurs prior to the product testing phase.

Commercialization

My students say that commercialization is what is left to do after subtracting all the other phases from the process! This is not too far from the truth. But a few items are "specifically redundant" to earlier phases discussed. For example, the business forecasts and estimates made earlier must now be considered actual (*i.e.,* raw material acquisition, unit price, inventory units). Production which began on the heels of testing must now be "ramped-up" in order to inventory product for deployment at market "rollout." Earlier, we considered the viability of physical distribution; now, we must put in place the actual channel members, devise their incentives, and develop/provide any product-specific training required for capable sales and shipment of the product.

The components of an effective promotional strategy must begin with the development of the campaign theme (objective). Next, create the message, develop the copy and graphic materials, select and contract for the mediums to execute the strategy television, news print, magazines, billboards, radio, handbills, brochures, trade shows, and others.) We will include packaging here, although an argument can be made that today, packaging is a part of three of the four "P's" marketing mix areas (physical distribution, product, and promotion).

The package can serve many purposes: (1) to protect the product, (2) to showcase the product, (3) to provide exterior shape consistent with economical pallet or break shipping requirements, (4) to educate and inform, (5) to add value to the product by providing a secondary use (*i.e.*, a refillable container or some other after-market use), or (6) simply to indicate international symbols for shipment instruction to channel carriers. The students are essentially correct: commercialization requires a vigil over any remaining details before the next step—market introduction and product rollout.

Certainly not a detail, but just prior to or during the commercialization phase of the PPLC, the marketer may be faced with multiple product survival. Suppose that more than one new product satisfies all of the requirements for entry into the market. Decision theory will improve the manager's ability to select the product which will yield the greatest return by constructing a tree representing the chronological decisions and events of probability. Let's examine our two surviving products, 1 and 2.

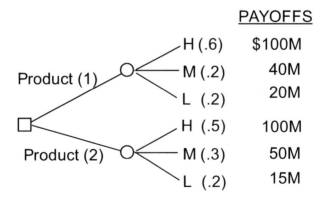

PAYOFFS

H (.6)	$100M
M (.2)	40M
L (.2)	20M
H (.5)	100M
M (.3)	50M
L (.2)	15M

Product (1)

Product (2)

Notice that we can decide by choice which product to produce. But events associated with probability are occurrences beyond our control. (It is important to note that any event fork possibilities must sum to 100%.) In this example, Product 1 has a 60% chance of high market penetration, a 20% chance of moderate market penetration, and a 20% chance of low market penetration.

In order to determine the product payoffs, the marketing manager must "fold" back the payoffs by multiplying each payoff by its respective probability and then add each result to reach a 100% probability of that total event. For example, the first product's total payoff = [(0.6 x $100m) + (0.2 x $40m) + (0.2 x $20m)], = $72 million. The second product's total payoff = [(0.5 x $100m) + (.3 x $50m) + (0.2 x $15m)] = $68 million. Therefore, the marketer would select the upper fork—Product 1.

This decision analysis is a very simplified example. More than two surviving products could be included, and serial decisions or events in any natural number or order could be represented. Further, event probabilities have been assumed here, but certainly each pre- and posterior probability would be carefully calculated from our fundamental understanding and diligent application of statistical probability formulae. Also, payoffs and market penetration estimates come from the business analysis performed earlier in the PPLC. Yet, even simply applied, the market manager can see the advantage of a payoff analysis to help select the most capable market entry.

The Product Life-cycle and Demand (PLC)

Product life cycle as a concept provides a model for logical treatment of product sales demand and stages of product acceptance[127] among consumers. When plotted on a one-dimensional graph, the PLC displays the correlation between the quantity of product demanded and time, where sales demand is the dependent variable and elapsed time is the independent variable (see preceding graphic).

The logic is that time goes on, the demand for a product will change. By separating the demand into stages, the market manager can anticipate and make certain strategic decisions and resource allocations more effectively. While opinions vary among professionals regarding its application, timing, and even number of stages, the Product Life Cycle provides for a logical framework to anticipate and consider management action during a product's entry into and exit from the marketplace.

The steepness of the slope (incline or decline) of a demand curve is based on how rapidly a product is purchased by consumers, once it is "launched" or rolled out into the market. The idea for this acceptance rate was developed by Everett Rogers.[128] He referred to the phenomenon, the "diffusion of innovation," later to be more commonly known as "the adoption curve." (See graphic in the Segmentation section of this book.) The PLC will emulate the adoption curve, as both are based on consumer demand. As products or services enter or leave these life cycle stages, the manager will be faced with different threats, opportunities, and challenges.

Most researchers and authors consider these four basic stages of introduction, growth, maturity, and decline. Others have included as many as seven stages, adding rapid growth, competitive turbulence, and exit to more specifically delineate strategic management decision points or specific issues related to the timing of markets. It is for the latter reason that competitive turbulence will be included in the analysis that follows. In this model, the shape or skew of the curve for a particular product is determined by the relationship between demand and time. Irrespective of the shape the curve takes, it will include all PLC stages.

Introduction Stage

The introduction stage begins as the product moves from the commericalization stage of the PPLC or the strategy of "ramping up" to the actual "rolling out" of the product into the marketplace for sale. This is the first opportunity that the product has to be purchased—it is now "in the market." The sunk costs accumulated during the PPLC continue. Resource allocation remains high during this phase.

The transition from commercialization to introduction requires continued advertising to inform and educate the prospective consumer. Finished goods and inventories must be developed. While sales levels will be minimal during this stage, soliciting customer feedback is important from those who do purchase. These feedback allow corrective actions, such as product changes, safety improvement, and necessary recalls while market penetration (retail customers) and install base (business customers) remain low. A new product introduction can anticipate some sales activity in the form of revenue, but break-even is unlikely during this stage, and the continuing sunk cost of the PPLC remains a deterrent to profitability. A new product entry at this stage can anticipate little or no competition from other firms.

Growth Stage

Sales begin to increase at an increasing rate. Revenues will begin to reach and pass break-even. Profitability will be reached during short-run monopoly and the enjoyment of high pricing. Product awareness by the market will begin to stabilize increased demand. Inventory, channel relationships, and physical distribution begin to normalize. Increased sales volumes should translate into production efficiencies and economies of scale. If the market demand increases sharply, the beginning of additional market entrants can be anticipated and competition begins. Increases in overall market size allows for competitors to grow their market shares simultaneously.

Page 199

Competitive Turbulence

In markets where sharp increases of sales occur during the growth stage of a product, the initial manufacturer can benefit from large rates of return with high prices, very high, or even "obscene" pricing. Large numbers of competing firms will enter the market to also take advantage of the demand created by the first entrant. The turbulence created by this intense competition will tend to dramatically force down prices and profit for the initial entrant. Remember, successive competitors do not have to overcome the startup and development costs incurred by the first market entrant, and, therefore, can reach profitability at a much lower price point. Also, it is likely that the short-run incidental monopoly position enjoyed by the firm first entering the market will be lost as well.

Maturity

During the maturity stage, demand decreases at an increasing rate. Prices among competitors continue to fall, further reducing profit. A few competitors continue to enter the market, further eroding revenues until saturation of the market is reached.   Marginal competitors begin to leave the market. Large manufacturers will have short-term benefits of large-scale production efficiencies and inventories. Branding and promotional activities will be essential to survival. Extreme price competition will continue as product proliferation creates reduction in market shares. The market now becomes a zero sum game, so for one competitor to increase market share, another one must lose penetration.

Decline

This stage begins with long-term stabilization of sales volume and then a decline.   Demand is reduced and price reductions will become severe, if not predatory. Profitability will be very difficult to maintain, and inventories should be closely monitored and reduced. The decision to abandon a product altogether must be considered and is a normal evolution of the life cycle process. Migration from what the Boston Consulting Group termed a "cash cow" during growth and maturity can just as rapidly become a "dog" or liability during decline.

Short-Run "Incidental" Monopoly

It should be no surprise that when Chrysler was going bankrupt in the late 1970s, General Motors factored some of Chrysler's accounts receivable and saved the struggling company from going out of business. Did this act occur from an altruistic gesture of camaraderie? No. As we have discussed, GM's decision was calculated to keep the Justice Department from viewing the domestic auto industry as monopolistic. In our current mixed economy (monopoly, oligopoly, and free competition), monopoly is regarded as not in the best interest of the consumer and illegal as a restraint of trade. Chrylser again faced bankruptcy in 2009. This time, to avoid a monopolistic auto industry (due to a major company being forced to leave), the Obama Administration and the Democratic Congress voted to provide stimulus monies to Chrysler to make certain the company did not fail.

However, short-run positions of "incidental" monopoly are sought by certain companies and are tolerated by the Justice Department. Notice that as the pre-product curve decreases over time, an associated "negative profit" curve develops below the zero demand axis and grows more negative as time and the PPLC develop toward market rollout and slightly beyond. This relationship clearly demonstrates that firms which develop truly new products incur unique and heavy costs to bring new product offerings to the market.

These costs are avoided by the competing firm that waits until market rollout, then emulates the original product or, worse, "reverse engineers" the concept and competes with the originating firm. Realize that the "knock-off" or illegitimately competing firm has relatively little investment if they join the process after the originating firm deploys and rolls out the product or service.

The originating firm does have the advantage of being in the marketplace first. And, depending on the shape of the demand curve, that firm will have an incidental monopolistic advantage in the short run. The advantage may last quite a while if (1) no firm chooses to compete quickly; (2) the barriers to entry are high; (3) patent or copyright protection is available; [This possibility is quite low in competitive markets like technology, fashion, trends etc. because the length of time required to secure a patent will far outstrip the "half-life" before the next generation of product in that type industry is developed.] or (4) the firm has experience in developing the product. This characteristic offers an economy of scale and application development advantage. This latter situation may continue to provide a significant advantage in warding off serious competitive threats, creating a monopolistically competitive environment.

While it is true that the originating firm must have the incentive of short-run competitive advantages (or no firm would risk new product development), in order to overcome investment disadvantages, one of two things is certain. Either competitive turbulence "settles" the market imbalance, or the Justice Department ultimately will.

Demand Curve Myth

It is refreshing to see that contemporary introductory Marketing texts are beginning to discuss demand curves. The product life-cycle is, of course, a demand curve. It is a graphic representation of a demand schedule.[129] Yet, traditionally, we expose students early-on in their study of marketing to the classical PLC. This classical curve often becomes imprinted in our minds as the only possible demand outcome. The "classical" demand curve is really the anomaly. It suggests a series of averages: an average company, an average product or service, an average price, an average customer, etc.   In reality, each of these characteristics will be unique in most situations, thus causing dissimilar outcomes (shapes) of the curve.

Consider, measure, and forecast your potential demand curves. That's what all that econometric machination and calculus was for! Today's plethora of statistical software routines can help. Keep the methodology simple. Remember, the object is to explain as much as we can about demand by using the fewest number of variables possible (a fact too often forgotten as we construct and apply forecast formulae). The two most important forecasts to notice in the product life-cycle are the initial increase during introduction and the initial decrease during decline. (See the shaded deltas on the PLC illustration presented earlier.)

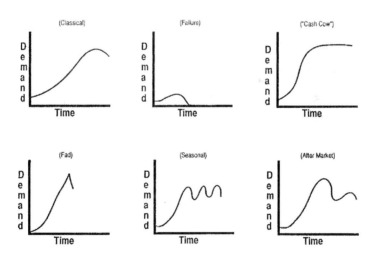

While it is true that curvilinear regression is prevalent for setting demand curves, it is also true that by observing increases (or decreases) in regression coefficients, together with the slope (R positive or negative), even simple regression can be useful to help observe diffusion of innovation in the form of forecasting life cycles and demand curves. (See "Forecasting for Market Management" in this book.)

Summary

Are you developing a truly new product or not? What are the chances of the "idea" surviving to roll out? What is the shape, trajectory, and slope of the demand curve? How long can a monopoly and monopolistic competition be expected to last? How much "unfair" competitive advantage can be counted on before the Justice Department takes an interest?

The consideration of these and the other questions raised are essential to skillful and effective market entry applications. Remember, build carefully the pre-product strategy and then deliver the product with conscientious post rollout tactics.

For sample study questions, see Appendix J.

This presentation was first delivered as a professional development seminar to Memorex Corporation and was entitled, "Where Do I Make It and "Moor It, and How Do I Move It?"

Channels and Physical Distribution

Probably the simplest way to begin a discussion of channels and physical distribution is to first simplify the definitions of each and then "rebuild" each definition from its piece-parts. In the most general of terms, think of channels as being made up of the members or people of a logistics network, and think of physical distribution as the means of storage (warehousing and inventory) and movement (shipping and freight) of products.

Channel Members

Channel members in typical retail consumer environments would appear as follows:

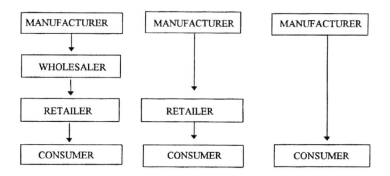

Clearly, each member of the channel is compensated for the value that each adds in bringing the product to the marketplace (*e.g.,* fees, commissions, mark-ups, etc.). It might appear at first glance that the most efficient delivery system for the manufacturer is to sell direct to the consumer. However, as we consider selling regionally, nationally, and internationally, it becomes apparent that in order to increase the size of the market or to more fully penetrate an existing market, channel members provide a valuable service to the manufacturer.

Troy-Built used the direct-to-consumer approach when it first made rototillers as a small manufacturing company in Troy, New York. As Troy-Built increased its product line and wanted to expand its market share nationally, channel members "came with the territory" and are now sold nationally by Lowe's and Orchard Supply Hardware. Some companies, with the help of the Internet, such as Dell Computers, successfully compete nationally direct-to-customer. As the size of the company expands and the number of units sold rises, a direct channel becomes increasingly difficult to maintain.

The **wholesaler** assists its manufacturer by facilitating the sale of large quantities of bulk into a more manageable volume of sales to one or more retail outlets. A common example of wholesaling occurs in the cosmetics business where stylists, salons, and beauty boutiques purchase products wholesale for application and resale.

Wholesalers are used in the industrial and commercial markets when sales are not generally made to an account on a regular basis but, rather, many smaller sales are made in a more random manner in the market. Wholesalers also contribute in developing assortments of products, maintaining inventories, providing faster restocking capabilities, helping with retail financing, taking title, dealing with shrinkage, and discovering new products and services for their customers (retailers).

Residential construction firms such as Shea, Citation, and Chappel use regional lumber wholesalers to supply their raw material needs. The **retailer** acts as a conduit or reseller to the end user. This part of the sales process is generally fulfilled by boutiques, independent stores, and chain stores. Nordstrom,

Neiman-Marcus, and Macy's are good examples of retail resellers in the consumer apparel market.

Channel members in typical commercial industrial environments would appear as follows:

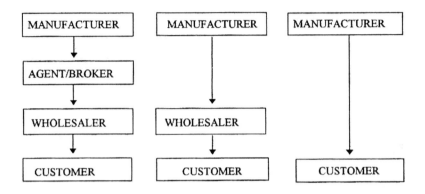

The **agent** provides a sales force for the manufacturer, which, many times, cannot afford one or does not feel that its expertise lies in the actual sale but, rather, primarily in the efficient production of the product. Apple and Hewlett-Packard use agents to resell their computer products. In these cases, the agents act as value-added resellers or VARs. The agents for Apple, for example, may bundle peripherals, products, compatible hardware and software, or provide product service and training to wholesalers and end-users. These are valuable enhancements to the customer and provide a substantial contribution to the manufacturer's sales effort.

A **broker** may be used when sales are made in large lots or when sales are in an international market outside the manufacturer's host country. An agricultural example is a domestic farming cooperative that uses a broker to sell its wheat crop to Russia. (Very large commercial or industrial construction firms such as Hyundai or Bechtel might use a lumber broker to deliver in large lots from sources thousands of miles away.)

Whether a short or long channel is selected is based primarily on the type of product, its value, the sales capability and financial position of the manufacturer, as well as the market share and profit desired. It must be remembered, however, that the longer the channel is, the less control the manufacturer has over its product and the relationship with its customer base.

The typical channel member relationships presented here can be and are modified in length from time to time. Chewing gum, for example, is nearly a "commodity" (relatively inexpensive, reasonably generic, and widely available) by definition and is found in almost every food, confection, and drug store, as well as in most restaurants in the United States. The physical distribution of this product requires a long chain of channel members to complete. On the other hand, as an example of a short channel, Cartier manufactures custom, one-of-a-kind pieces of estate jewelry (the opposite of a "commodity") for an individual. The channel is very short because it requires sittings, drawings, and personal trials with the end user—and the price may well be in the $100,000's.

Further, some manufacturers vertically integrate and possess an ownership or financial interest in their channel. Irrespective of their ownership, manufacturers should re-evaluate the channel relationships from time to time. The elimination of non-productive (irresponsible) members and venues as well as the addition of new (responsible) members and venues based on profit motive will improve market share and return on investment.

Channel Member Responsibilities

Decisions regarding the increase or decrease of channel members must not be made lightly, and, when the decision is made, the selection of the right channel member should be based on several factors:

1. How rapidly is the prospective channel member capable to fill customer orders?

2. How willing is the prospective channel member to fill special orders or emergency requests of customers?

3. How willing is the prospective channel member to oversee "shrinkage" (breakage, loss, and theft) of the product?

4. To what extent will the channel member carry deep inventories of the product?

5. How anxious will the prospective channel member be to take back defective, exchanged, or damaged product on the customer's and manufacturer's behalf?

6. Will the prospective channel member carry necessary replacement or maintenance inventory?

7. Will the channel member accept the responsibility to train, to service, and/or to install the product for the end customer?

8. Can the channel member be trusted to assure goodwill with the end user?

9. How interested is the channel member in reselling the manufacturer's particular product as opposed to others which the channel member may also stock?

10. How capable is the prospective channel member to remain in business and remain fiscally responsible to follow price guidelines, pay invoices, and manage EOQ (economic order quantities)?

When evaluating potential or existing channel members, remember that each of the previous requirements (from the manufacturer's point of view) may very well be looked at as burdens or liabilities (from the member's point of view). The channel member makes money very differently than does the manufacturer. The member is most efficient if s/he "handles the product only one time" for a sale. It is for this reason that channel incentives or demand "push" in the forms of "spiffs," promotions, or cooperative advertising may be necessary to motivate the channel network.

Physical Distribution

When manufacturers consider the larger definition of physical distribution, it must include strategic decisions with regard to location of production facilities, location of warehouse facilities, freight options, inventory policies, and packaging applications.

Decisions regarding the location of **production facilities** may include local, state, or national restrictions concerning heavy, medium, or light manufacturing requirements. There may be income tax incentives (*i.e.,* duty-free trade zones) or decentives (school, sewer, and/or emergency services bond requirements). The availability, quality, and cost of labor, proximity of raw materials, and cost of real estate (lease or purchase) must be considered. Further, the political, special, and general public interests may have a substantial bearing—each can be a positive or negative influence on the business decision.

The manufacturer must consider where to locate its **warehouse facilities**. Many of the considerations here are similar to those evaluated for production location but are usually less volatile due to the "lighter industrial" zoning restrictions for warehousing facilities. All things being equal, the manufacturer will want to locate its inventory as close to its first channel member as possible. If, as we saw earlier, the manufacturer uses a direct selling approach, the inventory should be kept as close to the customer as possible.

Check to make certain that movement of the product is both legal and possible. For example, in California, local, state, and regional restrictions have been levied in terms of GRVW (gross rated vehicle weight) on roadways, freeway off-ramps, and bridges. Further, if a major change in road access or perhaps a rail spur will be required, unless each already exists, it will be almost impossible to build, due to cost, easements, and right-of-ways.

Efficiency is the cornerstone to effective **freight policies** and is based primarily on cost, type of product, value of the product, and availability of the freight medium. When the relative efficiency of freight options (based on weight and bulk) are considered, pipeline is the most cost effective, then waterway, next railway (for example, rail can carry a ton of freight 500 miles on one gallon of fuel)[130], then motor carrier, and the least efficient is airline. Electronic multi-media in the forms of 56 KB land line and satellite must be considered viable means of product and service delivery systems. This high-technology delivery system is clearly the most cost effective means of physical distribution.

When a manufacturer considers the energy that goes into its market mix decisions, positioning strategies, and AIDA effort, it cannot afford to make errors in **inventory policy**. When the combination of these strategies results in customer propensity for the product, all can be lost—the sale, reputation, add-on sales, and repeat sales—if the demand cannot be met due to low/no inventory. Here is an opportunity for the manufacturer to apply and require channel members to apply economic order quantity procedures.

$$EOQ = \sqrt{2SO/ip}$$

<u>where:</u>

S= annual quantity sold in units   O= cost of placing an order

i=carrying cost as a percent of   p= dollar price per unit
   selling price

Packaging applications have become a major added value to the sale of almost all product offerings, whether due to "political" damage control (*i.e.,* the Tylenol incident), shrink packing of "bundled sales," reusable containers (ecology), commercial containers (tractor/rail/air), bulk pallets, physical damage control, or advertising. No longer can a manufacturer think of packaging as a perfunctory necessity to the movement of goods. Packaging is and will continue to be a strategic part of the sale to the end user of the product.

Conclusion

The relationship between manufacturers and channel members is a complex one, sometimes resulting in cooperation, sometimes resulting in conflict. While it is true that there are clear and different, even competing, business "agendas" among the logistics of product manufacturers, resellers, and consumers (customers), each also has a unique and selfish reason to effect the final sale of a product.

As individuals, we cannot understand why, for example, in 2011, the National Football League (NFL) found itself in the midst of a labor dispute and a player lockout threatening the 2011 season, or why the National Hockey League players and owners had a work stoppage in 1994 causing the disruption of season play as well as the all-star game.

Not until early in the 1995 playing season were their differences worked out. Their commissioner said, "...finally each side has realized its common goal and recognized that each individual interest could be met only through common agreement (salaries and ticket sales) concerning the product—to skate for the fans." And so it is in the channel and physical distribution area of business and industry—<u>no</u> <u>one</u> profits unless the customer makes a purchase.

For sample study questions, see Appendix J.

This article was first published in the California Business Education Journal *and was entitled, "Program Evaluation Review Technique: A Physical Distribution Application."*

Physical Distribution: An Application

The PERT (Program Evaluation and Review Technique) concept for decision making is not a new tool, particularly in the quantitative methods. PERT was developed in the 1960s by Booz, Allen, and Hamilton, Inc., for use by the United States Government Defense Department in research and development. The current approach is to adopt PERT as a reasoning discipline model for students and practitioners in market management. PERT is used to schedule and anticipate component and successive steps of a project.

The steps are represented by circles (O) and ordered by their relative importance and necessary sequence. James March and Herbert Simon have expressed the decision dilemma as a study of three states: certainty, uncertainty, and risk. Certainty is the basic assumption that all relevant facts are known. Uncertainty is the assumption that there is a significant field of variable unknowns. And risk represents the area between the two.

While it is true that network analysis is more practical for complicated problems, it provides logical, systematic, rational, and quantitative guidelines to communication, projections, resource consumption, and scheduling, allowing valuable feedback for corrective action to deviations.[131]

Management of Time

A PERT analysis is concerned with time management. A systematic schedule of events is determined; and, collectively, the network allows a strategy selection based on statistical probability of project success. The basic PERT chart is organized from the logical steps of the procedures which comprise the total project. Each step to be accomplished is defined as an event. The resources to accomplish the event are expended on the path or route to the next logical event. An activity is the accomplishment of the work necessary to achieve the completion of an event along the PERT path. PERT considers that the scarcest resource to be exhausted is time.

A Single Path Model

Consider an example of shipping product by truck from San Francisco if your customer is based in New York, and they need the items in five days. A simple network for this problem might consider only one route: San Francisco (1st event) to Salt Lake City (2nd event) to Des Moines (3rd event) to New York (4th event). We make three estimations of time between each of the four events/activities on the path.

We first need to determine the optimistic time (T_o), or the least amount of time under optimal conditions we believe it will take the shipment to reach Salt Lake City from San Francisco. The second time estimate or "most likely time" (T_m) is determined assuming there could be inclement weather, a flat tire, or some other minor delay. The third time determined is "pessimistic time" (T_p), or the worst of all worlds under Murphy's Law.[132]

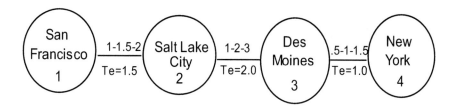

We now have three educated guesses which will be refined one further generation to a single time estimate for each portion of the path, expected time (T_e). The expected time formula is the next attempt in refine our network. These PERT formulas display constant weight factors of 6 and 4, which are so defined but will not be proven here. Loading of the factors creates a weighting which favors "most likely time."

The PERT formulae depend on constant factors of "6" and "4." The "4" weight in the numerator of the T_e formula favors the most likely time estimate in the calculation. The "6" in the denominator represents the number of standard deviations in the distribution. The yield of the T_e formula is affected by the time estimate of the mid-range carrying two-thirds weight. (Therefore the optimistic time and the pessimistic time estimates are each weighted "1," and the most likely time estimate is weighted "4.")[133]

The "6" in the denominator is based on the assumption that the standard deviation of the distribution is 1/6 the range of possible time estimates. (This assumption presumes that both tails of the probability distribution lie three standard deviations from the mean—three above the mean and three below the mean.) The T_m weight is based on the fact that 95% of a normal distribution falls within two standard deviations above and below the mean.

$$T_e = \frac{T_o + [T_m(4)] + T_p}{6}$$

On this basis, expected times are calculated for all remaining segments of the path or activities. Suppose then that we have established T_e's for the path segments: 1.5 days, 2.0 days, and 1.0 days, respectively. Following PERT procedure, we now make an adjustment for the variance (V) or area of uncertainty in our estimates of expected time. Using our original time estimates between each event, we establish a variance for the individual segment and account for any error generated by T_e (a point estimate):

$$V = [\frac{T_p - T_o}{6}]^2$$

By summing all of the individual T_e's and variances, we are able to use the last formula to determine the probability that product will reach our customer by the contract time.

Where T_s = Time Constraint

$$Z = \frac{T_s - \sum T_e}{\sqrt{\sum V}}$$

Calculating the respective variances to be .03, .11, and .03, then:

$$Z = \frac{(5 \text{ days}) - (4.5 \text{ days})}{.41} = 1.22$$

This final number, z = 1.22, is the measure of success of our entire problem.   By locating this number on a table of areas for standard normal probability distribution (area under the normal curve), we determine that the corresponding probability that our shipment will arrive on or before the deadline is approximately .3888, or (.5 + .3888) or 88.88%.   Remember that if you are using a standard Z table, the areas listed are only for one half of the distribution—so add .5 (which represents the other half of the curve).

The Z table (found in the last pages of any basic statistics text and in Appendix C of this book) provides the area in the lower tail for values of the normal deviate (Z).

An interesting feature to note is that if it is possible for the client to accept the shipment three hours late, we can increase our probability of success to 94%:

$$z = \frac{(5.125 \text{ days}) - (4.5 \text{ days})}{.41} = 1.52$$

If, on the other hand, the customer wishes to have the product three hours earlier than five days, our probability of delivering them diminishes to approximately 82%.

$$z = \frac{(4.875 \text{ days}) - (4.5 \text{ days})}{.41} = .91$$

The significance of these manipulations becomes acute when applied to management procedures such as personnel evaluations using management by objectives (MBO), manpower utilization, requisition, budget, and many other applicable areas.

A Multiple Path Model

Now that we understand the mechanics of the single path model, let's move on to a bit more complicated but realistic model—a multi-path configuration (in this case, a two-path example).

In this example, we will examine an internal logistics problem of preparing a hardware shipment together with the corresponding technical documents in order to meet our customer's demand. The contract for delivery in this example stipulates that both the hardware and supporting documents must be delivered FOB to the customer in 35.5 hours.

The PERT program which follows provides the events, their order, the path segments (activities), and the respective forecast of times (optimistic, most likely, and pessimistic).

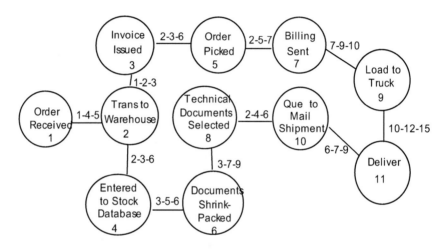

Notice that in a multi-path program, it is now possible to deploy our resources more efficiently by performing tasks simultaneously. In order to determine the probability of success for the sales contract, the same steps performed in the earlier single-path problem must be repeated for each of the activities on **both** paths. Following are the expected-time calculations for the upper and lower paths.

Expected Time: Upper Path

$$1 - 2: \quad T_e = \frac{1 + 4(4) + 5}{6} = \frac{22}{6} = 3.67$$

2 - 3: $\quad T_e = \dfrac{1 + 4(2) + 3}{6} = \dfrac{12}{6} = 2.00$

3 - 5: $\quad T_e = \dfrac{2 + 4(3) + 6}{6} = \dfrac{20}{6} = 3.33$

5 - 7: $\quad T_e = \dfrac{2 + 4(5) + 7}{6} = \dfrac{29}{6} = 4.83$

7 - 9: $\quad T_e = \dfrac{7 + 4(9) + 10}{6} = \dfrac{53}{6} = 8.83$

9 - 11: $\quad T_e = \dfrac{10 + 4(12) + 15}{6} = \dfrac{73}{6} = 12.17$

$$\underline{\sum T_e = 34.83}$$

Expected Time: Lower Path

1 - 2: $\quad T_e = \dfrac{1 + 4(4) + 5}{6} = \dfrac{22}{6} = 3.67$

2 - 4: $\quad T_e = \dfrac{2 + 4(3) + 6}{6} = \dfrac{20}{6} = 3.33$

4 − 6: $\quad T_e = \dfrac{3 + 4(5) + 6}{6} = \dfrac{29}{6} = 4.83$

6 − 8: $\quad T_e = \dfrac{3 + 4(7) + 9}{6} = \dfrac{40}{6} = 6.67$

8 − 10: $\quad T_e = \dfrac{2 + 4(4) + 6}{6} = \dfrac{24}{6} = 4.00$

$$\textbf{10-11:} \quad \mathbf{T_e} = \frac{6 + 4(7) + 9}{6} = \frac{43}{6} = 7.17$$

$$\underline{\Sigma \ \mathbf{T_e} = 29.67}$$

By calculating the respective expected times and then summing the T_e on first the upper path and then the lower path, they may be compared. The comparison of these two numbers will provide the answer as to which one of the paths is the "**critical path**."

When a program has more than one path, the critical path (the path which takes the longest) must be determined before we continue the problem solution. (This step was not necessary in the previous single-path model.) By observing the total T_e for upper and lower paths, we quickly see that the upper path (34.83 hours) is longer and, therefore, the critical path in this particular program. The logic of the term "critical" is that if the longest path is determined, then all other paths will necessarily require less time to complete.

As in the first example, we now wish to identify the point estimate error for the expected-time calculations themselves before continuing. It is important that this error is enumerated, but, more than observed, it must also be calculated and used to influence the final probability of success or failure in the answer.

However, because we have determined the upper path to be "critical," we need only calculate the error (variance) associated with the T_e on that path. (Again, we are assuming that all other paths will be completed in less time and, therefore, will not influence the basic probability outcome.)

Using the same formula applied in the earlier example, the following are the variance calculations for T_e along the upper path.

Variance: Upper Path

1 - 2: $V = \left[\dfrac{5-1}{6} \right] = \dfrac{4}{6} = (.67)^2 = .45$

2 – 3: $V = \left[\dfrac{3-1}{6} \right] = \dfrac{2}{6} = (.33)^2 = .11$

3 – 5: $V = \left[\dfrac{6-2}{6} \right] = \dfrac{4}{6} = (.67)^2 = .45$

5 – 7: $V = \left[\dfrac{7-2}{6} \right] = \dfrac{5}{6} = (.83)^2 = .69$

7 – 9: $V = \left[\dfrac{10-7}{6} \right] = \dfrac{3}{6} = (.50)^2 = .25$

9 - 11: $V = \left[\dfrac{15-10}{6} \right] = \dfrac{5}{6} = (.83)^2 = .69$

$$\underline{\Sigma \ V = 2.64}$$

With the summation of variance calculation on the critical path complete, it is now relatively simple to complete the probability calculation and determine the % chance of completing the delivery on time:

$$z = \frac{35.50 - 34.83}{\sqrt{2.64}} = \frac{.67}{1.63} = .41$$

The probability for a "Z calculated" of .41 (reading from the Z table) is equal to .16. Again, remember that a standard Z table provides only one-half of the total area under the normal curve, so, as in the first example, add .5 to the solution.

$$.16 + .5 = .66$$

Therefore, the probability of delivering the hardware and technical documents to our customer within 35.5 hours is 66%.

Observations

While the virtues of network programming are many, there are a couple of caveats to consider. First, the summation of expected time determines the critical path in PERT. The determination of the critical path is based on the time estimate assumptions—if these times prove inaccurate, a different path may become critical and, in effect, change the probability of success. (Simulation might help here. Monte Carlo simulation, for example, involves many repetitions of the same path calculations.) Second, select only a network program that is probability-based (stochastic). These applications will yield percentage chances of success or failure of the project. Third, do not accept the responsibility for estimating T_o, T_m, and T_p. Depend on historical observation, experienced colleagues, or consultants.

Statistical Approximation

Students have asked if the entire PERT network isn't a guess. It is true that PERT analysis yields an approximation; however, it is based on sound statistical assumption and adjustment for error. A decision maker is far better off with a probable project success of 89%, 94%, 82%, or 60% than to seek risk or be averse with no probability at all. This example is an elementary look at the basic calculations.

In the course, we discuss more complex multi-path models, dummy activities (used to order dependent chronological activities), slack time (calculated to determine the difference between the earliest possible time an event will occur and the latest possible time an event will occur), crash activities (brings the expected activity time completion to its minimum with less regard to cost or efficiency), and other facets of the network necessary to predict success for complex problems. While it is true that marketing is not a course in statistics, and that this quantitative method does not create fail-safe decisions, there is a strong correlation to the systematic application of logical steps and planning in PERT theory and practice.

In the courses, we dwell on logical planning and corrective action to the deviations uncovered. It is the discipline of this logical thought which PERT develops. Consciously or unconsciously, we find ourselves eliminating erroneous steps and discovering neglected ones. PERT is not a panacea for marketing management; however, its structure provides valuable assistance for market decision making.

Bibliography

Lapin, Lawrence L., *Quantitative Methods for Business Decisions*, New York: Harcourt, Brace, Jovanovich, Inc.

Laufer, Arthur C., *Production and Operations Management*, 3rd ed., Cincinnati: Southwestern Publishing Company.

Thierauf, Robert J., Robert C. Klekamp, and Daniel W. Geeding, *Management Principles and Practices*, New York: John Wiley and Sons.

For sample study questions, see Appendix J.

Part Four

Marketing Communications

This article was first published in the California Business Education Journal.

"Two Plus Two Equals Three". [sic]

The statement "2 + 2 = 3" is no more or less incorrect than the statement that periods and commas sometimes are placed within quotation marks. The fact is, two plus two equals four, and periods and commas are always placed inside quotation marks. However, the way these statements appear here, both are equally wrong. Unfortunately, many people mistakenly assume that words are somehow less precise than numbers. The question as to which—words or numbers—have more precision, and therefore "value," arises from a power struggle between English academics and Math academics.

Both seem to be competing against each other for a "power of legitimacy." The struggle between English (a "words" field) and Math (a "numbers" field) stems from the competitive feeling in academia that the various fields of study are all part of a zero-sum game: in order for one concentration or school of thought to be legitimate, valuable, or "right," the others must be, by definition, illicit, less valuable, or "wrong." So far, numbers appear to be ahead in the struggle because many people mistakenly believe (perhaps are taught?) that quantitative methods produce precise answers because they are based on what looks like exacting and intricate formulas. The truth is that many times the answers to even very intricate formulas are merely an educated guess.

Sometimes words, too, tend to be given more legitimacy than they deserve. Many people believe that if something is stated in print, especially in a textbook, it must be true. On the other hand, words sometimes suffer severe legitimacy problems. For some reason, people have a much harder time believing that words can be as legitimate when compared to the legitimacy of numbers. As we interpret and explain something with only words, the explanation is thought to be weak, comparatively, because words are not scientific—they are chosen somewhat randomly by the writer. To compound the problem, words can often have different meanings, depending on the context in which they are used. With these inherent language difficulties, then, words are often thought to be "vague and insupportable."

Interrelationship of Words and Numbers

A faculty member of Temple University suggests "...a basic feature, if not the human condition...is that while practically everyone is in favor of progress, problems are our most important product."[134] He maintains that "there are...many divergent, even passionately divergent, views of what is to be done about these problems."[135] Perhaps it is easier to think of the problem (whatever it might be) as one big elephant which no one field of study can see the whole of. Each academic area sees a part: one field sees the tail, one sees the ears, one sees the large feet.

However, with each field trying to support the idea that it alone has all the answers, each field has a tendency to describe the elephant based on the part they can see. They don't realize that they are seeing only one part of the whole elephant.

If, however, all fields worked together to describe the elephant, the description (and therefore solution to the problem) would be much more complete and accurate. The question is not one of choosing new over old or sciences or arts, but, rather, a realization that we need both for more accurate and complete answers. With the contribution of both words and numbers working together, we will produce solutions and approaches greater than either could provide separately.[136]

The following matrix shows the interrelationship between writing (words) and statistics (numbers).[137] As you can see from the model, the combination of the two (words and numbers) produces an outcome greater than the individual inputs. The assumption of this model is that its area is ever expanding, but only as the two—Mathematics and English—work together. The value of their use together has been and is now clear.

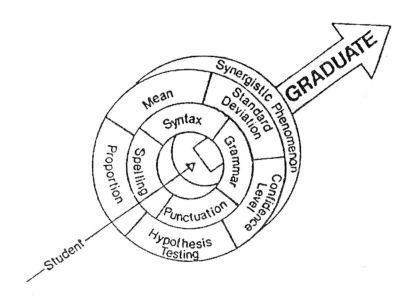

Because we have not wedded the two to date in academia, students have expressed boredom with the subject matter in both "words" courses and "numbers" courses. Because real-world applicability is also missing in many of these courses, students have expressed frustration in attempting to understand and conceptualize, for instance, many statistical concepts—for example, mean, standard deviation, proportion, confidence level, and hypothesis testing.

They suggest that current approaches to the subject matter are classical and only theoretical, that the framework and models only approximate real-world practice. Similar feelings of boredom and lack of applicability are expressed by many students of English about parts of their field of study. These students maintain that the study of grammar, punctuation, spelling, and syntax do not stimulate their interest in developing good writing habits. English students suggest that the isolated repetition of writing is dull, only an exercise of explanation, not creativity.

Graduate students in all fields are then asked at the end of their individual course work to develop theses or dissertations that demand the mixture of both numbers and words. This task proves to be very difficult for many students who have never before been asked to work with both words and numbers together. Faced with this problem, why do colleges wait until late in the candidate's progress toward the terminal degree to require the union of words and numbers? They ought to be requiring the use of the two throughout the curricula!

Realizing the problem that exists for students in using the two simultaneously, colleges and universities are now beginning to develop and require courses that combine the need to write intelligently and creatively with the calculation and explanation of numbers. The challenge to the academic environment is to realize the strengths and weaknesses of both "English" and "Math" and to foster the blending, interdependence, and growth of the two, rather than a competition between the two. One suggestion to effectively blend the two is to have students take a course in communication research early in their course of study. Courses such as this one would develop student awareness of the relationship among analysis, presentation, mathematics, and methodology.

Summary

Both words and numbers when used separately are criticized (by the opposite camps, of course) for being merely "guesses" and containing "vagueness." However, academics are now seeing that a very positive synergy is created when words (prose) and numbers (quantification) are combined to explain the solution to a problem. We need to continue in this same direction—education has the obligation to develop the use of the two simultaneously into initial courses of study. As educational curricula meet this challenge, we will find the solutions to problems both in academia and the real-world to be more complete.

For sample study questions, see Appendix J.

This paper was first presented at the Western Marketing Educators' Association Conference and was entitled, "A Study of Student Writing Weaknesses in Marketing: Does Anybody Know It, Care, or Have a Solution?"

Student Writing Weaknesses in Marketing

Abstract

Employers are lamenting that our Marketing graduates have inadequate writing skills, but university education is no longer providing enough classroom opportunities for students to develop their writing proficiency before graduation. This article examines Marketing students' fundamental writing problems, based on a study done of over 3,500 student Marketing papers. The article then suggests a form-specific pedagogical approach that has been effective to shore up students' writing problems. With the addition of a few targeted writing assignments and some changes in class procedure, Marketing students will be better prepared to handle the writing that will be required of them in Marketing positions.

Introduction

Employers in the Silicon Valley have been giving feedback to our College of Business on a regular basis for many years, stating over and over that our Marketing graduates cannot write adequately for today's corporate environment and have weak thinking skills. Given the intense criticism from these Business professionals over a lengthy period of time, I decided to evaluate in more detail the particular writing weaknesses of my

Marketing students, so that I might design class assignments to not only strengthen these weaknesses but to also better prepare them for on-the-job writing to achieve success in their Marketing positions after graduation.

Methodology for this data collection was simple. The student writing tabulations included my evaluation of over 700 undergraduate Marketing students, sampling some 3,500 Marketing writing assignments accounting for 15 per cent of their course grade. Each writing assignment was based on the students' ability to conceptualize, present, and explain a Marketing principle previously presented in class lecture and discussion or prerequisite material or material from their current Marketing text.

No specific algorithm or measurement scheme was used for grading these assignments, other than my own 33-year history of grading similar assignments. I based results on a non-curved standard of "A" (excellent) through "F" (failure), "A" equaling a 4.0 grade point and "F" equaling a 0 grade point, with my standards being what Junior level university students should be capable of, as well as what the business environment will expect of them upon graduation.   Therefore, I graded on each of the following elements that are required in any business deliverable: content, clear and logical presentation, following directions, and mechanics. The result was a mean grade of 1.8 or "D+" with a standard deviation of .52, or one-half letter grade.

Writing Weaknesses

Below are described the four major weaknesses I found in student writing and suggestions for shoring up these problem areas:

Using Poor Mechanics

Students were very weak in the mechanics of writing (Flateby, 2005)[138]. I decided I can at least address the most basic writing weaknesses that can be readily and profoundly improved. (Identify the mechanics they will be responsible for in their writing assignments, and make these a significant part of their grade: grammar, punctuation, spelling, and syntax. If these mechanics aren't graded, the students are left to believe that the mechanics really aren't that important after all.)

Not Articulating Knowledge

Because my students have never been "Marketing practitioners," they tend to state principles by rote definition or memory rather than articulate knowledge of skills associated with the principle or its actual practical Marketing application and so had great difficulty in explaining these Marketing principles from the textbook in their own words (Labat & Bilorusky, 2003).[139] Their understanding may be there, but they haven't had much experience explaining concepts in prose. So I decided a good exercise to develop this writing ability was to have students explain in writing some of the skills required to apply Marketing principles discussed in the textbook and in class lecture. (For example, I ask students to explain in writing the "workings" of market mix allocations to positioning or why the normal curve of the "Diffusion of Innovation" is skewed in reality, or the logic of the Market Concept, etc.)

Difficulty Explaining Mathematical Formulae in Prose

Students had great difficulty explaining mathematical outcomes in prose. In math classes, they have been used to providing a numeric answer only, but never being challenged to explain what the relationship is among the components of the formula, how they impact each other, and what the answer means in a real-world applied sense (Rosen, Weil & Zastrow, 2001).[140] I now teach students how to understand the formula-driven and numeric Marketing applications (what each variable means and how each affects the outcome), then I ask them to explain their results in understandable prose, not just in numbers. (I assign sample size, forecasting, or break-even problems, etc. and then require the students to explain the algorithm and the meaning of their quantitative Marketing answer in writing.)

Not Writing Succinctly

Students have a difficult time writing succinctly (O'Regan & Mackenzie, 2005),[141] so I purposely put a limitation on the length of their answers to 50 words or less. They need to understand that in Business Marketing, less is more and time is money, so they need to learn how to write clearly, quickly, and to the point. In most college courses, students have not been taught to write with brevity, but instead, have usually found themselves working hard to extend what they've written to meet a document length requirement by adding fluff and extraneous material resulting in wordiness.

Additional Problems

I also found in my recent work that poor student performance on writing assignments, aside from weak content, can be divided more broadly into four procedural areas: not following instructions accurately, "delegating upward," [142] substituting guesswork for knowledge, and offering personal opinion when not asked for.

Not Following Instructions Accurately

Students were, number one, very poor at following the directions for assignments. It would appear that in past courses, they have been held to few, if any, specific formatting instructions or other specific requirements, so, predictably, there was much variability in the finished output. In business, most correspondence and reporting is rather standardized by comparison. Departments and companies have certain ways they want things done or protocols, so few things are left up to entry level employee discretion to change.

Sometimes, I found, their not following instructions accurately was due to lazy listening. Thus, students picked up only a fraction of the significant elements involved in an assignment or misunderstood the directions in other significant ways (McHugh, 2007).[143] Lazy listening, surprisingly, can occur among students with the most capability as well as those with less.

Unfortunately, faculty do not often penalize students for lazy listening and actually give them at least partial credit or sometimes full credit, despite their not following directions. As a result, students often have no incentive to improve their listening skills, since basically they are never made to suffer any significant consequence and learn from this bad habit. In a classroom is the best (and cheapest) place to learn how to improve listening skills, so when faculty do not make students pay a price for lazy listening, students leave the university still incredibly weak in this skill. They arrive, then, in their first job after graduation still thinking that they will never be made to account much at all for not following directions accurately and that therefore they can continue to pay little attention to assignment specifics.

In a Business classroom, students are also often offered the opportunity to re-write an assignment to improve their grade, whether the poorly written product was due to misunderstanding the directions or simply from giving an overall poor initial effort. Such well-meaning rewards on the part of faculty, unfortunately, simply encourage students to continue in lazy listening and other poor writing habits, because they believe they will always have time to do it over and, most importantly, get rewarded for it.

Sadly, once they obtain their first job after graduation, they will soon learn, and will probably be quite confused about the fact, that in a business setting they will be given no "points" for a mediocre first effort as they were often given in the classroom. Business simply cannot give any points for effort alone. Effort is automatically expected; after all, that's what the employee is getting paid for. The employee is also getting paid for doing the job right the first time. Since time is truly money in a business setting, students in their first job after graduation will quickly find that the classroom practice of "rewriting your way to an 'A'" tragically did not train them in how to produce their best effort the first time nor in how to listen carefully at the beginning.

The sense of rushing in a business environment is nowhere to be found on a college campus; students have ample time to complete assignments. In a business environment there is often a sense of rushing and little time in which to complete the task, so understanding the instructions accurately and knowing how to work accurately and quickly is a must. Any work that has to be re-done wastes precious time because it reduces employer profit and reduces personal success. Thus, employees who can't do things right the first time may, sadly, become too costly to keep!

Delegating Upward

This situation occurs in business when an employee is assigned a task to accomplish, but lacking understanding of what exactly to do or where to get the needed information, returns to the manager or supervisor and asks for help with the assignment from this person, such that the supervisor is actually doing the work assigned to the employee (Oncken & Wass, 1974).[144] A supervisor expects the employee to look elsewhere for answers and ideas, not to return empty-handed (Setty, 2005).[145] Where do these recent graduates now on their first job get the idea of returning to their boss constantly for personal help? Delegating upward occurs frequently in university classroom settings. Students are taught, in fact, to go to the professor as a resource, if need be. They will often go to the faculty member's office to request help, even to get explanations concerning fundamental prerequisite course knowledge they lack that is needed for the assignment.

Many university faculty welcome the opportunity to help students far more extensively than they should. Faculty should give general guidelines for students as to where to find information but also tell students at the outset of an assignment that they will not be providing extensive help and answers to the students. Weaning students from the upward delegation habit takes time and compassion (a "tough love" of sorts) but creates strong, capable and viable students who will, by graduation, have developed independent work habits.

Substituting Guesswork for Knowledge

This strategy occurs to many students as an acceptable effort. Again, there are several dangers to this approach when used in the workplace. (1) Guesses are rarely correct, contribute nothing to the work product, and can be outright dangerous, creating at the very least company embarrassment and, worse, possible charges of misfeasance or malfeasance, which sometimes results in costs to the company to pay court judgments if lack of specific performance can be proved. (2) For reasons mentioned above, guesses are not rewarded.

Unfortunately, guesswork is often rewarded in classrooms, particularly on short answer and essay exams. Students have often been rewarded for "writing something," even if it was quite off the mark. They get some points, in other words, for making an attempt, even if it is entirely guesswork. Sadly, this kind of "reward" has encouraged students to guess, a habit they will likely carry into the business world until they face a different, more unpleasant outcome for guessing. The employee is far better off admitting he doesn't know the answer; the manager will then put someone on the task with the employee, someone who does know the answer or at least who knows how to proceed intelligently. This "bailout" will not, however, happen without cost to the employee, because the manager will believe this is information and skills the employee should have had.

Offering Personal Opinion

This is what students usually do when asked to analyze something and provide conclusions. In entry-level Marketing management, of course, personal opinion is almost never asked for, and, in any event, personal opinion is not the basis for a conclusion (Blackford, 2004).[146] Employees will, however, be asked to provide a careful analysis of data and facts plus, possibly, conclusions. Unfortunately, in many of their academic assignments, students' personal opinion or "creative thinking" is what was solicited.

They are simply asked how they "feel" about a topic, or to write about a personal experience. Rarely are students taught to look at data and rigorously analyze a topic. So instead of being trained in the rigors of analysis and logical thinking, their assignments are watered down to be a matter of simply forming their own opinion of something, which, conveniently means there is no longer any "right" or "wrong." They have thus grown up completely unprepared for the business world in this regard, believing that their opinion will be solicited and does matter.

I'm not sure why educators have found this type of assignment worthwhile, since it doesn't prepare students for the real world, and it teaches students that their opinion is hugely important to others, which it usually is not, at least in an entry level work environment. So once students begin university life and later job settings, it is difficult for most of them to understand what it means to simply be a "data gatherer," analyst, and presenter, contributing to a capable management decision. In particular, undergraduates must be helped to understand that not only does their opinion not have much place in business writing, but also the idea of drawing conclusions is usually not called for at an entry level either.

The only useful conclusions they will be allowed to draw will be very elementary ones, and only after they have presented the appropriate history and data from credible secondary sources. They do not yet have enough personal experience to offer meaningful "gut-level" intuitive opinions. Their job is to objectively and thoroughly present secondary findings and let management take it from there. As a result of this early education that focused more on opinion than research, students often give short shrift to the importance of doing secondary research, thinking their own view is more important than documenting real experts and don't really know how to approach, let alone organize, a research assignment.

These four problems (not following instructions, delegating upward, substituting guesswork for knowledge, and offering personal opinion) seem unimportant and fairly trivial to a generation of self-indulged young people. So perhaps one of the greatest practical gifts faculty can pass on to serious students is to spend some time teaching students about the gravity of these weaknesses in the workplace and how to correct them. A few initial faculty prompts can go a long way to stimulate and build stronger student solutions to these fundamental writing problems.

A portion of the grade of each assignment is allocated to fulfilling the specific directions and fulfilling management's directive. Require students to write real-time, in class, short but frequent assignments so that they realize and demonstrate proficiency and knowledge without the aid of spell- and grammar-check software, dictionaries, notes, textbooks, or editorial help.

Provide ample initial dialogue when students receive the assignment to answer their questions. Then hold them accountable for lazy listening and the assigned deliverable without further "delegating upward."

Hold students' grades accountable for guesswork. A wrong guess in business is, at best, the acknowledgment that a student doesn't understand or know two things: what the correct answer should be or an understanding of the "guess" that they substituted, which is also clearly wrong. Lower the grade for unsupported and undocumented opinions, provided by students in their answers, thus helping students to understand that in a business setting an opinion is a privilege, not a "rite of passage," based simply on their attaining a college degree.

Conclusion

As one might expect, students differed in their areas of writing weaknesses. The writing problems examined in this study are not the sole culprits. But these basic difficulties occurred regularly and in nearly the same proportion, albeit to differing degrees among three-fourths of the student papers. My expectations for this pedagogy was not to turn marginal communicators into "Ernest Hemmingways," but I did find that grades, even in the short run of a semester, improved over 0.5 of a grade point, or one-half letter grade. These data do suggest that the attention to detail that Marketing faculty can provide can be instrumental in raising student academic and professional competencies.

Therefore, there is much that we can do to help prepare students more effectively for real-world Marketing positions, far more than we're generally doing now. It doesn't have to take a lot of additional faculty or student time, but, rather, a slightly different focus as professors of Marketing. The rubric to a form-specific pedagogical approach is to require students to write short but frequent in-class explanations of two types: (1) quantitative, and these would include writings about sample size, break even, forecasting, etc. and (2) qualitative, and these would include writings about market mix, positioning, diffusion of innovation, etc. And then evaluate their assignment deliverables for mechanics, articulation of true knowledge, explanation of quantitative applications, writing succinctly, following specific instructions, resistance to "delegating upward," eliminating guesswork, and avoiding opinions, making each a substantial factor in the final course grade.

We need to add to our pedagogy these proficiency requirements for effective Marketing communication, skills that will not only transition students to a job in the Marketing field but to a Marketing management career as well—remembering that Businesses are our customers, not the students. The students are our "product" and our reputation.

For sample study questions, see Appendix J.

This manuscript was first presented to management at the San Jose State University Career Center.

Business Writing and Academic Writing

Introduction

Most business students today have done a fair amount of academic writing but almost none in a business setting; therefore, they have limited experience writing for success in this very different environment. Significant differences exist, and teaching these differences to our students will help them more effectively make the transition to writing in their first career position after graduation. As business faculty responsible for one concentration or another (Accounting, Marketing, Management, etc.), it is all too common to conclude that teaching these writing skills is not necessarily our responsibility, or to believe that these subtleties in communication are already obvious to students or that student environmental proficiency will be achieved somehow later after the student is hired, but we would be wrong.

My observations for this article are based on a 30-year career that includes M.B.A. Director, Associate Dean of the College of Business, consulting to many Fortune 500 firms in business and industry, and professor to over 10,000 students. Other data and conclusions enumerated in this article came from corporate recruiters who attended the Expo '09 Job and Internship Fair held at San Jose State University[147] and the National Association of Colleges and Employers, who found that the #1 personal quality that business seeks in new hires is communication skill. [148] Also significant in demonstrating the overall weaknesses in student writing skill were the high failure rates on university writing skills tests as well as alumni observations regarding their own writing weaknesses.[149] This article not only explains major differences between writing in an academic environment and writing in a business environment but also offers practical suggestions as to how to create assignments in the classroom to better prepare students for real-world expectations and business audiences.[150,151]

Business Writing Purposes Differ from Those in Academia

To begin with, the purpose for writing in an academic environment is vastly different from the purpose for writing in a business setting. Students write in classes, fundamentally, to demonstrate knowledge of a course subject in order to earn a grade; people write in business, however, solely for the purpose of conveying precise information to others who need it to make business decisions. With this major difference, as one might expect, comes a whole host of subtle and not so subtle aspects that need to be understood.

Students Will Represent Something Larger than Themselves

In writing for college assignments, students represent only themselves; in business, however, the writer represents both himself and his company. Based on feedback from corporate recruiters at the recent Job Fair I attended, this was one of their biggest problems with new hires. New hires simply do not understand the huge importance of this fact—that everything they do in the workplace reflects either positively or negatively on the company. This is a very important point for students to understand because of the legal implications for them as employees. Suddenly, exactly what the new hire says and how he says it become very important.

Obviously, employees should guard against saying anything in letters and emails to customers and clients that can cause the loss of customers or otherwise get the company into legal trouble or other problems. A recruiter from one of the largest mainframe manufacturers in the United States offered an example of a situation that occurred at their company when a new hire made an errant statement to a customer that cost the company the account, even though management apologized and attempted in several ways to compensate the customer and woo them back. In this case, the damaging remark did not cost the new hire her job, but it did have a chilling effect on her opportunities for advancement.

Sentence Structure and Correct Spelling Become More Important

Suddenly now as well, sentence structure and correct spelling become important because (1) writing to the public affects company image, and (2) one's own credibility is at stake both inside and outside the company. Unfortunately, students have been told virtually throughout their high school and college careers, "Don't worry as much about grammar, spelling, and sentence structure; just get your thoughts down on paper." It is primarily content that counts and are graded accordingly. When, then, do they think about the mechanics of writing?

Now they find themselves in their first serious job and finally told to think about it, but, unfortunately at this point they have, usually, only minimal skill development in the written word. So they now find that, while their faculty gave them a "pass," their readers aren't so charitable, because they do expect basic, competent use of English. And customers certainly cannot believe in a company that boasts of excellence and then sends out a letter or email that is carelessly written and contains serious spelling errors.

Luckily word processing software is available to check some grammatical constructions and spelling errors. However, students need to be made aware that spellchecking software cannot catch some rather basic mistakes, such as the use of "two, to, and too," because spellcheckers as yet cannot understand sentence context or help a student craft a well-thought-out statement. An employer services consultant attending the '09 Expo expressed frustration that while students recognize the importance of a well-presented resume, they frequently fail to realize the same significance in preparing company memoranda and customer emails and other correspondence on a daily basis.

Guessing May Now Be Frowned Upon

Because students are writing basically to demonstrate knowledge to earn a grade in the classroom, students will often choose to guess when they have no idea what a correct response would be. Especially when taking essay or short-answer exams, they've learned that they're better off to write something than nothing because they are often rewarded with partial credit for guessing, even if their answer is entirely off the mark. Sadly, this kind of "reward" has taught students that to guess is perfectly acceptable when they aren't sure of the facts.

They will logically carry this belief into the business world until they face a different, more unpleasant outcome for guessing. Because the purpose of writing in the business world is to convey information (which must be as accurate as possible), the employee is far better off admitting he doesn't know the answer or have all the facts; the manager can then put someone on the task with the employee, someone who does know the answer or at least who knows how to proceed intelligently. There is simply not time in business to spend any effort proceeding along a wrong track or, just as serious, misleading readers with guesswork.

This "bailout" help provided by another employee will not, however, happen without cost to the writer, because the manager will believe this is information and skills the writer should have had. Because bluffing one's way can be such a serious mistake in a business environment, students need to learn while still in college that to guess may come at a very high price. They will quickly learn this by being penalized for guesswork, rather than being rewarded with partial credit—if it's wrong, it's wrong. There should be no credit given for an incorrect guess, and students should be told specifically that they will not be rewarded for a "guesswork" approach in the real world. The irony to a guess is that it demonstrates that the writer lacked knowledge in two areas—first, he didn't know the primary data, and, second, neither does he understand that the "guess" is also wrong.

Following Specified Procedures Will Now Become Very Important

Writing in academia, students are often allowed the freedom to design their own layouts for, and approaches to, their writing assignments. However, even if they are given specific layout and formatting instructions by the professor, they are often not penalized for ignoring the instructions or for following some but not all of them. In contrast, not following instructions for layout, design, or protocol in a business document, however, would carry serious penalties.

Because the purpose of writing in business is to convey information and do it quickly, writers must follow predetermined and existing formats. To save reader time in going over reports of a repetitive nature, many formats stay the same so readers can find the information they need very quickly. Therefore, the business writer may be given very little personal discretion in choosing the layout and design of the document. To prepare students for these realities, they need to be given specific layout instructions and penalized if they do not follow them.

When they are not penalized, students often have no incentive to improve their listening skills or attention to detail, since basically they are rarely made to suffer any significant consequence for ignoring instructions. In a classroom is the best (and cheapest) place to learn how to improve listening skills and how to pay particular attention to specific directions. So when faculty do not make students pay a price for these mistakes, students leave the university still incredibly weak in this skill. They arrive, then, in their first job after graduation still thinking that following instructions isn't critical and that they will never be made to account much at all for not following directions accurately. In a business environment, however, penalties can be severe, including dismissal from the job for being a lazy listener or for not having adequate attention to detail.

Ability to Analyze Will Be a Major Focus

Another major difference between academic writing and business writing involves the substance of the document. In high school and some college classrooms, few assignments involve thorough logical analysis of data. Instead, students in many classes are asked to do rather simple things these days, such as writing their feelings or opinions on a subject. This kind of assignment does not develop students' critical thinking skills, let alone their ability to do rigorous research, collect, document, and organize data. Also important to note here is that with an "opinion piece," there is no right or wrong and, at the very least, should be supported by some experience. Since many assignments are mostly about personal opinion, the subtle message to the student is that their opinion in the real world will matter. Unfortunately, in a business setting, it may not until a few years of experience have been acquired.

Understandably for a recent graduate writing on their first job, a business's lack of interest in their personal opinion is perplexing and confusing. They've been assigned and rewarded throughout their education for giving their personal opinion, and now, as a "newbie," their proactive and unsolicited opinion could actually damage their credibility. Sadly, not only do they tend to give their opinion when not asked for because they may not know any better, but they also lack the skills to research, organize, and analyze data, skills they will desperately need in a business environment to form meaningful opinions.

Because most college students tend to lack these analytical writing skills, if asked for an analysis of something in a college assignment, their analysis will often be superficial and incomplete, and they will almost always tack on an unsolicited personal opinion at the end, as if that sums it all up.   In entry-level positions in business, personal opinion is rarely asked for. Employees will, however, be asked to provide a careful analysis of data and facts plus, possibly, conclusions. How can they possibly do this with no training in this kind of assignment? They have thus grown up completely unprepared for the business world in this regard, believing that their opinion will be solicited and does significantly matter.

Such assignments inadvertently teach students that their opinion is hugely important to others, even in their early work environment. So once undergraduate students enter university life and later job settings, it is difficult for most of them to understand what it means to simply be a "data gatherer," analyst, and presenter, contributing to a capable management decision. In particular, undergraduates must be helped to understand that not only does their opinion not have much place in business writing, but also the idea of drawing conclusions is usually not called for at an entry level either.

The useful conclusions they will be allowed to draw as an entry-level employee will be very elementary ones, and only after they have presented the appropriate history and data from credible documented sources. They do not yet have enough work experience to offer meaningful "gut-level" intuitive opinions on the job. Their primary task is to objectively and thoroughly present secondary findings and let management take it from there. As a result of this early education that focused more on opinion than research, students often give short shrift to the importance of doing analysis, thinking their own gut-level opinion is more important than carefully documenting real experts.

New Hires Will Be Expected to Give Their Best Effort the First Time

Because faculty want to encourage student learning and improvement, students are often offered the opportunity to re-write an assignment to improve their grade, whether the poorly written product was due to misunderstanding the directions or simply from giving an overall poor initial effort. Giving students the opportunity to re-work their writing is understandable, because the purpose of these writing assignments is an educational one, designed to build their writing skills. Such well-meaning rewards for revised work on the part of faculty, however, simply encourage students not to work hard to give their best effort the first time, because they know they will always have time to revise and resubmit the paper and, most importantly, get rewarded for it by receiving a higher grade if they make a few small changes that improve the paper.

The problem with this is that it doesn't help students develop the kind of writing skills they need for the workplace because in a business setting "do-overs" can cost the company money and time, as well as clients or customers. Sadly, once students obtain their first job after graduation, they will quickly learn and will probably be quite confused about the fact that in a business setting they will be given no "points" for a mediocre first effort as they were often given in the classroom. Business simply cannot give any points for effort alone.

The purpose of writing in a business setting is to convey information—quickly, concisely, and accurately. A solid first effort is automatically expected and expected to hit the mark; after all, that's what the employee is getting paid for. Thus, students will quickly find that the classroom practice of "rewriting your way to an 'A,'" tragically did not train them in how to produce their best effort the first time. In a business environment there is often a sense of rushing, so there is little time in which to complete the task once, let alone multiple times. Thus, the extensive revising and editing allowed in many college courses would be seen as an impossible luxury in a business setting.

Any work that has to be re-done on the job wastes precious time and therefore reduces employer profit. Thus, employees who can't do things right the first time may, sadly, become too costly to keep!   To better prepare students to give their best effort the first time, faculty should record the original grade. If faculty want to strengthen students, they could tell the students that the original grade will be entered into the grade roster but only after the paper is resubmitted with noted corrections and other improvements made.

Some Business Documents Are Kept Virtually "Forever"

Lastly, because writing in college classes is done to demonstrate one's knowledge to earn a grade and for learning purposes, these specific classroom assignments lose their value by the end of the semester, once the course grade is recorded. So when students have an assignment returned to them in a college classroom, they can throw it away or simply keep it until the end of the term with no further implication.   The instructor rarely keeps a copy, so what the student wrote is soon forgotten by all. In business, by contrast, documents as well as emails may be kept for an indefinite period of time, oftentimes for legal reasons but often just to maintain the "history" of ongoing operations.

When storage space on the job site is filled, companies rent space elsewhere in town to store old documents ("long-term storage") or store them electronically. So, conceivably, any business person can get his or her hands on nearly any document written in the department or company, should there be adequate reason to do so.   Students will need to quickly get an understanding of this as soon as they enter the workplace: their written correspondence may "live forever," or at least outlive their employment with the company.

What does this difference mean to the student? It is a significant one. In a college setting, students can be rather careless in what they write, especially politically, because the assignment loses its value quickly and can be destroyed by the student as soon as it's returned by the professor. In a business setting, with many documents being kept virtually forever, business writers must be very careful in what they write, and they must be very careful not write anything in anger.

Even if a writer sent an angry email to only one co-worker, that co-worker could keep the memo and use it against the writer at a later time. Also, if the employee believes that possibly politically dangerous statements must be made, they should be done orally if at all, but not in writing. A good question students should ask themselves on the job is, "Would I want this read by my boss's boss or to the entire department or by a customer?"

The Writer's Business Audiences May Have Less Subject Knowledge

Students write in classes usually only to the professor, and this person always has more formal education than the student and so generally knows more about the subject than the student does; in stark contrast, business documents are often sent to readers within the organization who have less formal education than the writer and oftentimes is someone who has less knowledge about the subject. What does this difference suggest is needed here by the writer?

This difference means that business writers have to write with far greater clarity than they ever thought about doing in academic assignments. With no real thought to being understood when writing to an instructor, writing in an academic environment is comparatively much easier because instructors will often, as they read the student's paper, consciously or unconsciously fill in missing information when the writing is unclear.

Instructors know what a student meant to say because they originally gave the student all the information in the first place, or they are at least very familiar with the subject. This "filling in the gaps when reading" may be intentional or unintentional on the part of the faculty member, but, nevertheless, a drawback for the development of writing with complete clarity.

Business readers, on the other hand, simply cannot fill in the gaps of a poorly written message because the reader may have little or no knowledge of the subject of the writer's message, so they cannot predict what the writer meant to say.   A manager, for instance, might give an assignment to an employee to research a new type of software that might be useful for company needs. The employee would then research the pros and cons of the software and write a report for the manager. The manager, then, must rely totally on the employee's ability to write a clear document, since the manager knows nothing about this new software and its possibilities.

This suggests that for business writing, students will have to work much harder to make each point clearer than they ever had to do for college writing assignments. Faculty, then, when reading and grading student papers, should ask themselves, "If I knew little or nothing about this subject, could I understand what this student is trying to say?

If I were completely ignorant of the subject matter, is it now crystal clear? If it isn't, am I guilty of reading in what isn't really here because I know the student and the topic so well?" If something isn't crystal clear, faculty need to deduct points for lack of clarity and, unfortunately, be rather brutal about this if they are going to adequately prepare their students to write with greater clarity for on-the-job assignments.

Business Readers Don't Have to Read the Message

In business, no one has to read a writer's documents, not even the person the document is addressed to. Being very busy people with an overabundance of written correspondence to read every day, business people are, therefore, much more likely to read a document if it is well written (clear and concise), and if they think there is something of importance in it for them. Otherwise, a poorly written document may be put on the bottom of the stack, skimmed over lightly, or simply tossed into the wastebasket. What does this mean for the student writing to such busy people? It means that their writing must be good—it must catch the reader's attention quickly, state its importance for the reader up front, be easy to understand, and to the point. Students write in classes to someone who must read their work in order to assign a grade, so students generally don't learn in academia the importance of getting the reader's attention and how to do it.

Unfortunately, conciseness in classroom assignments often tends not to be stressed either. In fact, the bad habit of wordiness actually develops in its place because students throughout middle school and high school often have been asked to meet a length requirement specifically assigned by their teachers. Instructors, being well-meaning, give such requirements to encourage thorough coverage of the subject; however, in an attempt to meet length requirements without having done the research necessary to legitimately fill that number of pages, students learn how to insert "fluff" when necessary, In doing so, they are able to generate a document of the required length, but unfortunately a very cumbersome and overly wordy one. Wordiness in college assignments must guard against inadvertently rewarding this failed approach.

In a work setting, busy readers get very impatient having to read documents containing a lot of fluff and fill because either the main point of the message is missing, or it is difficult to find quickly. In frustration, such readers are just as likely to throw a wordy memo into the wastebasket as to make any effort to re-read and attempt to decipher it. People who get a reputation for wordiness in their writing will have a difficult time getting others to read their documents. So the objective in business classroom writing assignments should be to cover the topic thoroughly in as few words as possible. Students should be rewarded for conciseness and taught that in business writing, "less is more." Even though they can't experience a rushed environment on a college campus, they need to be taught what working in one is like and the changes they will need to make in their writing to succeed in a very fast-paced environment.

Business readers, also to save reading time, want messages they read to have a clear point, preferably one related to them and their interests! When a reader picks up a memo or report, he or she is going to immediately ask, "What's in this for me?" "Why should I take my valuable time to read this?" Writers must work hard, then, to get their business reader's attention and to keep it.

Students are often never taught how to put themselves in the reader's frame of mind as they prepare to write. In fact, if there is any accommodation, it's the instructor accommodating to the student—the instructor trying to figure out what the student meant to say. A couple of applied lessons here would be helpful. Students preparing for a business environment should be taught to first think, "What is my reader responsible for in the company? What are my reader's business concerns right now?"

Students also need to be taught to determine a main point. Having taught Business Writing for many years at the university level, I remain amazed at how difficult it is for students to read a sample short report and determine its main point. Given that they have trouble even understanding the concept of a main point (and being able to ferret through lesser points), their writing is often very muddled as well, with the main point either unclear, buried at the end of the document, or lacking entirely.

Their writing assignments, therefore, ought to include skill development in isolating and making very clear a main point, with everything else in the message written to support the main point. Skillful analytical thinking, planning, and drafting, then, should precede any writing.

The Writer's Business Audiences May Not Even Know the Sender

Another fact about a business environment that impacts writing is that reports and memos will often be read by people who do not know the sender at all. The writer may need to send his or her report to certain people in the organization because of other people's positions or levels of responsibility; these may be people the writer has never met. If the correspondence was sent to a known receiver, the receiver may choose to send the memo or report on to others the writer does not know. What students need to understand about these aspects of the business environment is that business readers who know little or nothing about a writer they've never met will have only the written document with which to judge the employee. Thus, readers who do not know the writer will form opinions about the writer's competence based solely on what the writer says and how he says it.

If they find the writing contains muddled thinking, is wordy and redundant, or has several grammatical and spelling errors, they are very likely to form a negative opinion of the writer's abilities and of the content of the message. Since first impressions are lasting, as the saying goes, their initial negative view will often be very difficult for the writer to overcome, hence another reason to develop one's writing skill—to gain an initial positive impression with readers they have not yet met.

Lead Times for Business Assignments Can Be Very Short

In business, because resources are precious, employees will often be writing under extreme time pressure, and due dates usually cannot be extended, at least without severe penalty to the employee and/or the company. A veteran manager from a high-technology firm pointed out that due dates and meetings with clients and customers must be met. "There are heavy consequences to the organization for less than on-time performance." Employees often feel rushed because they receive assignments with (what they consider to be) unrealistic due dates. Due dates, however, will not be the employee's to argue or negotiate. So the new hires who survive in business are those who are able to complete the assignment within the time period allowed. In college assignments, students often have plenty of lead time to complete an assignment and in many cases are allowed to submit assignments after their due date and with no penalty.

Students, therefore, need to learn to work to deadlines in their college classes as well, and, yes, that often means being able to juggle several assignments and other commitments at once. But this is the real world too. This will teach them how to budget their time or suffer the consequences if they don't. Letting students "off the hook" and allowing them to turn in work late with no serious penalty is not preparing them for a company's expectations.

"Politics" and Power Relationships Become Critical in a Business Setting

Part of the problem for the new hire in learning about how to function successfully within the power relationships in a company is the fact that nothing has been written down about this; the new hire can't go to a company manual to determine the operating procedure or nuances of how to write up and down the chain of command, so oftentimes, new hires have to learn the hard way. If this were to be taught on the college campus, new hires could at least enter the workplace with a much greater understanding of how they must speak and word their sentences. "Make other people important, and do it sincerely."[152]

For example, word choice becomes critical when writing upward to one's manager, not so critical when writing down the chain of command. For instance, students should be taught that we do not "command" people above us in the hierarchy by writing something as innocent as, "I would suggest that you look into this." Instead, we might write: "If you would like, I can look into this." These subtleties are beyond students' cognition, and so must be carefully taught to them. Writing downward, it's perfectly appropriate to say, "Please look into this and get back to me."

Writing in a college environment, students do not have to deal with the politics of the organization or consider carefully the power relationship they have with their reader (the professor). So in a classroom setting where writing is required, students should first be taught about an organization's hierarchy and the politics of this hierarchy—what is appropriate to write when writing "up the chain of command" and what is not appropriate or could get the employee into trouble.

Communication protocol, because of the business hierarchy in which the new hire will be writing, is also another "sticky" issue that should be taught in advance. When writing in college, there is never any question about who should receive the assigned document. It goes to the instructor, of course. In business, the answer is not so simple. Besides the initial receiver in a business setting, the writer has to consider who else should get a copy of the message and in what order their names should appear on the distribution list. Offending people in business can happen inadvertently when the person finds out from someone else who did get the memo what is going on, so knowing who to send the memo to is critical. Employees should be taught to ask their manager for his or her advice first concerning how to write sensitive correspondence and also to ask their manager who should be on the distribution list before sending it out, at least for a while as a new employee.

Help and Mentorship May Not be Forthcoming in a Business Setting

Students need to be told that submitting their work in a business environment may be very different from the kind of feedback and help they enjoyed in a college classroom. They may not be given the positive praise or patient help they were used to getting from their professors, because their relationship to their manager will not necessarily be one of a mentor or helpful guide. Managers will expect good work and often without giving praise or much comment at all. It can get much worse than this, however, because some employees, especially those senior to the writer, may care not at all for the writer's feelings and offer very blunt criticism.

Students will usually find in a college setting that their instructors, will, on the whole, be encouraging and helpful. Faculty, having more of a mentor-like role in the classrooms, will therefore usually offer positive and constructive suggestions to students for writing improvement. I'm not suggesting that faculty give harsh criticism of students' work as a new hire's future manager might, but I am saying that the more we can describe to students the sometimes harsh realities of the business world, the easier it will be for them to adjust to these realities. Supervisors will come in many forms, from administrators to managers to leaders, so not all will see mentoring as useful or necessary.

There may also be readers who, for whatever reason, want to harm the credibility of the writer and will criticize the writer's document in front of others. Students need to be told about these harsh realities of life in a business setting. To them, once leaving the safety and "cocoon-like" nature of the college campus, they will often feel like they've been thrown into the deep end of a swimming pool, and into icy water at that!

In business, when an employee is assigned a task to accomplish, a supervisor expects the employee to be resourceful in looking for answers and other ways of accomplishing the assignment, and if he doesn't know where to look, ask another employee for help, but definitely not to return empty-handed to the manager and give that person an "assignment" to help. This could run the gamut from needing assistance with formatting a document to making elementary-level decisions as a trainee. An observation from a division manager of a large retailer found that many new hires in the management training program "just don't get it. Part of learning to manage is to evaluate, be resourceful, and act. At some level, not all decisions are crises to be returned to your supervisor." In business, this is often referred to as "delegating upward."

This can be very difficult for the new hire, because most students have been used to having professors who were more than willing to offer help all along the way. Students generally have learned that whenever they have a question or problem with an assignment—how to get started, where to go for information, needing a review of concepts from previous courses now needed for this assignment, etc. they can always find a helping hand from the person who gave them the assignment with little or no resistance or "cost" to them personally.

To better prepare students for the business world in this regard, faculty should consider giving general guidelines, in some cases, for students at the beginning of an assignment as to where to find information but also tell students that they will not be providing extensive help. The student needs to learn how to find sources of information and answers for himself or talk with other students about the assignment. Weaning students from the upward delegation habit in a university setting takes time and compassion (a "tough love" of sorts) but will create strong, capable and viable students who will, by graduation, have developed independent work habits.

Conclusion

Even if the popular argument is made that effective writing skills are not as critical in today's casual culture as they once were, it is still true that promotions, careers, and executive succession in the corporate culture will be dependent on effective communication skills. Having both worked in corporate America and taught in college classrooms, I have always kept my "mind's eye" on the eventual place my students would be doing their most important writing—on the job site and so, therefore, carefully structured my classroom environment and writing assignments with this end in mind.

The changes to class assignments and general structure I recommend above are really quite small ones to make but offer huge rewards for the students. It has been very encouraging for me, as well, to watch students' general growth in maturity and writing skill development as I modeled the classroom setting and assignments to be closer to what a company environment will require, while specifically preparing them for real-world expectations and success—teaching them the difference between classroom assignments and business deliverables and how to successfully produce documents for a business setting.

With these changes I've made in pedagogy to better prepare my students for real world writing expectations, it has been gratifying to see them grow and develop, not only in communication acuity but also in their self-confidence. They're better prepared for the real world than they would have been otherwise, and they know it.

For sample study questions, see Appendix J.

Page 265

This manuscript first appeared in Writing in a Business Environment, *by Susan G. Thomas.*

Writing Weaknesses in Business Deliverables

Much of what students will do on the job once they graduate is communicate, certainly in emails and often in letters and reports. Employers tend to be shocked and often times frustrated with the inadequate level of their new hires' writing skills. One problem is that students simply do not do enough writing in their college years, and when they do it is often not critiqued rigorously enough to do the student any good. Another problem is the type of writing students do in college courses. The writing skill of getting to the point quickly and clearly tends not to be taught to students.

Employers complain that this is a major writing weakness in the graduates they hire. This is a fairly easy problem to correct, once students have thought about what their main point is. Other writing problems, however, are every bit as serious and not as simple. They have great trouble as well with content-related problems: expressing themselves coherently, logically, and analytically. This article, then, addresses this larger issue—that of helping our students develop content-related skills in their writing.

Being able to think coherently, logically, and analytically depends, to a great deal, on how strong and developed the student's thinking skills are, and this skill largely depends on how large the student's knowledge base is. A knowledge base, of course, takes years to develop. So are there, then, things students can do in the short run to improve the logic and analysis of what they write now? I think so. Let's look first at thinking mistakes and how students can correct them to improve the content of their messages. These content problems can occur in all types of business writing—memos, advertisement letters, contracts, reports, etc.

Common Content Problems and Solutions

Problem #1: The main point is unclear. A very common problem in much student writing and on-the-job writing is that many writers do not have in mind a clear main point to their message. Many writers, even after being questioned as to what their main point is, cannot say for sure. To a more mature person with good thinking skills, such a problem seems almost incomprehensible. How could you not know what your main point is?   What are you asking for? What do you want of the reader? What is the most important thing you want the reader to know as a result of reading your message?   But it is true that many writers new on the job and those who have been employed for quite some time but with weak thinking skills definitely do have this problem.

If the writer is unclear himself about the main point when he wrote the message, the reader will have tremendous difficulty figuring out what is being conveyed in the document as well. Most business readers will become quickly frustrated and will not spend the time necessary to try to figure out the main point.   Many of these documents end up in the "round file."

If students cannot learn how to define their main point in a message, the rest is a waste of time, so I spend some time in class helping them to learn how to "get a feel for" a main point. I have devised a dramatization to help them learn how to crystallize their thinking in this. To help them find the main point in a message they've written, I ask them to picture this: picture that you've been working on a project for some time, you walk to your manager's office to turn in your report, and you're told you just missed her.

She left two hours ago for the nearby airport to board a plane. Since she was supposed to have taken your report with her to work on while away but didn't because you didn't have it ready, you now quickly get into your car and rush to the airport to try to catch her before her plane leaves. You arrive, unfortunately, just in time to see her walking through the security checkpoint. You rush to this gate but too late. You then realize that you have time to shout out one sentence to her before she's out of earshot. All the work you've just completed for this report is swirling around in your head, but as you see her quickly disappearing in the distance, you realize that you have time to shout out to her only one sentence from this report that she will hear before moving out of earshot.

You catch her eye for just a second. Now, which of all the sentences you wrote would you pick, if she had the time to hear only one? This dramatization often helps students prioritize in their minds rather quickly, thinking, "What one sentence would I shout to her?" Putting a severe time limit on it, as in this scenario, helps students immensely to crystallize and prioritize their information.

Problem #2: The focus is too broad for the assignment. Unfortunately, students in classes often write to fill a page requirement rather than cover a topic, or at least are tasked to do both. So they usually aren't rewarded for narrowing a topic down and staying on point. To fill a large number of pages when they don't have enough related material, they will often include only marginally related information. Unfortunately, more is usually <u>not</u> better when it comes to business writing. When the focus is too broad and too much irrelevant information is included, the report can easily become confusing for the reader. With tangential information being only barely alluded to and largely undeveloped, the reader is left confused as to their relevance to the topic. The document now develops a superficial quality as well.

In an academic environment, students would often be praised for a lengthy report, even if many of the pages contained relatively superfluous information, so learning to narrow a focus is not something taught or necessarily rewarded in their academic writing. In business, superfluous words and pages create impatience in the reader, at best. Most business people are overrun with far too much paperwork to slog through in any one day.   So a 1-page memo that gets right to the point is far better than a 5-page memo that includes unnecessary information.

Students need to quickly learn that less is better in business and they need to be rewarded for it in the classroom. They should write exactly what has been asked for, no more and no less. Writers who have crystallized in their minds their main point before they start to write as well as generated a short outline or rough plan to follow will have a much easier job of developing a document that is properly focused.   It will contain enough information to bolster or prove their main point but will leave out all information that doesn't directly help.

Problem #3: Inadequate explanation of ideas. Messages containing poorly developed ideas are frustrating to read and take additional reader time to try to understand.   Students need to be sure to explain fully whatever they discuss, particularly when they cite numbers or suggest an idea that may meet with reader resistance or rejection. To adequately explain something, they must think about it from all angles and consider all the parts of the problem or issue, particularly from their reader's point of view.   This ability to explain fully and clearly is often undeveloped when students graduate because faculty sometimes "fill in the blanks" automatically for students when they read and grade student papers.   Letting students off the hook in this way causes students to leave the university not having had to do the hard work to create complete understanding. They tend not to go over their own papers to be sure they have written with total clarity and completeness. This is most important in business because many of a student's business readers will be ignorant of the subject written about and/or will not even know the student personally.

An area that students usually fall short in explaining adequately is that of presenting numbers in a report. For most university writing, students don't have to lay out an analysis and explain the numeric "answers" they arrive at, so they are generally very weak in this. They often will pull a number, seemingly, "out of nowhere" without explaining how or where they got it. If they think there is any chance a business reader would be confused or raise a question about a particular number or how it was arrived it, they need to explain that. If the number was generated from past activity, they must state where they obtained the figure. If the number is a projection of future performance, they need to tell how they arrived at this estimate, step by step. Most business readers want to "do the math" themselves, so it is critical that students learn to explain all their work.

When making numeric estimates to be used in a report, students need to understand that all estimates are made based on one or more assumptions. Usually, readers will want to know what assumptions the writer used to arrive at their projections so that they can decide for themselves the validity of those assumptions. Students spend so much time with textbooks at the university that they come to believe that if it's in print or from a professor's lecture, it must be a fact. They are used to being given numbers as fact, such as in a math problem from a textbook.

The problem will typically include given variables to be "plugged into" a formula. Students do not realize, however, that many formulas require the use of numbers that are based on assumptions or predictions about how the "world" will likely (or hopefully) play out. In a break-even formula, for instance, students are expected to "plug in" the costs associated with producing a product. In a textbook, these numbers are not even discussed; they are simply supplied to the student.

In the real world, however, the costs to produce a product are simply estimates, based on assumptions that, for instance, suppliers will not raise their prices within the next six months for the needed materials, there will be adequate availability of the materials so that a more expensive substitute doesn't have to be made, utility costs will remain the same over the short run, etc. Not much, if any, time is spent on this aspect with students, so they are not used to recognizing assumptions, let alone explaining them.

When presenting solutions to a problem in their writing, students should be taught to suggest more than one solution. The student may have in mind a preferred solution and may not even want to seriously consider any others. However, if their manager is the type of person who likes to explore several possibilities, they should suggest alternative solutions and then tell why, in their judgment, they think the other alternatives will not work or will be less effective.

This strategy is much more effective in situations where other viable solutions do exist and, particularly, if the reader is probably holding to or even leaning toward one of these other solutions. Optimal solutions may not be possible due to constraints related to time, financing, human resource, etc. Alternative solutions are also important as possible backup strategies if the "world changes" in some way, rendering the first solution inoperable or if the first solution should fail.

Problem #4: The arrangement of points is confusing or distracting. This problem occurs when the presentation of ideas does not proceed clearly and sequentially but either jumps around or places ideas in an illogical order. There are only a few ways to order information effectively; there are, on the other hand, many ways to order information ineffectively. If the writer jumps around or does not use a logical approach to present information, the reader will end up confused and may never get the point of the message. At best, poor organization of information will slow the reader down and likely reduce comprehension of the message (as well as create frustration and reader resentment along the way).

Students need to be taught how to order information in a report, to make it easiest for the reader to follow. For business reports of a non-sensitive nature (that is, the reader will not argue with or be upset by the outcome), information is usually "bottom-lined," with the main point appearing in the first sentence or two. In situations that are considered sensitive (the reader will not be particularly happy with the main point), then the main point would not be bottom-lined or put up front.

Rather, in this case, background or history may come first, followed by the relevant facts that build to the writer's final conclusion. (Most of the information students need about how to organize non-sensitive messages and sensitive messages should be covered by the required basic Business Writing course for majors taught at the university.) Probably at least 80% of all business writing will be of the non-sensitive type, so students should be taught how to order information quickly for this most common type of writing situation.

Students need a lot of practice in developing a logical flow of information in their writing because they tend not to do enough writing (with complete critique) in their academic years. Because they tend not to develop any great amount of confidence in their own writing, they often rely far too much on the structure of the printed sources they are consulting for their assignments (textbook, books, or magazine articles). Most good writers were taught how to outline the structure of their document in advance of actually doing any writing.

While this approach would likely seem overly cumbersome to today's student, it is often the best way to develop a sound structure to the document and a clear flow of logic. I often tell students it's like consulting a roadmap before taking off on a long trip. Most people don't just get in their car and start driving to a place they've never been to before.   If you wanted to save time (and gasoline), you would plan out your route first. Such is the value of a written outline for a report or paper.

Problem #5: Emphasis weak or misplaced. Documents usually contain many points, but they are certainly not all of equal importance. Students should be taught how to format their document to highlight the important information. Putting the main point first in non-sensitive messages is a good first step, as was already mentioned. But the sentences to follow are also important in creating a coherent and clear document.   What is most important for the reader to understand should be made obvious; what is of lesser importance should also be evident. One way to accidentally create prominence for everything within a message is to devote the same amount of space in the document to all ideas.

Readers assume that the space allotted to an idea determines its importance. If the writer discusses one thing for 5 sentences and another thing for 25 sentences, the reader assumes that what was discussed in the 25 sentences is more important than what was discussed in the 5 sentences. The amount of time and space devoted to an issue, then, indicates to the reader its relative importance in the message, whether you meant to convey that or not.

Student writers need to decide exactly which ideas they want to give the greatest emphasis to and devote more physical space and prominence within the document to these ideas, giving less space to lesser ideas.

Added emphasis is also created by doing any of the following, as appropriate:

- underline, CAPITALIZE, or **boldface** important words, numbers, or sentences.

- indent the margins of important information, such as in a table, chart, or paragraph.

- itemize important information contained in a list with either asterisks, dashes, numbers, or bullets.

- put important sentences in visually prominent places— the first sentence or the last sentence of a paragraph or report.

Common Logic Problems and Solutions

Along with improving the five basic writing skills discussed above, students must also be taught to improve the logic of their writing. Most academic writing students does next to nothing to develop logical writing skills, since much of what they write in K-12 and Freshman English in college lets them get by with writing about their opinion of something. They almost never have to write to persuade anyone logically or develop an argument of any kind. But in business, aside from writing quick information memos, most other documents students write will require them to apply some logic to the situation.

If a writer is able to analyze clearly and provide clear conclusions, he or she will quickly develop a reputation of having excellent skills in both logic and analysis. If a writer is unable to do this, he or she will create the reputation of having very weak logic and analytical skills. There is nowhere to hide. Below I have defined four types of poor logic as found in student papers and how students can develop the skills to correct these problems.

Problem #1: Rushed Generalization. This problem occurs when the writer bases a conclusion on too little evidence. Let's say the human resource manager asks the employee to do a survey of the company's 300 employees to assess the level of interest in having a set of training and development seminars on several upcoming Saturday mornings. Of the first 30 people the student asks, 20 say they would like to have such seminars. The student therefore concludes and reports that interest is sufficient. Can it reasonably be concluded that 20 out of 30 is an accurate representation of all 300?

Statistics, of course, provides formulas to determine the proper sample size if one is doing a study, because, generally, one does not have the time nor money to poll the entire population in question. If the writer did not use statistical formulas to arrive at the proper sample size to be able to draw inferences about the whole, he must say so.

No matter how many people were polled, if that number was not arrived at statistically, the report should state that the number of people polled may not be the proper sample size and that it will be important to draw conclusions about the whole very cautiously. Usually everyone within a company could be polled; however, when working with predictions about the general public, it would be impossible to question everyone in the relevant market.

Problem #2: Faulty Cause-Effect Reasoning. When writers attribute a result or effect to a particular cause or causes, it is important to try to verify that the causal relationship is sound. Businesses constantly look for causes to problems. Why did our market share drop? Why is department morale low? What caused the breakdown on the assembly line last week?

The student writer may be accused of faulty reasoning if he or she simply looks to causes that took place before the effect to explain the problem. "Our morale problem began after Jim became manager." Jim's becoming manager may have nothing to do with the problem, so it's important that we teach students not to simply look to obvious events as the probable cause unless they have more proof.

Another aspect of faulty cause and effect reasoning is what is called a "chicken and egg problem." The age-old unanswerable question is, which came first—the chicken or the egg? Answers to questions like these are often impossible to determine. As an example, corporations usually prefer to hire people with college degrees. Why? Are these people always smarter? Do they have better thinking skills than people without college degrees? Corporations must believe that college-educated employees can make a more substantial contribution, or they wouldn't be willing to seek them out and pay them generally more than those without college degrees.

But analyzing why this is so is a "chicken and egg" question and impossible to answer: do smart people gravitate toward college, or do people become smart in the process of getting a college degree? It would be foolish to assume that college automatically makes all students smarter. It could be that the smart people choose to go to college—smart people are not afraid of class work, studying, memorizing, etc. Or, the answer may be a combination of the two—smarter people tend to go to college, and the experience also increases their thinking and intellectual skills. It could also be a matter of upbringing and early encouragement from parents and have nothing much at all to do with intelligence. In many cases, where causes cannot positively be determined, the student is better off to state all the relevant factors he or she is aware of, then let the reader draw his or her own cause-and-effect conclusions.

Problem #3: Either/Or Reasoning. Student writers may be accused of either/or thinking if they suggest that only two options exist or when they suggest that all situations or people are either one way or another—usually at the opposite end of the spectrum. Many such student descriptions include words such as " good," "bad," "right," "wrong," etc. This extreme kind of thinking suggests immaturity or undeveloped reasoning, because life is not black and white but, rather, shades of gray, as we all learn as we gain more life experience. The mature person eventually learns through often-difficult experiences that life or the people in it cannot be this neatly divided or explained. Students should be taught to consider a statement such as the following: "If we do not expand into this particular geographic market, we have no chance of remaining competitive."

To a business reader, a statement such as this sounds like something a desperate person would say. It also is not very believable—we have <u>no</u> chance of remaining competitive? It is much more believable and persuasive to calculate an estimate of how much market share (or whatever measure is being used to calculate competitiveness) would be lost. A quantified outcome (even if it is only an estimate) looks much more objective and rational. Then let the reader determine—after all the numbers have been presented—whether this decision truly means that you will have no chance of remaining competitive.

<u>Problem #4: Judgment flawed</u>. This logic problem occurs when the writer assumes that a certain conclusion must follow from a certain kind of evidence presented. But in fact, it may not logically follow at all. An example of automatically assuming a certain conclusion is in forecasting sales based on historical observations alone. Many events occur—both inside and outside a company—to affect next year's sales: the state of the economy, the entrance of new competitors, etc. One must first examine the entire picture before coming to quick projections based simply on last year's data.

To avoid flawed judgment problems, students need to be taught to review the evidence they plan to present to support their judgments. They need to consider what judgments are logically possible, given that evidence. They need to examine the judgment(s) in question, looking carefully for unwarranted assumptions, and whether they have ignored other important information. Working on case studies in class are is one way to help students develop adequate judgment as they work with case specifics and consider all the aspects that affect or may affect a company at a point in time.

Fact or Perception?

As students write, they must constantly be on guard against writing personal opinion in business documents unless this has been asked for specifically, and usually it won't be. When a document includes a lot of personal opinion, the writer will be accused of lacking objectivity. Since objectivity is critical in business writing, if a student's writing does not appear to be objective, it will be discounted or dismissed altogether. Students need to read through their documents carefully to make sure they haven't accidentally or purposely passed off a personal opinion as fact.

This is a challenge for most students because most of their writing assignments through their classroom years, as I've said before, usually have solicited their personal opinion, so it's understandable that they would be most comfortable writing from their own point of view. This approach will have to come to a screeching halt once they enter a business environment. Their opinion will no longer matter or be solicited, at least until they have years of work experience in their field. Even then, opinion as defined in business is at best one's "gut" feeling about a direction to go, but even then their logic would be asked for, and that logic must be based on fact and a few solid business assumptions that can be defended.

Students must also guard against introducing a perception or opinion with the words, "The fact is..." when what the person is about to state is still really his or her perception or opinion of something. Students need to be taught that a fact, by definition, is a piece of information that can be verified by other people. The statement, "Paris is the capital of France," is considered a fact because it can be verified easily by anyone, and no one can come up with a different answer. "Paris is a lovely city," cannot be verified, however, in the same way by

100% of people; there could be difference of opinion on this; therefore, this is not a fact but rather a perception. So even though the sentence structure looks the same (both sentences beginning with "Paris is"), it's the idea of independent verification that determines whether a statement is a fact or not.

Students should be taught that their perceptions, on the other hand, are not based on fact at all, but rather on their emotional needs, personality preferences, and life experiences. When they express their perceptions, they often reveal a great deal about themselves and are merely revealing their own needs, and this has nothing whatever to do with objectivity.

For example, a person's behavior can be seen quite differently by different people. This difference of opinion is due to the evaluator's needs and expectations rather than the individual's behavior, *per se*. Tom tends to keep most of his communication to on-the-job issues. He shares very little with co-workers about his personal life. Two of Tom's co-workers see this behavior very differently. Rebecca, who likes a great deal of social conversation in all her dealings with people, describes Tom as "cool" and "aloof." Tiffany, on the other hand, is a solo performer, needs little interaction with others on a daily basis in the workplace, so she describes Tom simply as "businesslike." It could be assumed that Rebecca is not particularly happy with Tom's behavior because she used rather negative adjectives ("cool" and "aloof") to describe him.

Tiffany, however, does not seem to hold the same negative opinion of Tom because she used a more neutral adjective ("businesslike") to describe him. And, as said before, she doesn't see his behavior as negative because what Tom presents to Tiffany in behavior is just fine with her. So who is correct about what Tom is really like—Tiffany or Rebecca? The answer is, neither one because this isn't really an issue of correctness at all; this is an issue of perception. The adjectives used by both Rebecca and Tiffany are valuable, but only in that the words they choose to describe Tom actually reveal more about each <u>woman's</u> personal needs and expectations than they tell about Tom.

What we can say about Tom that would be considered fact is the kind of thing that would appear on his résumé—where he has worked, the titles of the positions he has held, the particular company projects he has worked on, the awards he has earned, etc. His daily comings and goings is also verifiable fact—what time he goes to lunch and what time he returns. But to draw conclusions about what these goings and comings mean about Tom (and his motives and values) is entering the area of perception, perception from the viewer's perspective. And the viewer's perspective is based on that person's values and needs. Such resulting conclusions the viewer may draw, again, are subjective.

They can't help but be because of the human emotional and value-laden perspective involved in all human perceptions. Such perception-laden value statements are made often in business: "Tom is a good manager." "Tom gets along well with people." "Tom has great analytical skills." Or, "Tom has trouble taking advice." "Tom is an impatient person." These statements are simply perceptions made by different viewers of Tom's behavior; but they are <u>not</u> facts about Tom.

Now, if in past performance appraisals, several people have written that Tom appears impatient, then the most that could be said is that for the environment Tom is working in, such speed is not rewarded or appreciated. In an environment where speed is rewarded, Tom would get gold stars for the same exact behavior. To underscore the point once again, students need to remember that the choice of one's adjectives to describe another person tells more about the needs of the person doing the describing than the one being described.

Because our perceptions play such a major role in our thinking, oftentimes without our being aware of it, business writers need to learn how to guard against subjectivity in their thinking and writing.

When asked to make a judgment about something, students need to develop the following:

1. Be sure that preconceived ideas or prejudices do not confuse one's judgment. Preconceived ideas or prejudices are developed either from experience or steady influences from other people, such as from parents. One preconceived idea, or what we might call prejudice, is the assumption that people of the same ethnic group or social class have the same traits. The danger of this kind of prejudice is that the writer has already determined how he or she will treat this person—without adequate evidence, he has already decided that he will treat the person in a positively prejudicial manner or negatively prejudicial manner. People who are prejudiced toward favorably receive things they have not really earned, such as an excessively positive performance appraisal or approval to implement a plan that does not make good business sense.

If a student's preconceived notions cause her to see a person in a negative light (without the appropriate evidence), she will tend to make unfair judgments against that person: unfairly negative performance appraisals, for instance. She may also withhold approval of a plan that makes good business sense, simply because she does not want to see this person succeed. The real reason people do not like someone often has nothing to do with the individual's performance but, rather, with his ethnic origin or religious preferences or an aspect of the individual's personality that is difficult to accept.

The preconceived notions human beings carry inside of them can be totally subconscious. Our students may be unaware that they harbor any prejudices. They may be stunned to learn that these under-the-surface notions actually cause them to make decisions or judgments without adequate logic or evidence. Students need to be taught that they must work hard to modify those ideas that are causing them to make judgments (too positively or too negatively) that cannot really be backed up with solid evidence and logic.

2. Be sure that one's approach does not simply serve one's own needs. Many people tend to judge issues and ideas narrowly, in a way that serves their own interests first. The business environment, with its pyramid-like structure, unwittingly encourages competitiveness and self-centeredness, with competition becoming keener as the available positions up the pyramid become fewer. Students must realize the tendency to be self-serving in their thinking, and work to make their ideas and analysis fit the needs of the situation and the department and company as a whole, rather than selecting only the facts that will support the outcome they personally desire. Ignoring pertinent facts will never work in the long run and in actuality could be very dangerous, because the business world is a very economically unforgiving one, as anyone with a fair amount of business experience could readily attest.

3. Be sure judgments are not made too quickly. Given the short time allowed for many assignments in the fast-paced world of business, it is tempting to try to push for solutions and answers very rapidly. A judgment arrived at quickly is not necessarily an inferior judgment; yet, the odds are against its being correct or best, especially when dealing with a complex issue. Given the time allowed for the assignment, students need to be taught to try their best to (a) get the most facts they can in the time they have and interpret them carefully and (b) examine the arguments on both sides of the issue (if there happen to be two sides) and honestly consider a number of possible options before settling on any one judgment. If they have run out of time and know there is more that ought to be researched, they should state that specifically in their paper: "Had additional time been possible, I would look into the viability of establishing markets in the Phoenix and San Diego areas as well."

4. <u>Be sure to avoid too many assumptions.</u> In most cases, an assumption must be supported by facts before a reasonable judgment can be made. For example, many decisions must be made about production levels, Marketing plans, etc. Certain assumptions must always be part of these decisions. Since production decisions are made on demand projections, one such assumption could be, "Demand will remain constant." This is not a fact but an assumption. What proof does the writer have that this assumption will likely happen? Is this a valid assumption to make? What are the economic indicators that demand will likely stay constant?   If they believe it will remain constant, it's still best to using hedging words, since no one has a crystal ball and therefore this cannot be stated for sure.   It would show more writing and thinking maturity to state, "Demand will likely remain constant." Then it is important to state why they think it will, in other words, build a case for the reader to be able to agree with this prediction.

5. <u>Be sure logic makes sense.</u> The most logical judgment is the one that fits the facts of the situation. When the facts will not support a firm or final statement, students should be taught to make their conclusions appropriately tentative. If they cannot speak with certainty, and in some cases they will not be able to, they are much better off admitting that. For instance, if they are presenting a plan to change something that they hope will increase productivity, the most they can logically say about future productivity is that it will <u>likely</u> increase. They cannot say that it <u>will</u> increase—that is not logical.

Tentativeness is especially important when they are predicting results that will involve the cooperation of other people. Since they cannot control others' behavior, they cannot predict with certainty anything that requires others' performance for success. In these cases, they must be taught to use hedging words to make promises. Appropriate hedging words include "likely," "probably," "should result in," etc. If they are predicting an increase in productivity with the purchase of a newer, faster piece of equipment, they do not have to hedge their prediction. They can say with more certainty, "If we buy the TR7000, we will be able to produce 9% more widgets per hour than with the current equipment."

6. Be sure not to oversimplify a complex issue. This occurs in many cases when writers define things as either good or bad, right or wrong, etc. In the real world, most situations cannot be this easily categorized. Most choices are not between the best and worst. In fact, with most business decisions, writers must decide which is the lesser of two evils or the greater of two goods. Since many alternatives are possible in most business decisions, writers can open themselves up to a greater number of solutions and more creative thinking if they do not see everything in black-and-white terms. Such dichotomous thinking usually stifles creativity and effective problem solving.

Summary

It is abundantly clear to faculty teaching any subject, but certainly any Business concentration, that the students' lack of fundamental literacy is a "competitive disadvantage" to them when they graduate and attempt to compete with applicants who have far better communication skills. And while it is true that most "hard" subject teachers do not want to or don't feel capable to grade writing assignments, it is essential that to improve, students must practice and hone their practical and logical communication skills.

The six problem areas enumerated in this article can be improved considerably by simply raising the consciousness of importance to students, then requiring assignments that address each problem area. Relating them directly to "hard" subject matter of a particular concentration fosters in the student a sense of importance and relevance. Faculty should require these assignments in class so that there is no "third party" editing opportunity.

Grading

These assignments don't have to be long or arduous to grade. A writing of just a few sentences or short paragraph over a semester dealing with each of these six major writing flaws can have a huge impact on student acuity. Grading of such short assignments is fast, doesn't require a degree in English, and can actually help endear students who see in a faculty member someone who cares about creating a competitive advantage for them among their peers and an on-the-job relevant skill. If time constraints for grading are a problem, consider "sampling" of student work: selecting a small portion of each assignment to be graded in full. Make writing a small portion of a larger quantitative, accounting, management, MIS, or computer-related core problem.

What is important here is that the student has to write, it must be a part of the course final grade, and there must be faculty feedback. If we are honest, most teachers' expectations have let student writing requirements fall into the areas of obscure or unimportant. If students see this low priority in our attitudes and syllabi (and they do), we are complicit in their competitive mediocrity. There was, after all, a very sound reason that each of us had to write a thesis or dissertation: Knowing the subject matter in an applied field isn't enough. A practitioner has to be able to articulate his or her knowledge through the written word. The students know they need improvement, we know it, and employers say it every year in the Wall Street Journal and in other polls. Or just ask a major company executive where writing ranks on their agenda of importance in student job interviews.

For sample study questions, see Appendix J.

Understanding Market Communications

Significance

Most of us take for granted the ability to communicate. Sort of like eating or breathing, we feel it is a natural ability—it is not. Effective communication is very hard work and must be manifest in all mediums of market documents, programs, campaigns, and others. In short, communication is essential to the sale of any product.

Remember the basic elements of any sales transaction: (1) there must be a product/service which has value to both parties, (2) there must be a medium of exchange (currency, precious metal, barter, etc.), and (3) the parties must be able to communicate the transaction.[153]

Communicating in marketing is not only the basis for effectiveness but it is also the cornerstone of personal and company credibility. Lack of ability in spelling, punctuation, and grammar is inexcusable for a college graduate and practitioner. If your documents include these mechanical flaws, many of your readers will wonder about the quality of your education and how much time you spent in school really trying to improve your skills.

Business readers are very unforgiving when they see words misspelled, errors in possession, capitalization, and other such errors. Readers are always consciously or subconsciously asking themselves how much "stock" to place in the writer. They often will ask themselves, "What is the chance that this writer really knows what he or she is talking about?" If they spot communication errors, they are likely to discount the content of the document or discount the company—which means credibility suffers.

For one thing, the use of poor mechanics shows a lack of attention to detail. After seeing such poor attention to detail in the simple mechanics, your reader is likely to seriously question your overall capabilities.[154] It doesn't matter whether the error is inadvertent (a typo) or due to ignorance. The result is the same—you lose. Give yourself every chance to be listened to and respected by your business colleagues.[155]

It is difficult to over-estimate the value of the written and spoken word in effective marketing communications. In prose, the layout; use of color; graphics; and white space each play a significant role in the appearance of the document. Even correct grammar, punctuation, spelling, and syntax are each critical to "reaching" our customer. In oral delivery, our personal grooming and appearance must be considered. Grooming makes a statement about how we feel about the receiver, and about how we feel concerning the material being presented, and perhaps most important, our grooming tells something about how we feel about ourselves.

In order to effectively communicate with customers and potential customers, the communicator must speak in their language. Consider first just how different the potential customer segment may be from our own. Each customer has his or her own profile which includes education, family background, ethnic origin, values, beliefs, political and religious affiliation, customs, etc. When market communications are developed, each must reflect a consideration of the characteristics found in the prospective or current customer segment.

Effective market communication begins with primary and secondary investigation of these elements. Developing understanding of the customers' profiles requires a great deal of effort and in some cases complex survey techniques as well as data base evaluation. Once we have "profiled" the customer segment, we can begin to communicate on their terms.

One factor to consider when communicating on their terms is your language. Are the words you are using easy enough to be readily understood by your target audience? The reading level of a document can actually be calculated. Robert Gunning created the Gunning Fog Index—a mathematical formula of sorts to calculate the reading level of a passage. Created in 1952, it has become a classic approach to assess reading level:

Gunning Fog Index: [B/C + (A/B X 100)]   X   0.4

where:

A =   Number of "difficult" words in the paragraph (containing three or more syllables)
B =   Number of words in the paragraph
C =   Number of sentences in the paragraph

Look at the difference in difficulty between the following two passages. The first is taken from *The Reno Gazette Journal*, and the second is from *The Wall Street Journal*—both daily newspapers:

"The Reno <u>Municipal</u> Court set an across-the-board fine for wasting water at $600. Reno won't hire a full-time water cop until after city <u>employee</u> layoffs are approved Tuesday. That's so displaced workers have first dibs."

The calculation of the reading grade level for this passage is as follows:

[12.7 + (5.3)] x 0.4 = 7.2 or 7th grade

[Granted, this is a small sample from *The Reno Gazette Journal*. This level of prose, however, is common to almost all popular newsprint because it is so appropriate for the general reading public.]

Remember, the following *The Wall Street Journal* passage is intended for a much more narrow and educated "specific public" or readership than that of the previous publication:

"Increasingly, the American business community is coming to the same conclusion: it must get more involved with training young people. This is a concern not only for training your employees but for the youths themselves.

[17.5 + (17.1)] x 0.4 = 13.8 or Second Year of College

The first passage, obviously, takes much less effort to understand. The second passage would require much more effort for most people. In attempting to understand what the Gunning Fox Index really means, it is important to recognize that, since the time that Robert Gunning devised this formula and the associated "grade levels," societal literacy has dropped dramatically and scholastic test scores (ACT, SAT, GMAT, etc.) have declined.

Course content at all grade levels has become less rigorous, and grade inflation has increased. Therefore, most publications today are written far below an individual's academic year of education. Try calculating the grade level of a typical upper division college textbook (*e.g.,* Introduction to Marketing, Management, Accounting, etc.). You will find that each is written at about the sophomore level of high school, or the 10th grade level. Think about these same issues when evaluating the writing you do for market communications. The Gunning Fog Index is now embedded in Microsoft Word and other prominent software applications, making the analysis of reading level quick and easy.

Applications

Let's now look at six areas of marketing where communication plays a crucial role: Advertising, Sales Promotion, Personal Selling, Contracts, Data Collection, and Marketing Strategy.

Advertising: The objective of advertising is to concisely inform and educate your customer about your product or service. Whether the advertising is in visual, audio, or written form, the clarity with which it is delivered will determine just how much the receiver is able to "learn."

Sales Promotion: Effective sales promotion involves specific efforts aimed at getting the consumer to purchase the advertised product or service. These efforts can include promotional pricing, coupon development, free trial programs, sweepstakes, extended warranty and service plans, rebates, and others. The success of the promotional medium is directly related to our ability to effectively communicate the benefits to the consumer.

Personal Selling: Personal and direct selling are particularly applicable in the industrial and business markets, although there are applications in consumer product markets as well. The importance of communication skills here is just as critical. When we represent a product or service as a vendor, our individual ability to communicate with the prospective customer will often make the difference between a sale and a rejection. More importantly, the entire positioning of the vendor organization may be "on the line." The customer's first impression of excellence (or lack of) will almost always be through some form of communication.

<u>Contracts</u>: Contracts of all kinds are required with clients, customers, other manufacturers/vendors, channel members, and financial institutions. Many businesses are now leasing as well as selling their products, and these agreements must be clearly articulated. Particularly in the current litigious and caveat venditor environment, effective contract communication is critical to market success.

<u>Data Collection</u>: Effective communication is essential in consumer data collection. We must understand our current consumers, attempting to secure deeper market share as well as new market segments. From the simplest surveys to the most intricate data collection methodologies, we depend on the language and our communication skills in order to develop valid test instruments. Without the proper communication skills, we waste our clients' time and our own energy and resources.

<u>Marketing Strategy</u>: Imagine the number of internal marketing and sales meetings conducted daily. Communicating succinctly is essential. It seems easy enough—we know about the Gunning Fog Index <u>and</u> they are our peers, so we shouldn't have any problems being understood. Yet, think back to your basic statistics class and evaluate the number of possibilities for miscommunication. If you are in a meeting of seven market managers and combinations of three people are discussing, presenting, or arguing a position, there are 35 different combinations of three managers possible.

$$_nC_r = \frac{n!}{r!(n-r)!}$$

or

$$_7C_3 = \frac{7!}{(3!)(7-3)!}$$

where:

r	=	number of combinations
n	=	number of objects

C   =   total number of different combinations

$$= \frac{7 \times 6 \times 5 \times 4 \times 3 \times 2 \times 1}{(3 \times 2 \times 1)(4 \times 3 \times 2 \times 1)} = \textbf{35 combinations of 3 managers}$$

Implementation

Even if we understand the importance of communication in the marketing effort and even if we develop first-rate personal skills, we are not assured of the effective transfer of information. Following is a schematic of business to customer communication. In it you will see that transmission of data, even capable data, follows a pattern which can become confounded. This model becomes infinitely more complicated when more people are exchanging information (*e.g.,* the example of seven managers taken three at a time).

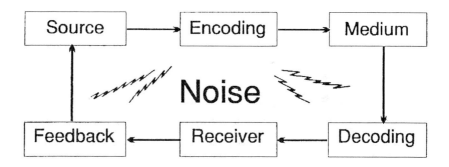

In order to fully understand the implications of the model, let's observe each of the elements and its contribution to the marketer's communication environment.[156]

<u>Source</u>: The source in this model is the originating entity or the business organization responsible for developing and promulgating the message. As we look back at the few examples of market communication earlier, we could recognize several different objectives for developing a client or customer

communication. Based on the firm's particular objective, a message is developed into a theme.

Encoding: The theme must now be developed in concert with the segment profile discussed earlier. The encoding step may be the most important of all in the process. It is arguably the step in which we can have the most influence over the effectiveness of the message. We are able to choose the syntax; the educational level; and the political, custom, or ethnic "twist." It is here that the validity of the message is developed. Is the objective of the message being met through our encoding process? Does the message mean the same thing to the customer segment that it means to us? Remember, once the encoding step is behind us, we have lost our control over the translation of the communication. "Try honestly to see things from the other person's point of view."[157]

Media: The firm may select from many different types of communication delivery methods in order to target its customers and convey its message. Among the most popular forms of media are television (public, private, and cable), radio, billboards, magazines, trade journals, trade shows, fliers, brochures, newspapers, point-of-purchase displays, direct mail, personal selling, search engines, and social web platforms. The significance of this choice is that certain mediums will be more effective than other mediums at reaching the specific market segment, and each medium is uniquely priced.

For example, "prime-drive-time" radio spots on CBS, NBC, ABC, FOX, and NPR news radio would not be a good selection to reach housewives, and this time spot is the most expensive on radio. This selection might, however, be very appropriate for reaching business and industry managers concerning a health program, financial investment, or vacation opportunity—even though the cost of exposure is high.

Decoding: Successful decoding depends on a common level of reference concerning the data presented. As discussed earlier, the control of the reception of our message is now totally under the influence of the receiver. How "correctly" the information is decoded depends heavily on the prior ability of the firm to properly encode its message within the customers' frame of reference (education, family background, ethnic origin, values, beliefs, political and religious affiliations, and customs).

Receiver: The receiver is, of course, the consumer, potential consumer, or the business to whom we intend to market. The individual or the entity will now cast its decision and "dollar vote." They will either purchase our product or service, not purchase the offering, or purchase/not purchase but request or present a response/expression back to the host firm (the source). Much can be learned by observing closely the receivers' reactions to the message they have decoded. This data is probably the least expensive and some of the most valuable market research that we can gain access to.

Feedback: Feedback can be measured in many ways. A fairly usual way is to evaluate the amount, quality, and consistency of the messages returned. Here is an opportunity to once again apply the AIDA model. Does the response indicate that the communicated message created ATTENTION? Was one of the results a generation of INTEREST? Did the communication develop DESIRE on the part of the consumer. And, most importantly, did the communication transmission create ACTION—a sale for our firm?

Noise: The stages in the communication model indicate the order, steps, and complete requirements to attempt successful and effective marketing communication. In each area, we have discussed possible advantages and a few of the pitfalls which can result at that particular stage. But there is a constant presence which surrounds all of the elements of the model— noise. Noise is the presence of any competing or supporting contribution which impacts the message itself. For example, if the message is an advertisement, noise may well be another ad which appears on the same page of printed copy. The ad need not be of another similar product. Any additional ad may attract the customer's eye. An interruption by telephone, a family member entering the room, a previous message provided by a competing product—there are almost limitless possibilities for contamination.

"Publics"

There are several public entities that may or may not provide additional interference with the basic communication model in business. A public is made up of a group of individuals or firms with the influence to provide distraction which may change the way in which our message will be decoded. This information may again be positive or negative and it may be directed at our firm specifically or impact the firm's market communication indirectly. Examples of such publics include the following:

Financial Publics: Financial publics are made up of institutions and individuals whose pronouncements regarding economic and financial data are respected (banks, brokerage houses, stock and bond rating services, etc.).

Media Publics: Media publics include newspapers, magazines, news services (UPI, Reuters, AP), television and radio broadcast news, public relations organizations, and others. Each is in a position to offer proclamations regarding both fact and opinion (editorial) regarding a myriad of subjects which might affect our consumers' interpretation of the original message.

Special Interest Publics: Special interest publics arise surrounding a certain common issue. For example, there are several special interest publics which address themselves specifically to consumer protection (Ralph Nader's organization, *Consumer Reports* magazine, etc.). Other types of special interest groups examine fine arts, education, unions, trade associations, MADD, and the list goes on and on.

<u>General Public</u>: The general public develops and molds opinion concerning general mores, values, ethics, social responsibility, human rights, and other issues. These positions may be manifest in the form of letters to the editors, public meetings, voting positions, committees, and company or industry boycotts.

<u>Legal Public</u>: Legal publics often make legal decisions, set precedent, make pronouncements, or interpret the law. Among the most common are law firms, courts, authors and publishing houses, judges, court television, and universities.

<u>Government Publics</u>: Government publics include the multitude of local, state, and federal agencies which evaluate and regulate just about everything. Among these institutions which may have a profound effect on market communication are departments of Health Education and Welfare, Transportation, Defense, Treasury, Justice, Federal Reserve, Trade, Food and Drug, and many others.

Conclusion

Communication touches every aspect of the marketing effort. In order to assure that our messages are effectively communicated, it is essential that the organization follow sound communication policies. No product, no matter how valuable or popular, will ever reach its potential in the marketplace without the well thought out development of a capable, surrounding communication strategy.

The model presented here indicates a sequencing of the communication steps. While these steps are related in specific sequence, you will be most successful if you consider them simultaneously, as a system/program, rather than stand-alone elements. Most important to recognize is that no element can or will function by itself.

Further, in market communications, and unlike the common software acronym, WYSIWYG is not always true. Here it is important to remember all too often the truism: "The large print giveth, and the small print taketh away."[158] And, as always, caveat lector (reader beware) is a very real responsibility.

For sample study questions, see Appendix J.

Advertising, Promotion, and Publicity

Introduction

Advertising, promotion, and publicity are sometimes confused with one another. The following is a concise and applied definition of each.

<u>Advertising</u> is a paid activity whose primary function is to educate by developing consumer awareness for a product or service. Advertising is clearly necessary. If the market observer considers the movement from the pre-product life cycle through the ramp-up and into the roll-out of the product, s/he recognizes that, for a truly new product, there is NO awareness of the product at all. What is the product? What does it do? What does it look like? These are simple but critical rudiments of a capable advertising message.

<u>Promotion</u> is a paid activity that attempts to persuade and influence potential customers and increase their propensity to buy. Promotion may not be necessary; however, it may well stimulate sales that otherwise would not be made. When promotional vehicles are considered (sampling, coupons, bonus packs, premiums, contests, lotteries, rebates, etc.), the market manager should evaluate carefully which among these possibilities offer the greatest "perceived" utility to the consumer, while at the same time requiring the least resource from the company.

Publicity can be defined as (1) a non-paid, uncontrolled dissemination of insignificant or significant information in the mass media or (2) a paid (company press or public relations) release of commercially significant product/service news to the mass media. Publicity, or the management of publicity, is, perhaps, more an art form than a fundamental strategic tool. It is for this primary reason that many organizations such as Emery Worldwide and DuPont have employed the large public relations firms of Ogilvy & Mather and Hoyt and Sudler & Hennessey, respectively, to assist them in positioning product releases and to give them advice on damage control, once adverse publicity has made its way into the mainstream media.

Because of publicity's "artful" nature, we may be well advised to retain a public relations organization. But, remember, they work for you. Your firm knows more about its company objectives, specific market, and product or service than a public relation organization does. These organizations and individuals are not journalists. They should be hired for their ability to influence public opinion, change minds, and get information printed in the mass media.

It is because of their third-party relationships and influence with principals among the mix of media that PR people are so valuable. Don't misunderstand. PR people can do many things that business does not do well, should not be spending their time on, and, frankly, are not trained to do (*e.g.,* press releases, exclusive editorial news features, press conferences and "kits," and invaluable assistance with trade "shows" and conference appearances and damage control of public disclosures).

Once the business unit understands the specific utilities of advertising, promotion, and publicity, it can then focus on objectives, theme, budget, media mix (mediums), allocation, and measures of effectiveness.

AIDA Model

In theoretical economic principle, the firm is expected to maximize profit and, therefore, should continue to increase spending in each campaign category until the point where the additional cost of encouraging the next sale is equal to the incremental profit received from that sale. Any self-respecting sales manager or marketing manager will tell you that the principle is more easily understood as "separating the consumer from his or her money." Whichever of these objectives you prefer, each must insure profit and not merely revenue increases.

Probably the best conceptual approach to apply in this "P" (promotion) of the marketing mix is the AIDA model.[159] The model assumes relative customer ignorance or indifference to the product or service and so follows a linear progression. First, advertising must be used to educate and provide exposure information to the prospective customer. Advertising can also begin to create interest in the product or service. Next, promotion attempts to assure interest and create desire by providing an incentive to purchase, which, hopefully, leads to action or to the closure of the sale. (See Appendix D.)

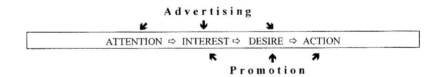

From a pragmatic point of view, the most significant element in the acronym is the second "A." Action is the closing of a sale, and, without this specific act, any investment in the other AIDA elements becomes a feigned meeting of the true objective. There are heavy sunk costs associated with advertising to raise attention, promotion, and/or personal selling to create interest and desire. If these costs do not "close" the sale, the market manager is worse off than before s/he started (lower profit).

The double-approach-avoidance conflict model from Psychology helps to explain the "powers" that must be overcome in order to convince the buyer to act favorably to make the purchase decision. The buyer vacillates between purchasing the new or better product and having to give up the required resource to do so (usually money). This vacillation in Marketing terms is called "dissonance." (See Glossary.) As an example of dissonance, the following graphic illustrates the student's decision (dissonance) between continuing to ride a bicycle to campus or enjoying the luxury of driving a Porsche.

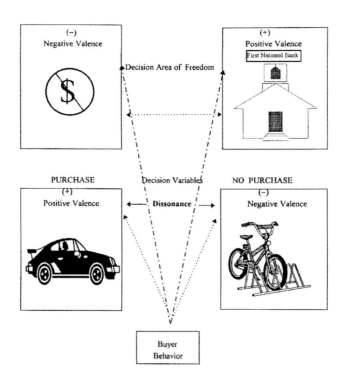

Trade-Off Dimensions
Purchase Decision

This type of tradeoff polarity occurs in both individual (personal) and business (industrial) purchases where the "stakes" are high. "Should I/we buy?" "Should I/we not buy?" If the purchase decision is made, then the question arises, "Was it a good decision?" If the decision was made not to buy, then we question whether another such product or service will exist in the future if we change our mind, or, we might also be afraid that we failed to capitalize on an opportunity that will no longer be available in the future. The combination of advertising, promotion (and personal selling), and publicity make up what is commonly referred to as the "promotional mix." (Take care not to confuse this definition with that of the marketing mix, media mix, or product mix [see Glossary]).

These elements can help the market manager to reduce the dissonance that the buyer experiences as s/he considers the tradeoff between giving up resources and fulfilling a want or need.

Objective

The fundamental objective among advertising, promotion, and publicity is to fulfill the AIDA model at a point above the economic diminishing return mentioned earlier. Any campaign should begin by complying with the overall strategy and positioning of the firm itself. If this is not the case, the campaign may well do a fine job of selling one product or service but at the expense of the consumer's perceived brand loyalty to other products offered by the company (for example, the changing of the "Classic Coke" formula and the consumer market debacle that followed).

Also, think about whether the environment may be strictly consumer-oriented or if it might be commercial/industrial. If the latter is the case, make certain that the objective is narrowed to reach the segment of qualified, prospective buyers or clients. In this instance, assure that the campaign is waged at someone who

1. has a need for the product (application).
2. can obtain the cash or credit (is able to buy).
3. has the authority to buy (is a decision maker).
4. will be reachable by a sales person (personal selling).
5. is eligible to buy (meets any legal restrictions).

It is important when developing objectives to consider a test for the "reasonable" expectations for strategies being considered. The same is true of budgetary constraints. Strive to enumerate specific and measurable (even soft-dollar) objectives. These objectives will establish a far greater probability of ultimate success in influencing sales than objectives not specifically enumerated.

Theme

With profit the main objective, there may be different themes (hopefully based on primary attitude research collected from among our potential customer base) or a combination of themes to be applied in the campaign.

1. The specific nature of the product or service
2. Competing products (if there are any)
3. Government regulations that could be used to advantage
4. Pricing
5. Guarantees and warranties
6. Utilities or applications
7. Superior service
8. High quality
9. Experience (install Base)
10. Prestige product
11. State-of-the-art distribution innovation
12. Emphasizing a trademark or brand
13. Positioning of goodwill
14. Highlighting unique features
15. Generating in-store traffic
16. Comparative advertising

It is difficult to overemphasize the need for specific attitude and behavioral market research from among the firm's prospective buyers. Buyer behavior is the direct link to customer propensity and close of the sale (the second "A" in AIDA). None among this entire list of themes is of value unless there is significant correlation between it and the willingness of the customer or client to actually purchase the product or service. Be as logically and operationally specific as possible here.

Budgeting

There are several methods for establishing a budget for advertising, promotion, and PR.

Per cent of sales is a common approach, basing the number of dollars to be spent on (1) a research forecast of product to be sold, (2) a level of past sales (if not a new product entry), or (3) an industry average expenditure of expected sales volume. The proponents of this budget style argue that some expenditure is necessary and a percentage of each revenue dollar is logical to assure sales. They further point out that the concept is easily understood.   On the other hand, some disadvantages are that it assumes that sales forecasts are accurate and that industry standards are relevant, and that all competing products are about equally "valuable."

Competitive parity is considered to be a defensive or reactive budget strategy.   A firm using this approach attempts to match the advertising budget of competitors.   This is a relatively accepted approach in certain industries like the cola and beer markets.   It is considered to be a "safe" option. Its proponents believe that the strategy will maintain relative market shares.   Opponents argue that again it assumes that there are no differentiated differences among products, that it is difficult to get accurate competitive intelligence, and it assumes that the competition know what they are doing.

<u>Marginal strategy</u> follows the economic theory that a firm should continue to spend on advertising and promotion, as long as revenues continue to rise. There is some fundamental logic to this approach; however, it is difficult to determine what percentage expenditure is most beneficial, particularly as competitors, consumer attitudes, product and employee environments, etc. change.

Per unit expenditure may be a viable option for an organization that produces or provides a variety of products or services. This approach sounds a lot like percent of sales, but it has a basic difference. The cost of production and market price are evaluated to determine a logical balance for each product. This method probably won't work very well for low-priced items. But where there is a substantial amount of difference between the production cost and the possible profit per unit (*e.g.*, the automobile or housing industries), it may make good sense to spend more "per each" to effect a sale.

<u>Objective or task approaches</u> use a program approach to assemble a budget. First the goals and objectives specified earlier are divided into tasks. Each is evaluated based on its individual or incremental cost to accomplish. Then all tasks are summed to determine the aggregate budget necessary to implement and achieve the initial objective of the campaign. This is commonly held as the most popular promotional budget technique. However, critics argue that its greatest strength of specific task elements is also its weakness—each element is difficult to fully evaluate in terms of actual cost to implement.

The most significant issue in budget allocation is not the method but rather the overall effectiveness of its success in terms of sales. Regrettably, this cannot be done very well until after the campaign has been put into action in the market place. Even then, the predictive ability of measurement models available is dubious with regard to the specific relationship between the campaign and increased sales. For this reason, we will see that the effectiveness of advertising, promotion, and publicity campaigns are often measured by means other than propensity or even actual sales results.

Media Mix

The media mix consists of a selection of possible mediums through which the firm can deliver its communication message. The following are common vehicles for transmitting the theme:

1. Billboards
2. Direct Mail
3. Magazines
4. Newspapers
5. Radio
6. Television
7. Trade "shows" conferences
8. Trade journals
9. Transit
10. Multimedia (Web, PC/CD/Video/Theater)

To make the most efficient selection of media, the focus must now turn to the target market and message strategy. What media do the potential customers subscribe to? What are their patterns of media behavior (traffic, visual, audio, print, etc.)? What is the most logical mix of media that will reach these constituents and be delivered at a "level" (style, tone, selection of words, format, and appeal) that they will find relevant and engaging? This may seem like an impossible task, but there is help.

Most of the major vendors of media (publishers, networks, agencies, etc.) have anticipated the business need. They have become very sophisticated in attracting advertising dollars, and, as such, make available "media packs." For the most part, these are very well done. Each consists of subscription or circulation data prepared by third-party research consultants. The demographics, psychographics, geographics, and behavioral characteristics of the media vendor's consumers are carefully examined.

Media Allocation

Once the objectives have been articulated, the budget determined, and the most appropriate vehicles for media selected, the issue now becomes how much of the budget would be allocated to a particular medium for maximum impact.   The decision of what mediums to use and the amount to be spent are all too often determined by the whim of executives in the organization, or the cost, or the type that appears most "creative" (*e.g.,* the CLIO awards).

It is simpler if only one media vehicle is to be used, but this is usually not the typical situation. Suppose some of your prospective customers read a certain magazine but do not watch television, while another group watches television but does not read magazines. A very capable algorithm is available to the students and practitioners of business—linear programming.

Linear programming can help to allocate resources, while at the same time considering restrictions and constraints of the organization.[160] The linear programming technique provides for a maximized allocation of budget, based on constraints of the media type and number of exposures desired. Consider the following example of a firm attempting to find the most efficient proportion of two competing media vehicles.

Based on the company's buyer behavior research and public relations data, television and magazines are the best way to reach their target market. Television commercials expose 20 million people per advertisement, and magazine commercials expose 10 million people per advertisement. Magazine ads cost $40,000 each, and television ads cost $75,000 each. The market manager has a media budget of $2,000,000.   The company's

CFO is a senior executive who insists that whatever the decision, there must be at least 20 magazine ads included if he is going to approve the funding. (This type of constraint may not be reasonable logically, but it may be a "trench" reality.) How many commercials of each type should be purchased to maximize the number of exposures, while at the same time humoring the CFO?

To set the objective function, let "T" stand for the number of television commercials and "M" for the number of magazine commercials:

1. $T \geq 0$ (It is illogical to have a negative number of commercials.)
2. $M \geq 20$ (We must have at least 20 magazine commercials.)
3. The cost of a television commercial is $75,000, and the cost of a magazine commercial is $40,000. The budget allocated is $2,000,000.

Therefore, the cost constraint (in thousands) is $40M + $75T ≤ $2,000

Following is the graphic solution defined by the cost constraints:

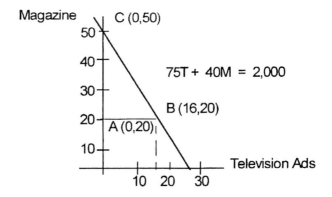

The preceding graphic solution is simplified to accommodate a "by-hand" graphic and quantitative solution; however, linear programming is capable of managing more complex problems involving multiple objectives and multiple constraints.

The smaller triangle (ABC) in the graphic is the region that is defined by the constraints. [Point 50,0) on the graph or 2,000/75T=26.7 television ads is not considered part of the media solution because of the chief financial officer's magazine constraint of M ≥ 20.] The market manager can find the point that yields the highest number of people exposed at the lowest price to the advertisement by applying a theorem of linear programming which states that the maximized point must be equal to one of the corners of the defined region.

[Corner A = minimum expenditure possible (0,20)]
[Corner B = 2,000 - (20x40)= 1,200
[Corner C = 2,000/40 = 50 or (0,50)]
         now: 1,200/75 = 16 or (16,20)]

4.   (0,20) number of people exposed
        = (20 million)(0) + (10 million)(20) = 200 million
        exposures

5.   (16,20) number of people exposed
        = (20 million)(16) + (10 million)(20) = 520 million
        exposures

6.   (0,50) number of people exposed
        = (20 million)(0) + (10 million)(50) = 500 million
        exposures

7.   Therefore, the best media mix, given the original constraints (1, 2, and 3) would be to have 16 television commercials and 20 magazine commercials. This solution would provide 320 million television exposures and 200 million magazine exposures for a budget which can provide 520 million combined media exposures.

Measure of Effectiveness

Once the campaign has been deployed in the prospective market segment, the question is, how effective is it?   This is an area in which market management has not been truly effective. There are several highly quantitative approaches that have attempted to measure outcomes but consider the variables.   If the relationship was simply a linear function, we could determine the current sales level (none, if a new product), spend, and re-measure based on sales. However, this approach does not consider other variables: consumer attitudes and beliefs, competitors, economic irregularities, cultural influences, or media dissemination, all of which we have no control over. Aggregate change is fairly easily measured. What is not as easily measured is the influence that caused the change in demand and to what specific extent.

Some practitioners have argued that rather than to employ copious formulae that at best approximate outcomes with little correlation to cause and effect, market managers should attempt to evaluate mediums and their effect "in advance," by more fully understanding what each can be expected or not expected to offer.

Five basic measures fall into this category:

Cost per thousand is a common means of establishing value of a media vehicle.   Cost per thousand equals the cost of one exposure unit divided by the quantity number of subscribers reached, divided by 1,000, or

Cost Per Thousand $=$	$\dfrac{\textbf{Cost of One Exposure Unit}}{\textbf{Number of Subscribers Reached / 1000}}$

For example, if a marketing manager was selling centrifuges, s/he might want to target wineries. Perhaps an ad in *Wino Times* would be desirable. If a single, full-page, national advertisement in this spirit magazine costs $25,500 and 2,003,000 vintners subscribe to the publication, the advertisement cost per thousand would be $12.73.

Reach is a calculation that helps to determine the significance of the message delivery in terms of potential impact to the target market. Specifically, reach is the total percentage of consumers exposed to the media once during a specific time period.

Frequency is based on, first, a calculation of the reach, and then a determination of the number of times that a potential consumer has been or will be successively exposed during a given time frame.

Gross Rating Points (GRP) is a relative measure of media effectiveness, based both on reach and frequency. In fact, it is determined by multiplying the two together. The gross rating point "objective" is also a relative term used in the media industry to attempt to justify effectiveness. To determine a gross rating point objective, let's go back to the *Wino Times* example and observe a relationship between reach and frequency. If the market manager wanted to reach 80% of the vintners during a specific time period (the industry standard range seems to be two to four weeks), say, two weeks, and the desired frequency was four exposures, then s/he would multiply [(4)(80)] to yield a GRP rating objective of 320.

Media Penetration must be considered by any marketing manager who is interested in objectively evaluating potential media performance and added value to a campaign. Vendors of newspapers and magazines will want to talk about their circulation numbers; radio and television purveyors will want to focus on watts of power from a logistical point of view. Sellers of direct mail will hype the quality and length of a segmented list, and so on. But, in an applied sense, the market practitioner should realize that these analyses can be flawed.

For example, many subscribers to news or magazine print read only the editorial, sports, or financial section, ignoring any of the pages dedicated to advertising space. Because a radio or television signal is strong geographically, it does not mean that the receiving hardware is turned on, or, conversely, if it is turned on that anyone is watching or listening. And, again, direct mail lists can only assure delivery, not whether the recipient will consider the piece as junk mail or worth their time to read.

For help in evaluating the true penetration numbers, Standard Rate and Data, Inc., A.C. Nielson, and Arbitron are consultants who evaluate news print, television, and radio, respectively, for this purpose. Also, the Direct Marketing Association (DMA) can provide some advice when considering how to evaluate mailing list effectiveness.

Summary

Any capable media campaign must begin with the premise that dollars spent without a clearly researched relationship between the design elements and the willingness of our specific segmented customer to purchase (propensity) is spurious at best. Further, a clearly delineated and practical understanding of advertising, sales promotion (including personal selling), and publicity is essential.

The program's objective should be clearly articulated in terms of attracting attention, developing interest, creating desire, and, most important, motivating the buyer to act by closing the sale (AIDA). Our market research should establish the characteristics of theme that will most likely influence the target market.

There will always be a budget constraint. But given a limited amount of resource within the firm, what is the best approach to compete effectively and justify an efficient campaign budget? Consider the alternatives of a per cent of sales, competitive parity, marginal strategy, per-unit expenditure, or objective/task approach.

Consistent with the objective, what are the media vehicles that can be logically expected to yield the highest results considering the target consumer?   Are billboards, direct mail, magazines, newspapers, television, etc., the most attractive, or some combination of the many other alternatives?   When attempting to make the difficult decision to optimize budget dollars among competing media vehicles, apply the power of linear programming to maximize dollars to be spent.

It is true that Marketing Management has not developed a fail-safe predictive model to evaluate campaign effectiveness, but it is also true that by evaluating measures such as cost per thousand, reach, frequency, gross rating points, and media penetration, the practitioner can "hedge the bet" before actual deployment of the campaign.

For sample study questions, see Appendix J.

This article was first published in Business Horizons *by Susan G. Thomas and was entitled, "Effective Oral Presentations: What Speech Classes Didn't Teach You about Presenting in Business Settings."*

Effective Oral Presentations

Because oral presentations are such a common and practical form of communication in business settings, you will likely have to give one or more presentations during your career. We cannot assume that people, having to present as part of their job, necessarily enjoy giving presentations. In fact, many people detest the task. Why? Partly because they have not had enough practice, and partly because audiences can be difficult—let us say, less than totally supportive.

This article is divided into two parts—(1) how to give an effective presentation and (2) how to deal successfully with audience members who will try to give you difficulty. At some point in your life, you may have already taken a speech class. Most speech classes do fairly well teaching students the basics of how to prepare and give an effective presentation, but they do almost nothing to teach students how to deal with the difficult audience members who may attempt to destroy the speaker's success. Such encounters are normally not a part of presentations in an academic setting. It is not until you attend (or perhaps give your own) presentations in the real world that you will discover very different "group" dynamics.

Unpleasant interchanges with difficult listeners are not rare occurrences in business presenting. Unfortunately, they are commonplace. Disaster can strike if you are unprepared for the difficult types lurking in business audiences. Let's look first at how to give a great presentation and then how to deal with the problem people in the audience.

Prepare Effectively

Visualize Your Audience Positively

You have been asked to speak because you have information that others need. This thought is both flattering and sometimes a little frightening if you have not done much presenting. The best way to approach the challenge is to begin by reducing your fears. The easiest way to do this is to re-frame your audience by trying to draw them closer to you mentally: think of the audience members as being in a partnership with you rather than as a solo performance on your part, a linkage rather than confrontation, coming closer, rather than pulling apart. Think of yourselves as a team. A "me versus them" mentality will only cause you to feel unnecessary nervousness. You are really all on the same team. Align yourself with them mentally even before you begin to prepare, and you will relax quite a bit.

Define Your Main Idea

Your first step in preparation should be to define the main idea that you want to get across in your presentation. If your presentation involves persuading your audience to implement something new, write out in one sentence the chief argument you will use to convince your audience to do what you will be asking.

If choice is involved on their part, persuasion is key to success. A main idea statement might be something like "Reorganizing the data processing department will lead to better service at a lower cost." Of course, the critical part of your presentation would be to convince the audience that better service is possible [after defining what "better" means] and presenting data that proves that lower costs are possible. Most main idea statements should (1) be stated in a positive way and (2) directly relate to the audience's interests or company goals.

If you cannot clearly define what your main point is, it is unlikely that your audience will be able to guess either. You're headed for a weak presentation. Audience members are likely to leave the meeting confused and unsure of how to apply the information you conveyed or what it all means to them. Defining your main point is not always easy; it may take an hour to work that out in your mind. The best presentations convey a crystal-clear thought process, not necessarily ALL the answers, but what is presented is clear, logical, well organized, and easy to understand. Creating a successful presentation takes a great deal of time.

Target the Audience's Needs and Concerns

Every presentation assignment is generated by a need—the audience needs something from the speaker, usually help—an idea, direction, motivation, information. As you now begin the process of gathering information to present and an approach to take, analyze what audience members NEED from your presentation. What are they supposed to leave the meeting with? Information to help them carry out a new directive? Motivation to do a better job? Are you going to ask their support for a new program? Perhaps in some cases there is not an audience need yet, but you plan to create one in their minds that you will then fulfill with your solution.

The closer you come to fulfilling their needs, the more they will meet yours. What kinds of needs do speakers have? Probably the most important one is the need for approval from the audience. Only the audience can give it, but it can be given in many forms—a vote, signature on a document, positive feedback to you or to others after the meeting, or even an outburst of applause.

Most speakers want to feel they have been successful. How will they know it unless they sense approval from those they have tried to help? You will be much more likely to get audience approval when you attempt to address THEIR needs. Even if what you are presenting is something **you** want, it's important to present it in such a way that audience members know they will benefit too—directly or indirectly—by complying with what you are asking for. If nothing is "in it for them," the idea becomes much harder to sell, and their approval probably will not be forthcoming.

As you have probably noticed witnessing both presentation successes and failures, the speakers who did well knew their audience's needs and targeted their comments to those needs or concerns. Knowing the composition of your audience is not really difficult for most business people giving presentations. In your own company, you would likely know quite a bit about those who will attend—their positions within the company, the projects or operations they are responsible for, and, perhaps, how they already feel about you.

As you analyze audience members, you should also consider their backgrounds, their educational levels, their general attitude toward the subject, and what they already know about the subject. The more ways the audience is dissimilar, the tougher your job is as a speaker. You need to reach everyone, give everyone something to take away from the meeting.

If people from other departments or people higher up the chain of command will be attending, it is important to remember that often these individuals are likely to be less knowledgeable about the specifics of the topic than those in your immediate department. You may need to give more background or "lay the groundwork" in these instances before you get to extremely specific information.

Your presentation can target audience needs even more directly if you address specific individuals during your presentation: "Bob, I think the new procedure we are about to discuss will particularly benefit your department." And then you proceed with a description of the new procedure.

If Bob was asleep, he will now wake up and pay particular attention to what you are about to say, since this appears to be information that directly relates to him and his needs. Either during this part of your presentation or at the end of it, Bob will likely either acknowledge that you were right and that the new changes will be a great help or, perhaps, point out some problems he sees with the procedure as you have outlined it. Bob's comments are valuable feedback, and you should not take this criticism personally [unless of course you really should have anticipated the very problem he now brings up].

Gather Relevant Material

Once you have clarified a main point idea in your own mind and analyzed audience needs and concerns, the next step is to prepare major and supporting ideas to prove your main point while, at the same time, addressing audience needs. In the preceding example, the speaker wants to convince the audience members that it would be in the company's best interest to reorganize the data processing department. While many attendees may think that sounds like a good idea, most participants would want some proof. What is your evidence that this is a good idea? In other words, what benefits would accrue?

On the heels of that question is always one involving the costs of implementation. What would it cost us to do this? [Effective presenters always anticipate and prepare for audience objections.] Both of these areas—benefits and costs—must be researched thoroughly. It is critical that costs be analyzed very carefully and accurately.

Since most participants can stay tuned only so long and remember only so much information, it is important to select, say, the three major benefits of reorganization. Do not list 20. If you hand out information to be discussed by the group, you can cover more and in more detail. If listeners, however, do not have the advantage of following anything written, then limit the number of points made and details given orally.

Keep in mind as you are preparing that your audience will want to know, basically, five things: (1) How do you know this? (2) Is that an accurate statement? (3) Does it agree with other sources? (4) What does it have to do with the subject, and (5) What does it have to do with me? Be prepared to answer any or all of these questions about any statement you make in your presentation.

An important rule of thumb when gathering information is to gather more material than you plan to use. In other words, know more than you give. Try not to speak to the edge of your knowledge [unless that's where everybody else is too]. It is too easy to get into trouble and become extremely nervous when you begin to discuss things you are not sure of. Try to stay away from the "edge."

This same rule applies to gathering data and figures as well—always have more backup figures and data than you plan to use. For example, when you are presenting an analysis of something, there is usually more than one way to show the numbers. If you plan to show yearly output of something, you could also have backup charts showing a quarterly breakout or monthly breakout or by department.

It can be very impressive when someone asks for information beyond the scope of what you have presented to already have the figures calculated that way ready to put on the overhead projector or jot quickly onto a white board. Such additional preparation makes you look thoroughly prepared. Many people who might try to make trouble for you during your presentation [we will talk about this specifically in a minute] might decide it's not worth the effort since you appear to be so thoroughly prepared.

Connect Ideas Carefully

Once you have gathered and selected the information you want to use, carefully organize it so that your message flows smoothly. To create a smooth flow, be sure that each IDEA logically follows from the last one. Also, be sure to use appropriate "connectors" between ideas so the audience can readily understand where you are going next.

It is very important to use connectors when presenting because audience members must rely solely on what they hear for understanding. Also, most people do not hang on every word. They mentally "drift in and out" one or more times during a presentation. To help listeners stay with us, then, we must carefully connect the parts of our presentation with transition words or phrases that prepare them for what we are about to say.

For instance, when you have three points to make, tell your listeners when you are moving on to the next one: "Now we come to the third point: what you can do as a group to help reduce cost overruns in the department." Sometimes a short summary is the best connector: "Now that we have reviewed the problem, let's take a look at some solutions." Always explain what you are about to show them: "I would like you to show you three slides that depict...." You will be able to see from these slides that...."

Make Appropriate Notes

Most presenters feel less nervous with a few notes. Speakers use various methods to jog their memory while speaking. Use whatever method keeps your thoughts flowing and creates a conversational style. You should know your material well enough that either a brief outline would suffice or brief phrases on cards. If you plan to hand out material to participants, sometimes just referring to that is enough to keep your thoughts flowing smoothly.

It is not a good idea, however, to write out every word of your presentation. If you are nervous, you may rely too much on the written document and end up reading the entire presentation. When speakers read their message, they usually lose their audience after about the first minute or two. Most written speeches become too tedious to listen to because they are too packed with information—much more packed than average conversation. Listeners usually begin to tire from attempting to absorb information that is this tightly packed. Conversational word choice is much easier to listen to and absorb.

Determine How You Will Handle Audience Questions

At some point during your preparation, you need to decide when you will allow questions and comments from the audience—during your presentation or only at the end. There are, obviously, pros and cons to each format. If you allow for questions and answers during your presentation, audience members may stay more involved; it also may be helpful for them to be able to get clarification on points as you proceed, in case there is something they do not understand.

Getting clarification immediately will make the rest of your presentation much more understandable and meaningful for them. However, holding questions to the end makes it difficult for the audience to sometimes remember their questions. By the time they do get to ask, you have covered so much more material, the question may be nearly irrelevant or they have forgotten precisely what their question was.

If you do allow questions and comments during your presentation, the previous problems are solved, but, in turn, you lose some control over the time element—some people can take five minutes to frame a question or make a comment.

Given your response and perhaps another question or comment from the audience, you can quickly find that ten minutes have elapsed and/or you and the group have gotten off on a tangent.

Probably the best guideline to help you determine the most effective approach for questions and comments is to consider the content of the presentation. If the material you are presenting is complex or very new information for the group, perhaps it's best to allow questions as you go. If the information is controversial or could generate considerable discussion, it's probably best to ask people to hold their questions and comments until you have finished.

How much time should you allow for questions and answers? It is difficult to give a simple rule of thumb for this because the answer depends on the type of topic, length of the presentation, and possibly the size of the group. A very interesting or controversial topic or information that is very new to people will usually require a lengthier question and answer period.

Another factor to consider is group size. People in large groups are often reticent to ask questions. Even if you allowed 10-15 minutes for questions when you present an interesting topic to a large group, it's doubtful all that time would be used, simply because people in large groups often become too inhibited to ask questions or make comments. A presentation given to a smaller group will usually elicit more response, simply because most people are much more comfortable in a small-group setting. A 45-minute presentation to a small group could easily use 10-15 minutes for questions, whereas a large group might not use more than 3 minutes of time.

Prepare the Setting

You often will not get a choice as to where you present. The room may already have been determined. Ideally, a few days before the meeting you should stop by the room where you are to present and check it for seating capacity, ventilation, furniture arrangement, and equipment you will need (white board, easel, slide projector, etc.).

As you check the room, be sure adequate ventilation will be possible. A room too cold or too hot can cause people to lose attention as they become more focused on either warming up or cooling down.

The furniture should be positioned to maximize audience members' attention. You as the presenter should plan to position yourself away from the door. If the door is near the front of the room, latecomers draw attention to themselves as they enter. If possible, have furniture repositioned so that the front of the room is away from the door, then latecomers can slip in the back, creating little, if any, disturbance. It's also a good idea to ask audience members to move to the front seats as they arrive so that space is left in the back for those who arrive late.

As you note the size of the room, be sure that adequate voice projection is possible. If all audience members cannot hear you, those who cannot will eventually give up trying to listen. If you cannot project your voice sufficiently without equipment, ask for a microphone a few days before the meeting. Generally, if the room is quite large, the need for a microphone will already have been anticipated.

If you plan to use visual aids of any kind, now is the time to stand in the back of the room to get an idea of how large the visual aids need to be so that they can be easily seen from the back row. Everyone in the room should be able to see the visuals easily and without straining their eyes.

If you are showing slides or overhead transparencies that cannot be seen from the back row, position the projector farther back from the screen. If you are planning to use an easel or white board in a very large room, those in the back will not be able to make out your writing. Only the first few rows can benefit from anything written at the front of the room.

Present Effectively

Plan Specifically for the First 60 Seconds

The first minute or so of any presentation is critical. You need to "win over" your audience as soon as possible. To be successful at this, to get them on to your side or at least to get their attention, it is important to "warm up" the audience. This simply means to soften the strangeness, defuse any underlying defensiveness you may sense in the group, and create an openness between you and the individual audience members. As you do your final preparations, think about what you might do to win over your audience.

It's an art to "unfrost" an audience—coaxing the face to smile, the senses to respond, the body to relax, the emotions to open up. To successfully warm up an audience, you, yourself have to be warmed up first. Your audience will reflect your attitude and manner. If you appear bored about your subject matter, your audience will be bored too. If you are excited and enthusiastic about your message, they can catch that feeling as well.

Unfortunately, many presenters think their job is simply to **build a case**. That's only half of their job. They should be **building a relationship** with every person in the room. And the relationship is not just for ten minutes or an hour; it is a relationship that has the potential to last—because it is based on a genuine need and a sincere desire to help.

A very easy way to get the audience to relax (and you, too) is to immediately involve them in a nice way by asking them something like, "Can you all see this chart from where you're sitting? How about the back of the room?. . . What if I move this easel forward a few feet? Is that better?" Of course, you should have checked out the meeting room well before your presentation. What you are doing now is making some slight adjustments to ostensibly accommodate your audience. You are also showing that you are not paralyzed by your own rigid planning; you are flexible. You are starting up a dialogue; you are getting a relationship underway. And you can reduce some of your own nervousness at the same time.

Another good ice breaker is to start with something of a human-interest nature. Any statement about PEOPLE is usually very interesting to an audience—people are vitally interested in people. If the ice breaker is not relevant to your topic, then keep it very short. Again, the point is simply to relax everyone and attempt to build immediate rapport with the audience so that they will be more receptive to your message.

In trying to think of something to say to get started, you may choose to say something about yourself. This is fine, but with three caveats: never admit you are not as prepared as you would like to be; never admit you are not feeling well; never admit you are nervous.

Audiences want to believe they are getting your best effort. They are giving up their time to listen to you, so, naturally, they want to feel their time is well spent. Telling them that you are not as prepared as you would like to be (with whatever justifiable excuse you think you may have) will not go over well. Some people will assume that you don't think they are very important, compared to your other priorities. If they were more important to you, you would be better prepared. Perhaps that's an unfair assumption, but we cannot prevent people from drawing assumptions based on the behavior they see. Audiences are sensitive; they pick up signals and react to them personally.

You should also never admit that you are not feeling well. Speakers often think that acknowledging a cold or fever will get them some sympathy or understanding, or, perhaps, create the rapport they want. Such an admittance usually backfires because audience members will quickly realize that they will not be getting your best effort. They will begin to feel that perhaps their time would be better spent somewhere else. If you have a cold or something obvious, say nothing about it. The audience will see that you are not in perfect health, but you do not have to admit that your cold is affecting the quality of your presentation.

It is also not a good idea to admit you are nervous. If you do, the audience will feel obligated to worry about you and be less focused on what you are actually saying. Also, presenters who cause worry do not inspire great confidence.

Consider Age and Power Differences

If you know the group you will be speaking to, you probably already have some idea of the age and power differences within the group. You will also know where you stand in terms of age and power relative to individual audience members.

If the audience on the whole is much older or much younger than you, problems can occur in breaking the ice and establishing good rapport with the group. If you're younger than your audience by quite a bit (more than ten years), you may find that many of your audience may resent you, assuming you couldn't possibly have THEIR wisdom and experience, and, yet, you're in a presenter's position attempting to tell THEM how to do something. On the other hand, if you are considerably older than your audience, your credibility can still be an issue, as the young audience wonders how "in step with the times" you could possibly be.

With both age gap problems, the authority of the presenter is being questioned. To deal successfully with the age gap problem, you may want to consider the following:

1. How you dress is very important in situations where your age could work against you. If you are older than your audience, dress less conservatively. If you are younger than your audience, dress more conservatively. Do not encourage negative stereotyping by what you wear.

2. Consider the age of your language. If you are older than your audience, go easy on the nostalgia and references to personal history. "Back when I was getting started in this business. . ." is an automatic tune-out for most audiences, particularly younger groups, no matter what the rest of the sentence turns out to be. Mentioning previous affiliations with now-defunct companies will only widen the perceived age gap.

If you are younger than your audience, be careful of phrases like "you guys" when addressing the group as a whole. Though it is meant to create familiarity and a relaxed atmosphere, it can make an audience of mature vintage **cringe**. Do not let your language contribute to negative stereotyping.

3. Do not patronize their age bracket. Do not give them the feeling that you are outside looking in. Just don't mention age at all. It's irrelevant. Providing solutions to problems is what's important and is the reason for the meeting. Once you get into answering their needs, it doesn't really matter how old you are. What matters is how effectively you help them.

Power differences are a problem, usually, in only one instance—where you the presenter have quite a bit less power than those you are speaking to. If you have quite a bit more power, that is, you are speaking to a group of people subordinate to you, there should not be any problems. Even so, it's probably best not to come across too harshly or authoritatively simply because of your greater power position.

If you have quite a bit less power than one or more individuals in the room, how you handle the situation is critical. If you have quite a bit less power, there is also a good chance that you are also quite a bit younger. For that reason, the superior in the room may purposely decide to counter something you have said, point out a flaw in your presentation, or bring up something totally irrelevant simply to reassert his or her power. Always be prepared for this. It's definitely not a good idea to argue with the boss!

Sometimes such confrontations or embarrassing situations can be avoided if you will acknowledge this individual at the start of your presentation with something like: "I am so happy to see Mr. Dawson here today. With his experience in _____, I'm sure he can add a great deal to our discussion." Any comment along these lines that acknowledges the superior's experience, wisdom, and intelligence may be all that's required. If you will publicly acknowledge the superior's power position up front and in a positive way, it's likely that he or she won't feel compelled to, sometime during your presentation in a way that may turn out to be negative or embarrassing to you.

Gauge Audience Reaction

As you speak, watch the audience for feedback. If you are speaking to a small group, it may not hurt to stop and ask Bill if you see a confused or puzzled look on his face at some point. If he is confused, maybe several others are too. Stop to clarify if necessary. There is no point in going on if everyone isn't "with you" so far.

If you see that your audience is bored—and that's usually obvious (yawns, sighs, doodling, whispering, etc.)—either end that part of your presentation if it's optional information, or think of a way to quickly involve the participants to get their attention back. If you cannot do either, simply proceed. After your presentation, ask an attendee what bored everyone (if you cannot already guess).

Try to ask someone who will be honest with you. If you are told it had to do with the information you presented, ask yourself whether the information wasn't really applicable to the group, was over their heads, or was presented in an uninteresting way. If the information had to be presented, ask yourself if you could have presented it in a more interesting fashion. Perhaps color charts or other visual aids? Could you have cut the numbers presented to the most important ones and kept the others for backup if needed?

Dealing with Difficult Audience Members

The last, but perhaps, most important issue to consider before presenting is to think about the difficult people who may attend your presentation. It would be nice, and certainly easier on presenters, if all who attended would be supportive or at least benign during presentations. Unfortunately, for several reasons, not all attendees can or will offer kind support and sympathy. In fact, as you have no doubt noticed, some listeners love to draw attention to themselves. Many times to get noticed they will find a place in the presentation to make a "jabbing" comment or pose a very insightful but impossible question.

I have termed these types of difficult people "hecklers" and "snipers." "Hecklers" are the individuals who will try to trip up the speaker to enliven the meeting and have a good time. They "play for the crowd." They want attention. The "sniper," the more dangerous of the two, has a much more serious intent: to publicly embarrass or discredit the speaker. Because your credibility is always on the line when you present, the last thing you need is to discover someone in your midst attempting to use you for his or her own selfish purposes.

What Are Their Tactics?

Both hecklers and snipers operate from a position of camouflage. They are not the types that like open attack, so they use more subtle methods. Since hecklers simply want attention and "play for the crowd," their comments or questions are designed to elicit laughter. Immediately after making a remark, the heckler will usually look at the other audience members and grin broadly. Often their comments are sarcastic in nature.

With both hecklers and snipers, your strategy should be, "Stand up but do not fight." Most of us cannot win in a confrontation with either a heckler or sniper. They are much too good at what they do and have considerably more practice in confrontation than the rest of us.

What Can You Do?

Since you cannot likely win against a heckler, what can you do to keep from losing? You should simply try to reduce the impact of their joke or sarcastic comment. The best way to do this in most cases is to laugh off the comment and look amused yourself. Other audience members may be laughing. But you must come back with something strong related to your presentation and its seriousness to bring the power back into your court and to bring the audience back to the seriousness of your message.

If you act bothered or upset at the comment or joke, the heckler's favorite retort is likely to be, "What's the matter, can't you take a joke?" or "You're just too sensitive." To prevent the first zinger from being tossed at you, it's important to laugh along with the crowd, or at least smile, and look unruffled. Do not respond defensively or your heckler may respond with the second retort—"You're just too sensitive."

Hecklers aren't looking for a serious answer to their comment or question. While their comment appeared to be related to something in your presentation, it really wasn't. It was simply a comment used to win attention. So do not expect to win your heckler over with logic—it's the other audience members you need to win back. If this person is someone who has heckled you during past presentations and seems unlikely to let up now or in the future no matter what you try publicly, it may help to speak to this person privately some time after the meeting.

Consider approaching him or her in private with the following: Remember, yesterday, Theresa, during my presentation you said "......" I knew you said it as if it were a joke and it was really very funny, but I thought I heard a "dig" in what you said. What I want to know is, did you mean it that way?" You are now presenting Theresa with a dilemma: she either has to come out into the open and admit she meant it that way, or she is going to have to quit heckling you in the future because you have now taken away her camouflage. She is not likely to come out into the open—hecklers do not feel comfortable in the open.

She is more likely to have to face the second alternative—to leave you alone in the future. You are proving to be too smart for her. She is much more likely in the future to heckle someone who will not give her any trouble. You have made her feel uneasy, and hecklers do not like that feeling. Keep a fairly "low-key" demeanor through this discussion. Remember, it's a game.

Snipers, on the other hand, have a much more serious purpose than merely to get attention and laughs. Because they are deadly competitive people, they are always looking for opportunities to get ahead of colleagues. Business meetings provide perfect opportunities for this. Their goal is to position themselves favorably with their boss or with others in the room. They believe they can do this best by discrediting you or by saying something more brilliant than anything you have said.

They might ask you something like, "Barbara, a minute ago you said we would be better off if we didn't open up sales offices in Michigan; now you're saying we need to increase sales in the Northeast." This is an attempt to snare you in your own logic. After posing the question, the sniper will likely stare piercingly at you, waiting for your response.

Preparing to deal with snipers takes much more preparation than preparing to deal with hecklers; however, the following suggestions should help you prepare for both of these trying and difficult audience members.

1. <u>Do your homework</u>. As you are preparing your presentation, ask yourself, "What is the worst question someone could ask me?" or, "What is the worst comment someone could make?" "What is the weakest part of my presentation?" Prepare well-thought-out, logical answers. Have backup figures ready.

Suppose you decide the worst comment someone could make is, "I think your analysis is all wrong." [This is a serious attack, so it's more likely to come from a sniper.] What do you say to a devastating comment like that? If someone attacks you with a general accusation, insist that he/she be specific. "John, can you give me a specific example...?" or, "Sandra, what point are you having difficulty with?"

Often, snipers throw out comments without much forethought, again, merely to try to position themselves publicly with superiors in the room. If John does have a specific example in mind, then at least you have a starting place from which to deal with his comment. Assuming you have done your homework, you will have additional data or comments with which to back yourself up.

2. <u>Circulate before the meeting starts.</u> When possible, arrive early enough to spend a little time informally mingling with attendees. This is especially important if you are speaking to a group you do not know at all or do not know well. The

important thing is that they get to know you a little. The more comfortable that audience members feel around you before you begin your presentation, the more likely they will be to support you and your ideas.

3. <u>Never look upset or show a negative reaction to a sniper's or heckler's comment or question</u>. Remember, sometimes their goal is just to irritate or upset you. If you get upset at their question or comment, they will see this as their victory. If you allow yourself to get upset, you are also likely to get too flustered to answer in a clear, logical way. You may also lose your train of thought for the rest of the presentation.

To keep from looking upset, immediately do a silent check of your facial muscles. Make a conscious effort to relax these muscles. Force yourself to put an upward curve to your lips. You may not feel like smiling, but try to look relaxed and approachable. Relax the rest of your body as well.

Be sure you're not standing rigidly with both hands on your hips. Such a stance is interpreted as confrontational. Instead, fold your arms at waist level. The others in the room are looking at you very carefully now to see how you are going to handle this. If you suddenly appear fearful of the heckler or sniper, your audience might think you have REASON to be fearful.

All of these body language "checks" can be made instantaneously, while your opponent is still phrasing the comment or question. If you sense yourself tightening up or frowning, make immediate changes, but do it imperceptibly. The more presentations you give, the more quick and natural this "body check" becomes.

4. <u>Do not refuse to answer the question or deal with the comment because time is short.</u> Time may very well be short, but if you use this reason, it may be perceived by your heckler or sniper and your audience as an avoidance technique. Snipers often have a wild kind of courage to ask the same question

that's running through everyone's mind. Others are too shy or too polite to ask it and put you on the spot. So, in fairness, your sniper's question may be a good one; you owe it to your audience to answer it.

5. <u>Answer calmly and politely, never defensively</u>. If you have done your homework as suggested in #1 above, you will likely be prepared for your sniper. Imagining the worst questions and rehearsing answers to them beforehand is certainly helpful in preparing for snipers. The real test, however, is in the moment of actual confrontation. In the "thick" of a real situation, your intentions of remaining calm can go out the window unless you remind yourself of the importance of staying calm.

Take a few moments to gather your thoughts before responding. Do not feel that you must "shoot back" an answer in a split second. Even allowing yourself a few moments can give you the time to better evaluate the implications of what you might say and to choose your words carefully.

Remember, everyone else is watching you very closely. They will remember how you handle this situation. If you get defensive—visibly tense, upset, or argumentative—your audience may think you are afraid of your heckler or sniper or that you have something to hide—they may assume that some of your material is not as strong as it should be. In your anger, if you attempt to "put away" your opponent, your audience may begin to fear you. They may even see you as ruthless. If they fear you, they likely won't support you in other situations. After all, when might you angrily turn on them in the same way? Do not risk losing their support and respect over one person.

But aren't we justified in showing anger in such an unfair situation? No. It may not be "fair," but there is no law against what your heckler or sniper is doing. So although you may not like it, visibly showing your anger will not help you.

Successful professionals remain in control; they train themselves to look at issues and data and keep personalities—or a reaction to them—out of the conference room. Some observers in the room will no doubt secretly envy your ability to remain calm, knowing that they might not be able to do as well if put in your place. Some may even personally compliment you afterward for "keeping your cool" under fire.

6. <u>Answer with assurance and confidence</u>. Always look your sniper or heckler in the eye, both while she/he is asking the question or making the comment and while you give your response. Do not be shuffling through your notes. You will look like he/she has you on the run or that you are ill-prepared. If possible, be so thoroughly familiar with your material that you have the answer to your sniper's question or comment in your head. If you want to show some backup figures, have those ready on an overhead transparency or in other visual form. Explain your logic as best you can. Do it assertively—looking calm, relaxed, and maintaining eye contact.

You may even want to move closer to your antagonist as you speak. Snipers are not used to such assertive body language in presenters they have attacked. You likely won't feel like moving toward your opponent. Here, though, you cannot allow yourself to act the way that feels most natural. If you did, you would likely frown, tense up, and move away. That's exactly the behavior your opponent wants to see and is probably most used to seeing. When your opponent is framing his or her question, consider moving TOWARD the person. This closing of the distance between the two of you shows your confidence.

7. <u>Keep your comment or answer brief</u>. Since snipers ask serious questions, you may feel tempted to get drawn into an elaborate answer. However, do not belabor the discussion because you can get yourself into trouble. The longer the dialogue, the greater the chance of escalating a minor skirmish into a major conflict. Once you respond to the sniper, accept maybe one more comment, then make one more brief response yourself, if

required. If your opponent still will not let go, state that you would be happy to discuss it afterwards. (Again, never sound as if you are running away. Then be prepared to continue a SHORT, cordial discussion with your opponent after the meeting.)

It's obvious to an audience that you can spend only so much time on any one point. In many cases you can simply end the discussion with your sniper by saying, "Steve, you may be right." Do not say this if his previous comment was something to the effect that you don't know what you're talking about, or that your analysis is all wrong! (To deal with a general attack of this sort, see #1 above.)

On the other hand, Steve may make a valid point. After all, you cannot know everything there is to know about the subject. You will actually look more self-assured and confident if you can publicly and graciously concede a (minor) point or two. This may be all your sniper wants—just a point or two. When you can do it at no serious cost to you, by all means, do it. If you must concede a major point, you have not done enough thorough preparation.

Graciously allowing others to make a few valid or helpful points during your presentation can also make you look objective and unafraid. It can also improve the overall impression audience members take away from the meeting. Often, audience members cannot remember who exactly said what. All they remember is that a good discussion took place and several good ideas came out of the meeting. However, if the meeting went poorly because you had a nasty confrontation with a sniper, they WILL remember that.

8. <u>What about the next time?</u> After an initial confrontation with a heckler or sniper, many presenters will purposely avoid eye contact with that individual for the remainder of the presentation, hoping not to be bothered again. You must remember that your heckler wants attention and your sniper

wants approval. If you proceed as if he isn't there, he will be all the more likely to remind you of his presence. Even if you continue to give him good eye contact, he still may not let you alone.

If he raises his hand a second time, and it's likely he will, follow the same procedures you used initially. Be calm; appear relaxed. Don't seem exasperated with a "here-we-go-again" look. Do not let your opponent think he is wearing you down. And do not let him! No matter how many questions he asks or comments he makes, look fresh and alert—as if each question or comment were the first.

Your audience will begin to lose patience with him, too. They will begin to resent his taking up their time to play games. If they are already very familiar with the sniper/heckler and his tactics from previous meetings, they will likely get impatient with his first comment to you, seeing he is up to his "old tricks" again.

9. <u>When you can, involve your heckler/sniper in a positive way</u>. This may sound like strange advice, but try it. It can do wonders. Not only will it surprise your audience, it will unnerve your heckler/sniper. He or she is, at best, used to being politely ignored. Snipers are used to out-and-out battles (which they usually win). They are not used to being treated with kindness and respect. When you can, show positive acceptance of snipers' suggestions and comments. All their comments aren't killers. Some are rather benign and harmless. When you can, follow up a sniper's good point or harmless comment with a positive statement: "George, that's a good point." "Bill, that's a great idea." "Barbara, you're exactly right." You can do a great deal to defuse their attacks by giving them the courtesy and approval they so seldom get and by helping them in positive ways to feel important.

What If You're Caught Off Guard or Outmatched?

Afterward, analyze your confrontation/s with the hecklers or snipers and what you did or said that gave him or her the advantage. Ask a co-worker, preferably another audience member, soon after your presentation, what you could have done differently. Continue to work to improve your ability to deal with people who publicly try to prevent your success. If you will consistently apply the principles discussed here, nine times out of ten you will render the heckler's or sniper's efforts ineffective. (See also Appendix A for oral delivery checklist.)

For sample study questions, see Appendix J.

This scenario was first printed in Managing Organizational Behavior *by Curtis Cook and Philip Hunsaker (Reading, MA: Addison-Wesley Co), adapted from the co-authored professional consultancy of Jerry Thomas, Marshall Burak, and Curtis Cook.*

Functional Versus Dysfunctional Interaction

Pauline Cotter, an upper mid-level marketing manager for a region within a Fortune 500 industrial firm, sat down with three consultants. They were meeting to talk through some of her ideas for responding to a new corporate directive. After preliminaries, Pauline began to identify her reason for seeking out the consultants.

As you're well aware, because of abrupt changes in the structure of our competitive environment, we're working through a major corporate reorganization. The corporate office has come out with a policy directive that all regional marketing divisions must develop and activate a plan for "force management" [a term used by this firm as a strategy for laying off employees] by the end of the year. Cutting through the verbiage contained in this white paper (she pulls a confidential draft of a 12-page directive from her briefcase), the bottom line is that we have to reduce our level of staffing by about 12 to 15%.

According to this white paper, regional personnel offices are supposed to help line management develop a scheme for managing the force reduction. I have the authority to hire two additional full-time staff professionals just for this project, but I'm thinking that for the same cost, we might be able to make a greater impact by using outside consultants such as you.

During the remainder of their initial meeting, the four exchanged a number of ideas about the objectives of the project and the techniques that could likely be used. Pauline also emphasized that she would "position" the consultants to secure cooperation of the marketing vice-presidents and other managers, who would both provide data and carry out any staffing changes. The four agreed that if Pauline's boss gave his okay to the concept, a formal contract would be negotiated and the first- stage investigative work would begin immediately.

The Organizational Design and Development Project

Pauline approached her superior, Jim Shortcut, suggesting the use of consultants to conduct a management audit of marketing personnel. Their purpose would be to determine skill needs and ways of better deploying human resources within the newly organized divisions. Pauline persuasively explained the rationale of the project.

You know, Jim, based on the changes in our business environment and our subsequent reorganization to cope better with competition, we really need to assess our management's capabilities to meet these challenges. What's more, this approach will provide a real service to the operating divisions within the region. A skills inventory conducted by the consultants could unearth a lot of things. We could find out where we had redundant resources, where our gaps are, and which people are and aren't qualified to fill newly created vacancies.

After hearing out Pauline, Jim Shortcut agreed and made the following suggestions. The line departments have a good deal of excess personnel that headquarters say must be eliminated. By offering them the services of seasoned marketing consultants, we could encourage and facilitate force management. Go ahead, Pauline. Bring in your consultants and have them develop a method that provides the necessary information and support for this project.

Pauline met a couple more times with the consultants to wordsmith the proposal and contract. The project design specified that an audit would begin through the three vice-presidents in charge of the key market areas, then fan out on a sampling basis to include managers within their divisions. "Organizational design and development" (rather than force management per se) would be the focus of the audit. It would include provisions for retirements and/or terminations, promotions or reassignments, new recruiting where necessary, and management training and development.

Delays in Getting Access to Line Departments

Almost from the start of the project, the consultants became frustrated at delays caused by Pauline's slowness in scheduling interviews with key executives. She insisted on the proper "positioning" of the consultants for each interview because of the "sensitive nature of the project and the politics and competition that exists among the three key vp's."

After talking with executives in two of the departments, the consultants finally went directly to the senior vice-president of marketing without waiting for Pauline's positioning, since they had other professional business to conduct with him. In all cases, the few respondents they did talk with were very candid and talked explicitly about their management problems under the new environment pressures and organizational structure.

The executives were excited about the possibility of using the consultants' expertise for a variety of organizational and manager development purposes. They all voiced ways in which the consultants could enable them to improve their operating management within and among departments. They all recognized that coordination was inadequate now that managers were expected to respond more quickly to environmental forces. But none of the line managers were particularly concerned about force reduction.

Several Months Later

Pauline is again in Jim's office. Jim appears visibly upset as he begins speaking.

> I've received a mid-project report and discussed it with the consultants. It seems that a couple of our departmental executives view us as meddlers in the management of their organizations. They say flat out that they aren't concerned about force management and are handling it in their own ways. But the line managers do want to go into greater detail with the consultants on a number of esoteric projects such as strategic business analysis, capital budgeting, executive succession, manager development, matrix management. This project seems to be out of sync with what line managers have in mind. Do you think we should have talked with them before we hired the consultants for this force management project?

Pauline stammers for an explanation as Jim continues.

> The direction of the original consulting study seems to be diverging from the direction the operating departments want to go. It appears that the consultants' document could put us in a position of conflict with the division executives, especially since the divisions didn't ask us to do this. In fact, from their vantage point, we seem to have concentrated on a problem that doesn't exist.

Pauline, I assumed you had done enough preliminary investigation to see if the divisional executives were concerned about force reduction. Now we've put the consultants in an awkward position, because they were led by us to believe that there was divisional support for the objective of force reduction. But, in fact, it appears to conflict with the goals of line management.

Pauline, we've spent a lot of money here, with almost nothing to show for it in the way of the original project intent. You seem to have stirred up a lot of problems here, in part because you restricted the consultants' access to people. We'll explain to the consultants why we have to terminate their contract prematurely. And, by the way, I've decided to give you the opportunity to see what you can do in line market management—I know you'll be challenged by your transfer to Cairo-Paducah.

For sample study questions, see Appendix J.

This article was first presented at a national sales and marketing education professional development seminar delivered to Genesis Electronics Corporation and was entitled, "Should I Keep My Eye upon the Doughnut or Focus Mainly on the Hole?"

Marketing Problems, Goals, and Constraints

The Decision Process

What are professional sales and market managers paid to do? Why, to separate the customer from their money, of course. Yes, O.K., but why will business and industry reward certain performances and not others? The answer lies in the definition of the difference between a "job" and a "career." A "job" can be filled with a "caretaker," but a career position must be filled with a decision maker capable to evaluate market problems/opportunities and to observe and accept the risk associated with certain prospects while, at the same time, recognizing inherent decision limitations. Problem solving can be defined as the process of identifying a difference between the actual and the desired state of affairs and then taking action to resolve the differences.[161]

 Decision making contains both "certainty" and "error." The distance in between the two is "risk," and successful management of risk is the reason that some professionals are rewarded with careers and others are relegated to spend their working years in jobs.

Let's think of the initial decision process as "peeling an onion." There are many layers from the outer skin to the innermost core.   Each layer has a specific purpose and order. The decision maker must decide if the observed threat or opportunity is of sufficient importance to require the time and effort of a formal decision analysis.

Perhaps the easiest way to make this determination is to ask yourself, what will be the "cost" of the analysis? For example, making a formal analysis will require time and resource (which might be seen as a small mistake), but not making a formal analysis that then leads to the loss of a significant client, contract, or personal bonus/promotion may ultimately be seen as a big mistake.

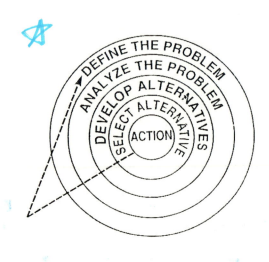

Define the Problem

The first "layer" is defining the problem.   At first blush, this may seem easy—even obvious. But care must be taken by the marketer. Most marketing threats or opportunities are not straightforward. Many are obscure. Put another way, most market challenges are heterogeneous in nature, not homogeneous. Rarely is a business challenge a single issue. Rather, it will be made up of several different heterogeneous parts.

Analyze the Problem

The second "layer" is analyzing the problem. The mission of the effective marketer will always be to isolate the "parts" and determine which are problem "symptoms" and which is truly the problem itself. Altogether too many times we find ourselves investing valuable resources only to find that we have pursued a symptom of the problem and not the problem itself. The significance of this error is not simply the expended resource but the strategic disadvantage of an "opportunity" cost or loss.

Develop Alternatives

The third "layer" is developing alternatives. An argument can be made that only one solution need be found—the perfect solution. But, upon pragmatic evaluation, the competent marketing or sales manager finds two things: first, that s/he may not be able to implement the optimal decision solution (discussed later as management freedom); and, second, that if the selected solution fails, it will be necessary to have a second "immediate action" to take its place. (There may be no time for further development of alternatives at that time.)

Let's begin with the premise that identifying the optimal decision solution is valuable, for it is by measuring all other alternatives against it that we can determine the best selection for our needs. Let's also remember that each alternative must be a "stand-alone" solution option and also able to be implemented. (Remember, the optimal decision strategy is almost never implemented due to constraints.)

Select an Alternative

The fourth "layer" is the selection of the best alternative solution. Remembering the segue from the preceding "layer," the likelihood is that we will not be implementing the optimal decision strategy. (Most organizations do not have the resources required to implement an optimal strategy even if they can find it.) The market manager must now search for a "mini-max" solution alternative. Again, we must find the alternative that provides the maximum solution while, at the same time, falling within the resource capability of the firm. Remember, when evaluating the firm's assets and abilities, to include extended possibilities such as debt service, stock offering, capital equipment lease, and other of the less obvious capital opportunities.

Take Action

The last "layer" of the onion to peel, or the core, is to take the action. Many practitioners consider this step to be the most significant and difficult to take. It's important to recognize that until this step, there may have been many people involved in the process. They may have included subordinates, peers, supervisors, staff, consultants, and others. Many opinions and much advice is usually generated during the "peeling" process. However, the ACTION step becomes very lonely. As a marketing or sales manager, you will now be in the position of actually making the decision, committing resources, and ultimately accepting the responsibility for success or failure of the outcome.

Everyone wants to be remembered for any contribution they made to the Apollo Mission project, but no one wants credit for the Columbia disaster. Yet, each marketing decision maker should feel comforted to take the necessary action, given the fact that s/he has taken the precaution to follow a scientific management approach to reduce the possibility of error—TAKE

THE ACTION WITH CONFIDENCE! This is not to say that we have eliminated all the error and have reached certainty. (The "value of perfect information" is almost always beyond reach.) But, it is to say that we should put the solution plan into effect and monitor its behavior.

Monitor Action

Leaders pay attention to, measure, and control on a regular basis.[162] Since we know that our decision process has served to reduce the distance between certainty and error but not eliminate the risk altogether, we must maintain a "vigil" over the deployment of our selected alternative.   The best way for a marketer to evaluate continued success or failure of an alternative is to develop a program to monitor the solution effectiveness.   A flow chart (preferably a stochastic one) to establish intermediate objectives can indicate successful closure toward the solution or quickly provide evidence that the effort is "off-track." This particular outcome may not be because the selected alternative was inappropriate but, rather, that the environment has changed to some degree. The marketing or sales manager's decision is complicated by the fact that business decisions must be made in a dynamic environment and not a static one.   Shakespeare said in his famous play *Twelfth Night*, "Some are born great, some achieve greatness, and some have greatness thrust upon them [sic];"

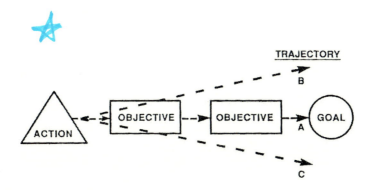

By observing the initial "start" and progress toward the first intermediate objective, we can determine goal congruence of the intended path and any possible errant trajectory. The significance of early detection is that the distance from the plotted deviate trajectory and the intended path may be fairly small, in which case the marketer may be able to correct the "action" or, if necessary, to select a "next best" alternative for deployment. Early observation and detection are the keys to the successful salvage of an action plan gone wrong. One effective algorithm that can be applied to more capably evaluate actions, objectives, and goals is Program Evaluation, and Review Technique (PERT). For a detailed PERT example, see "Physical Distribution: An Application" in this book.

Decision Freedom

What makes the market decision so complicated relates to the rare implementation of an optimal decision strategy (due to constraints). As students, we were free to develop fantasy decisions. A wag once said that the difference between a neurotic and a psychotic is that a neurotic "builds sand castles in the sky" and a psychotic "moves in!" As a matter of professional practice, I guess that all market managers can afford to be a little "neurotic" as they search for the optimal decision strategy, but none can afford the "psychosis" of actually accepting a decision solution that cannot be successfully implemented by the host firm.

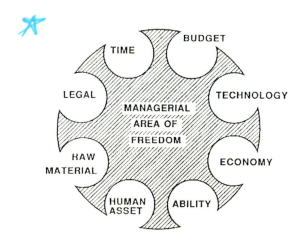

Constraints come in all forms, and this enumeration illustrates that fact. Each marketer must evaluate the respective decision environment before committing to an alternative solution. However, the most common constraints are time, budget, legal, technology, raw materials, human asset, the economy, and our own ability. The competent marketer considers the "fantasy" as having the entire "pie" with which to make the decision and "reality" as the decision freedom remaining only after the constraint "bites" have been removed.

As you consider the area of managerial freedom left in your particular application, think about other constraint issues of capital goods, supervisors' opinions, company SOP's, clients' prejudices, and the myriad of other limitations to an optimal applied solution. The successful marketing career is forged by a capable individual who is conscientious to use "due diligence" effort <u>each time</u> s/he practices the application of decision making. Also, do not underestimate the human condition—no matter how stellar the effort, you can only be as successful as those around you will permit you to be.

For sample study questions, see Appendix J.

Glossary

Many marketing terms were defined and developed in the preceding articles. Following are a few more of the most common terms used in the traditional market lexicon. The asterisks (*) next to some of the glossary words denote terms defined by the Committee on Definitions of the American Marketing Association.

Accelerated Cost Recovery System (ACRS) A depreciation routine that permits more rapid "write-off" of capital goods and equipment.

Accessibility Barriers to customers: Language, law, religion, culture, etc.

Actuary An individual who uses statistical techniques to determine the probability of events.

Advertising A paid activity that develops publicity for a product or service.

After-market Products or services that are developed to augment or replace previously created new products.

AIDA Model The promotion and advertising process of developing attention, interest, desire, and action.

Algorithm A specific mathematical method for solving a quantitative problem.

Altruism An individual's or organization's unselfish concern for the general welfare of society.

Anova A statistical test of difference among means of groups of data, allow "t" tests to be generalized to more than two groups, reducing Type I error.

A priori   A Latin term meaning "prior knowledge."

Arbitrage   The buying of currency in the denomination of one country and selling or exchanging it for profit.

Attention, Interest, Desire, Action (AIDA) A response model that attempts to put thoughts into the consumer's mind, change or reinforce their attitudes, and compel the consumer to act.

Backward Induction   The "folding" of a decision tree from its payoff to first decision fork.

Beta Distribution   A continuous random variable whose density is a function interpreted as having all values between zero and one equally likely to occur.

Beta Test The pre-trial of a product or service by a client company before actual roll-out in the market place.

"Boiler Plate" An analogy meaning the most basic element of a plan, concept, or idea.

Boomers The term used to describe the United States population generation born during the 1940s.

Brand Image A reputation associated with a particular product service or organization.

Busters The term used to describe the United States population generation born during the 1960's.

Capital Goods Items that are used in production to create goods for sale.

Caveat Emptor "Let the buyer beware." A tradition that suggests that a buyer has the responsibility to be knowledgeable about the product/service s/he purchases.

Caveat Lector Let the reader beware.

Caveat Venditor "Let the vendor beware." A tradition that suggests that the manufacturer of a product must be responsible for the product sold to any, even unsuspecting consumer.

Census The statistical process of measuring each element in a population.

Central Limit Theorem A statistical proof for the basis of a standard normal curve or distribution.

Channels of Distribution The "middlemen" or individuals associated with the delivery of the product or service to the customer or end user.

Chief Financial Officer (CFO) The principal responsible for fiscal accountability within an organization.

CLIO Awards International awards competition for advertising design. (CLIO was a mythical Greek "Celebrator of historical accomplishment.")

Coefficient of Determination (R^2) A slightly more pessimistic measure of error in a regression solution which may be found by squaring the correlation coefficient.

Cold Canvassing Sometimes known as cold calling. This is a technique of selling from lists of prospects you have never talked to or met.

Commodity In market terms, this is any good or service that is distributed or made available in mass to the market (*e.g.,* bread, milk, chewing gum).

Communality Analysis   Measuring the amount of variance each variable shares with other variables in factor analysis.

Confidence Level   The probability in sampling that the true population mean will be among the data that is sampled.

Conjoint Analysis   A statistical routine that evaluates independent product variables (attributes) relating to (levels of) customer interest (levels).

Consumer Price Index (CPI) A group of goods and services monitored by the federal government for fluctuations in relative value by the month and the year.

Cooperative Advertising A joint participation (creative or fiscal) in the development and application of advertising and or promotional efforts. Participation may be vertical or horizontal.

Correlation Coefficient (R) A measure of regression solution error. A perfect positive correlation solution equals +1. A perfect negative correlation solution equals -1.

Cost of Goods Sold (COGS) The dollar costs associated with producing an item or service.

Customer   Satisfaction   (See Appendix D.)

Data Analysis The coding, tabulation, and evaluation of market research data collection.

Demarketing   A systematic strategy to reduce current levels of sales.

Demographic   A measured variable that explains who a customer is.

Descriptive Statistics   Using graphs, charts, arrays, and visual displays of data.

Direct Reports   Employees who work specifically for you.

Discount Rate   (1) The cost of capital charged by the Federal Reserve to member banks; (2) determining the true value of primary and secondary information.

Discovery   Preliminary fact-finding for methodology development.

Discretionary Income   The amount of income that remains after paying for necessities and tax obligations.

Dissonance Sometimes referred to as "cognitive dissonance" the term indicates doubt concerning a purchase decision.

Dollar Vote   Each dollar spend by a consumer

Due Diligence A term designating the professional industry standard attention to detail for a particular task.

Durable Goods Products that are made from metal, woods, and long-term, hard plastics designed to have long usable lives of service (three to five years and beyond).

Economic Order Quantity (EOQ) The stock quantity to maintain to keep an optimal level of inventory.

Economic Recovery Tax Act (ERTA) Tax law that increased the incentive for lease arrangements of capital goods.

Economies of Scale   Large production allows efficiencies in utilization of capital goods, labor, raw materials, freight, etc.

Eigenvalue   The relative importance of each factor in a factor analysis.

Elastic Demand A demand function that occurs when changes in price have a substantial impact on the quantity demanded by consumers.

Error, Type I Rejecting a null hypothesis when the hypothesis is, in fact, true.

Error, Type II Accepting a false null hypothesis; that is, accepting a hypothesis as true when, in fact, it is not true.

Expected Value The calculation and combination of probabilities associated with an event.

Factoid   A snippet or abbreviated factual piece of information.

Factor Analysis   A data reduction routine to summarize and compare numbers of variables into common dimensions.

Factor Receivables   Buying a company's accounts receivable.

FASB   Financial Accounting Standards Board

Fiscal Policy Government regulation concerning tax, expenditure, and budgetary deficits and surpluses.

Free on Board (FOB) The term used to indicate that goods are being shipped at no charge to the customer.

Frequency A media term referring to the successive number of times that a particular subscriber is exposed to an advertisement over a given period of time.

Green Marketing ("Greenies") The production of goods and services specifically positioned for sale with regard to environmental demand and or impact.

Gross Domestic Product (GDP) The sum of all goods and services produced annually for sale inside the host country.

Gross National Product (GNP) The total of all goods and services produced annually by a country for domestic and international consumption.

Hurdle-Rate The arbitrary return on investment percentage below which a company will not risk involvement.

IASB   International Accounting Standards Board

Identifiability   Specific customer enumeration: Name, SSAN, Address, Etc.

Inelastic Demand A demand function that occurs when a change in the price has little effect on the quantity demanded by consumers.

Inferential Statistics   The use of probability to measure, approximate, and correlate data and variables.

Install Base   A term used to indicate numbers of products to business customers.

Inventory Raw materials Partially finished goods, and completed products for sale.

Investment Tax Credit (ITC) The income tax allowance for the purchase of a qualifying capital good.

Just-In-Time (JIT)   An inventory control system that attempts to coordinate goods in process closely to product demand in order to reduce inventory costs.

Knock-Off Product A counterfeit product designed to deceive the customer into believing the product is the "real thing."

Laissez Faire Economy without government intervention.

Line Extension Introducing a "new" product to the marketplace and naming it after an already marketed offering (*e.g.,* 7-up and Diet 7-up).

Linear Programming A systematic allocation model that provides a linear mathematical plan or solution to efficiently divide all scarce resources to arrive at a desired objective or business decision.

Loss Leader An item (product or service) that the producer or retailer sells at or below cost in order to attract the attention of prospective consumers.

Management By Objectives (MBO) A theory of management made popular in the 1980s relating specific task and reward relationships

Market Concept A consumer-oriented philosophy ascribing to find the consumer need and filling it.

Marketing Analysis* A sub-division of marketing research that measures the extent of a market and its characteristics.

Marketing Budget* A statement of the planned dollar sales and planned marketing costs for a specified future period.

Marketing Management* The planning, direction, and control of the entire marketing activity of a firm or division of a firm, including the formulation of marketing objectives, policies, programs, and strategy, and commonly embracing product development, organizing and staffing to carry out plans, supervising marketing operations, and controlling market performance.

Marketing Mix The proportional application of product characteristics, promotional efforts, place or distribution decisions, and pricing strategies commonly referred to as the four P's.

Marketing Planning* The work of setting up objectives for marketing activity and of determining and scheduling the steps necessary to achieve such objectives.

Market Penetration The extent (market share) to which a company sells into an existing consumer or industrial market.

Market Potential* A calculation of maximum possible sales opportunities for all sellers of a good or service during a stated period.

Market Saturation   A point where market demand is fulfilled.

Market Segment   A homogeneous group of customers sharing at least one common characteristic that directly relates to propensity.

Market Share The proportion of buyers in a specific market that purchase your good or service.

Mass Market A very large group of consumers who are very similar in a common characteristic related to their demand for a particular product or service.

Means of Capital   The sums of money available to business for investment.

Media Mix The various media vehicles available for news and information dissemination including billboards, direct mail, magazines, newspapers, etc.

Media Penetration The bona fide number of receivers for a particular media vehicle (*i.e.,* the number of people exposed to an advertisement confirmed by the demonstrated circulation numbers of a particular magazine publisher).

"Me"/"We" Products Products which stress being good to oneself or to a close significant other.

Millenials Another term for Generation Y, used to describe the United States population generation born between the mid 1970s to the mid 1990s.

Missionary Sales The distribution of literature, support materials and information about a product or service. This approach is not necessarily intended to "close" sales but to support that effort.

Money Supply (M_1, M_2, M_3) Available velocity of cash, based on liquidity.

Multicolinearity A circumstance where more than one independent variable appears to be explaining the same contribution in explaining a dependent variable.

Niche Market A unique opportunity to position a product for sale.

Noise Any distraction to a communicated message.

Non-Durable Goods Products that are made from materials other than wood or metal with the intent that these products should be consumed or worn out in a relatively short period of time (one- to three-year life).

Obsolescence A market phenomenon that occurs when a new product or service offering provides essential productivity improvement which the original product/service cannot.

OEM Original equipment manufacturer.

Operationalized Approach A plan that has been fully articulated in terms of specific managerial steps for implementation.

Opportunity Cost The amount of resource expenditure required to participate in a financial opportunity.

Overhead and Administration (O&A) A term used to designate general operating and management expenses related to a specific project or product.

Penetration The degree or percentage of customers who have purchased a firm's product out of the total market.

Physical Distribution* The management of the movement and handling of goods from the point of production to the point of consumption or use.

Positioning The use of product, price, place, and promotion to create a niche identity in the general market.

Predatory Pricing Pricing below the level of possibility for competition.

Pre-Product Life-Cycle (PPLC) The development curve of new product ideas including product "ramp-up" but not "roll-out." The phases of this decay curve are: idea generation, screening, business analysis, product development, testing, and commercialization.

Price Elasticity of Demand Indicates the price sensitivity (willingness to purchase) of consumers when fluctuations in product or service price increase or decrease.

Price Leader* A firm whose pricing behavior is followed by other companies in the same industry. The price leadership of a firm may be limited to a certain geographical area, as in the oil business, or to certain products or groups of products, as in the steel business.

Primary Data Data that is collected by the development of initial methodology and does not come from previously observed information.

Product Life-Cycle (PLC) The demand curve over time created at the "roll-out" of a new product or service. The curve includes the introduction, rapid growth, competitive turbulence, maturity, and decline phases of a product's life.

Product Line* A group of products that are closely related either because they satisfy a class of need, are used together, are sold to the same customer groups, are marketed through the same type of outlets or fall within given price ranges.

Product Mix* The composite of products offered for sale by a firm or a business unit.

Product Proliferation A situation where large numbers of competing products enter a market.

Pro-Forma Estimated financial values or predictions.

Promotional Mix Advertising, promotion, personal selling, and publicity make up the promotional mix.

Propensity A market term meaning the willingness of a potential customer to purchase a particular good or service.

Psychographic A measured characteristic that explains why a customer acts.

Psycholinguistic Scale A term referring to the combination of attitude and language techniques used to collect data from consumers.

Publicity* Non-personal stimulation of demand for a product, service or business unit by planting commercially significant news about it in a published medium or obtaining favorable presentation of it upon radio, television, or stage that is not paid for by the sponsor.

Publics Groups of entities that make pronouncements affecting business and markets.

Quality Control (QC) The effort to observe and measure defects in product or service rendered.

"Ramp-Up" A market management term referring to the production, inventory, promotion, and distribution development necessary to introduce a product or service to the market place.

Reach A media term used to describe and evaluate the number of exposures to an advertisement over a designated time period.

Regression Analysis Refining the "scatter" of data that predicts the correlation between predictor variables and a criterion variable.

Relevant, Accurate, and Timely (RAT) A business acronym used to describe effective data.

Request for Proposal (RFP) A document announcing a "for hire" project, including specific terms and deliverables required.

Retailing* The activities involved in selling directly to the ultimate consumer.

Return on Investment (ROI) A marketing term used to indicate the amount of profit required by a company in order to encourage it to accept a project/product opportunity.

"Roll-Out" A market management term referring to the actual new product announcement and offering of the new product/service to the market for sale.

Sales Forecast* An estimate of sales, in dollars or physical units for a specified future period under a proposed marketing plan or program and under an assumed set of economic and other forces outside the unit for which the forecast is made. The forecast may be for a specified item of merchandise or for an entire line.

Sales Management* The planning, direction, and control of the personal selling activities of a business unit, including recruiting, selecting, training, equipping, assigning, routing, supervising, paying, and motivating as they apply to the personal sales force.

Sales Promotion* (1) In a specific sense, those marketing activities, other than personal selling, advertising, and publicity, that stimulate consumer purchasing and dealer effectiveness, such as display, shows and exhibitions, demonstrations, and various nonrecurring selling efforts not in the ordinary routine. (2) In retailing, all methods of stimulating customer purchasing, including personal selling, advertising, and publicity.

Search Engine Optimization   Selection of Web intermediary or "carrier" that best fits a firm's business model.

Secondary Data   Data based on previously collected or published information.

Segmentation   Isolating and observing a unique sub-group of a larger market.

Segue A term meaning "transition" or moving from one topic to another, and pronounced "segway."

Selling* The personal or impersonal process of assisting and/or persuading a prospective customer to buy a commodity or a service or to act favorably upon an idea that has commercial significance to the seller.

Shrinkage Breakage, loss, or theft of products in physical distribution.

[Sic] Latin for "thus." Sic notation is used when quoting an original source in which there is an obvious error. The notation is placed directly after the direct quotation assuring the reader that the obvious error is attributed to the originating source and is not the writer's error. "Sic" may also be used when quoted material is flawed or questionable in some other way.

Social Responsibility A term related to the reasonable responsibility of a manufacturer or producer to the societal impact of the product or service being sold.

Soft-Dollar Value Intangible qualities that have a cost or value to either the buying or selling party.

SOP Standard Operating Procedure.

Spiff Market slang for a sales incentive or promotion.

Standard Deviation Measurement of the distance of one observation to its mean in a distribution of data.

Standard Industrial Classifications (SIC) A commonly published list dividing the most prevalent types of businesses into specific categories recognized by business, industry, and the U.S. government.

Standard Metropolitan Statistical Area (SMSA) A specific group of representative consumers geographically located in and around certain commonly designated cities.

Stochastic This term is used to indicate a relationship that is associated with probability as opposed to certainty.

Strategic Business Unit (SBU) Designates a self-contained division, product-line, or department that is autonomous with a specific market focus and responsible for its own business strategy, revenue, profit, and loss.

Strengths, Weakness, Opportunities, and Threats (SWOT) A problem/situational analysis approach which focuses on these four specific phases.

Substantiabiity Sufficient density by location of segment customers.

Supercession A product or service is replaced by another that has newer features and or applications.

Target Marketing The sale of a product or service specifically to a unique group of consumers (generally referred to as a segment).

Tax, Equity, and Fiscal Responsibility (TEFRA) Tax act that substantially restructured lease arrangements for capital goods.

Telemarketing A non-traditional, direct sales approach which includes: data base techniques, market research, telephone selling, and add-on selling techniques.

Testing, Alpha A term used informally in business and industry to indicate an initial, primary market test or research study.

Testing, Beta A term used informally in business and industry to indicate the re-test of a former market test or research study.

Total Quality Management (TQM) A program that attempts to distribute the responsibility for quality control throughout the organization before, during, and after production.

"Trench" Solution A fully operationalized and capable plan appropriate and ready for implementation (as opposed to strategy or tactics discussed in more general rather than applied terms).

Type I Error Occurs if the null hypothesis is rejected when in fact it is true.

Type II Error Occurs if the null hypothesis is not rejected when in fact it is false.

Universal Product Codes (UPC) These codes are a series of lines, differing in width, that are placed on merchandise. The lines are then electronically scanned to provide information to manufacturers and sellers about product, inventory, and pricing.

Utile A discrete measurement of data collected.

Value-Added Marketing The contribution which marketing makes to enhance the sales, application, or utility of a product or service.

Voice-Messaging Service (VMS) A computer-based PBX switching system that provides for interactive communication applications for call answering, call processing, and information provision.

Wholesaler A middleman who purchases good in large quantity and bulk or break ships, sells product in smaller quantities to retailers for ultimate sale to the consumer.

WYSIWYG A business slang acronym meaning "What You See Is What You Get" and pronounced "wizeewig." The acronym originated in computer terminology, referring to the capability of newer software to produce on screen exactly what the printer would print.

X Generation The term used to describe the United States population generation born during the 1970's.

Zero-Sum Game The principle that if a resource is finite and divided between or among individuals or firms competing for that resource, then in order for one proportion to increase, it must come at the expense of another.

> "More Pooh?"
>
> —An Anonymous Wag

Part Five

Appendices

Appendix A—Opportunity and Threat

A general misunderstanding about market plans is that they are generated as documents with the purpose of raising venture capital. In fact, a capable market plan is much more operational in nature with three main objectives:

(1) The process forces the principal(s) to take an objective, critical, and unemotional look at the situation or "landscape" in question.

(2) The market plan when completed will help to manage the business unit created and direct it successfully.

(3) The market plan will be the basis for communicating the analysis to others for emotional, managerial, and financial commitment.

Strategically, a situation, threat, or opportunity analysis has three specific components: the market plan, its executive summary, and the effective format for its oral delivery. Following are the basic requirements for the development and deployment of a successful market planning strategy.

Market Plan

A. Historical observations
    1. Product inception
    2. Market development
    3. List competitive "players" in the market
    4. Past challenges and opportunities
    5. Existing patents

B. Current product "landscape"
    1. Market Size
    2. Break-down of current market shares held
    3. Life-cycle period
        a. Brand names
        b. Price range and quality
        c. Emerging entrants

C. The product or service
    1. Proposed brand name
    2. Applications
    3. Added Values
    4. Unique requirements
        a. Raw materials
        b. Technology
        c. Barriers to entry

D. Data collection and research
    1. Secondary
        a. Literature review
            (1) Academic
            (2) Trade
            (3) Public Documents
            (4) Internet [excursion only]
        b. Existing company records

    2. Primary
        a. Descriptive statistics (test instrument)
            (1) Measures of central tendency
            (2) Empirical frequency
            (3) Descriptive graphics: data array,
                 Pie and bar charts, histograms, etc.
        b. Inferential statistics (test instrument)
            (1) Regression analysis
            (2) Conjoint analysis
            (3) Multi-dimensional scaling
            (4) Factor analysis

E. Competitive intelligence
1. Debt
2. Equity
3. Lines of credit
4. Location
5. Strengths/weaknesses
    a. Management
    b. Capital
    c. Production (Technology)

F. Customer profile
1. Demographics ("Who" characteristics)
    a. sex
    b. income
    c. age
    d. profession
    e. family size
    f. education

2. Psychographics ("Why" characteristics)
    a. attitude
    b. lifestyle
    c. behavior

G. Product Positioning
1. Attributes of demand
2. Locations of competition
3. Application of 4 P's

H. Product Pricing
1. Strategy
    a. Cost oriented
    b. Demand oriented
    c. Penetration oriented
    d. Skimming oriented

2. Tactics
    a. Cheaper Goods

        b.   Superior services

        c.   Prestige goods

        d.   Intensive Advertising

        e.   Product proliferation

        f.   Distribution innovation

        g.   Product innovation

        h.   Manufacturing cost reduction

I.   Promotion and advertising
1. Budget
2. Objective
3. Theme
4. Media Type

J.   Manufacturing plan
1. Specifications
2. Technology
3. Raw materials
   a. Availability
   b. Location
   c. Cost
4. Human asset

K.   Management
1. Current
   a. "Honest" skill assessment
   b. Experience
2. Required
   a. Educational
   b. Practical

L.   Channels and physical distribution
1. Channel members
   a. Education requirements
   b. Training requirements
   c. Channel length
   d. Commission structure

2. Physical Distribution
   a. Plant
   b. Equipment
   c. Inventory
   d. Shipping

M. Financial Analysis
   1. Company
      a. Retained earnings
      b. Lines of credit
      c. Quick ratio
      d. Profit Margin
      e. Return on investment
   2. Product or service "launch"
      a. Cost of capital
         (1) Venture
         (2) Stock
         (3) Loan
         (4) Mortgage
         (5) Lease
      b. Pro Forma Break-even analysis
         (1) Fixed costs
         (2) Variable costs
         (3) Price per unit
         (4) Market penetration
            (a) Initial
            (b) Growth
            (c) Tertiary

Executive Summary

Developing a Consultancy Approach

Evaluation

The object of any analysis or objective consultancy <u>should be</u> to first "wring out" every bit of information and data and, second, to consider the relevance of each piece. There is never enough good information. What information is provided is usually biased or slanted in a particular direction. The time provided is never enough. The organization is without sufficient resource. And we are usually asked to focus our attention on what may prove to have nothing at all to do with the problem.

Once all the relevant data has been assembled, look for the most significant problem. There may be many problems in a single situation. (Don't be naive and answer only "the questions asked," or attempt to solve more than one problem or follow the leads of discovery interviews with the principals.) Identify what you or your team feel is the most critical issue demanding immediate action. Have confidence. Focus specifically on the threat or opportunity you have identified—don't ramble or lose concentration!

Statement of the Problem

State the problem succinctly (no more than a single sentence—two if you must). This is not easy to do and will take considerable time and effort.

Development of Alternatives

Develop at least two competent alternative strategies for the situation. Remember, any solution must be a "stand-alone" proposal. Don't offer solutions which combine alternatives. By definition, these are not stand-alone options. Only offer alternatives that, in fact, will solve the problem identified. Only offer solutions which the company can afford (*i.e.,* consider talent, management, resources, markets, etc.). In other words, "Don't write a check that the host organization cannot pay." Provide specific applied and operationalized solutions which management can clearly implement. Think "RAT"—relevant, accurate, and timely information.
Recommendation

State it. DON'T RESTATE IT. All that is given here is the nominal selection among alternatives: "ALTERNATIVE B."

Support

The support section contains no personal opinions—NONE— nor does it contain any restatement of the obvious. (The principal already knows the general situation.) It contains no pros or cons regarding any alternative not selected.

The support section does contain all relevant analysis, facts, and conclusions regarding the literature reviewed, primary research accomplished, and analysis to arrive at the decision being promulgated. It also is complete with specific end- or footnote citations for all direct quotes, box quotes, and paraphrased material. This section should also provide the final resolve of any algorithm used to evaluate data (*i.e.*, regression analysis, sampling methodology proposed, break-even analysis, return on investment calculations, linear programming, expected value calculations, etc.).

Mechanics

1. All research will be secondary. NO PRIMARY RESEARCH is to be included unless prior arrangements have been made to do so.

2. The analysis is not to exceed two single-spaced pages of normal 12-point or larger print with normal margins.

3. Any amount of original but condensed (relevant) appendix material may be attached and referred to.

4. End- or footnotes are to consistently adhere to <u>one</u> major style guide of the principal's choice—Campbell's, Turabian, MLA, etc.

5. Deliverables will be evaluated first for literacy. (A "given" for university and industry standard level work is a very high

commitment to grammar, punctuation, spelling, syntax, and a professional level of neatness.)

6. Deliverables will be evaluated second, but equally, on content.

7. Expectations of a university or business researcher or practitioner are high. The expectations for a team of candidates are considerably higher.

Oral Delivery Checklist

Introduction

1. Did you state the purpose of your report?
2. Did you attempt to arouse interest?
3. Did you present the scope of the report?
4. Did you identify with the audience?

Body

1. Did the report seem to develop in an orderly fashion?
2. Was the report presented clearly?
3. Was the report well-developed and supported?
4. Were the transitions smooth?
5. Was the subject well-defined for time and purpose?

Conclusion

1. Was the conclusion logical and believable?
2. Was there a sense of closure?
3. Did you end on a dominant note?

Style

1. Suitable for audience?
2. Suitable for topic?
3. Suitable for speaker?

4. Short, simple sentences?
5. Imperative, interrogative, exclamatory sentences?
6. Was the presentation direct?
7. Were the important points repeated enough?
8. Did you hold the audience's attention?
9. Did you appear sincere?
10. Were you thorough?
11. Did you appear friendly?

Delivery

1. Was the presentation audible?
2. Was the rate of presentation varied enough?
3. Was the volume varied enough?
4. Were gestures and body movement sufficient?

Post Script

You will find that there is nothing easy contained in this appendix. The most difficult part of the required process is the executive summary. There are no shortcuts to due diligence in a business proposal. When you feel yourself beginning to falter on the slippery slope of <u>required</u> hard work, refer to the two short passages from footnotes 2 and 3 of the Preface to this book, which relate "The Munzer Theorem" and "The Dilbert Future."

Appendix B—Areas for the (F) Distribution

df for denominator	Percentile	df for numerator								
		1	2	3	4	5	6	7	8	9
1	.025	0	.03	.06	.08	.10	.11	.12	.13	.14
	.05	0	.05	.10	.13	.15	.17	.17	.18	.19
	.90	39.9	49.5	53.6	55.8	57.2	58.2	58.9	59.4	59.9
	.95	161	200	216	225	230	234	237	239	241
	.975	648	800	864	900	922	937	948	957	963
	.99	4,052	5,000	5,403	5,625	5,764	5,859	5,928	5,981	6,022
	.995	16,211	20,000	21,615	22,500	23,056	23,437	23,715	23,925	24,091
	.999	405,280	500,000	540,380	562,500	576,400	585,940	592,870	598,140	602,280
2	.025	0	.03	.06	.07	.12	.13	.15	.17	.18
	.05	0	.05	.10	.14	.17	.19	.21	.22	.23
	.90	8.53	9.00	9.16	9.24	9.29	9.33	9.35	9.37	9.38
	.95	18.5	19.0	19.2	19.2	19.3	19.3	19.4	19.4	19.4
	.975	38.5	39.0	39.2	39.2	39.3	39.3	39.4	39.4	39.4
	.99	98.5	99.0	99.2	99.2	99.3	99.3	99.4	99.4	99.4
	.995	199	199	199	199	199	199	199	199	199
	.999	998.5	999.0	999.2	999.2	999.3	999.3	999.4	999.4	999.4
3	.025	0	.03	.06	.10	.12	.15	.17	.18	.20
	.05	0	.05	.11	.15	.18	.21	.22	.25	.26
	.90	5.54	5.46	5.39	5.34	5.31	5.28	5.27	5.25	5.24
	.95	10.1	9.55	9.28	9.12	9.01	8.94	8.89	8.85	8.81
	.975	17.4	16.0	15.4	15.1	14.9	14.7	14.6	14.5	14.5
	.99	34.1	30.8	29.5	28.7	28.2	27.9	27.7	27.5	27.3
	.995	55.6	49.8	47.5	46.2	45.4	44.8	44.4	44.1	43.9
	.999	167.0	148.5	141.1	137.1	134.6	132.8	131.6	130.6	129.9
4	.025	0	.03	.07	.10	.14	.16	.18	.20	.21
	.05	0	.05	.11	.16	.19	.22	.24	.26	.28
	.90	4.54	4.32	4.19	4.11	4.05	4.01	3.98	3.95	3.94
	.95	7.71	6.94	6.59	6.39	6.26	6.16	6.09	6.04	6.00
	.975	12.2	10.6	9.98	9.60	9.36	9.20	9.07	8.98	8.90
	.99	21.2	18.0	16.7	16.0	15.5	15.2	15.0	14.8	14.7
	.995	31.3	26.3	24.3	23.2	22.5	22.0	21.6	21.4	21.1
	.999	74.1	61.2	56.2	53.4	51.7	50.5	49.7	49.0	48.5
5	.025	0	.03	.07	.11	.14	.17	.19	.21	.22
	.05	0	.05	.11	.16	.20	.23	.25	.27	.29
	.90	4.06	3.78	3.62	3.52	3.45	3.40	3.37	3.34	3.32
	.95	6.61	5.79	5.41	5.19	5.05	4.95	4.88	4.82	4.77
	.975	10.0	8.43	7.76	7.39	7.15	6.98	6.85	6.76	6.68
	.99	16.3	13.3	12.1	11.4	11.0	10.7	10.5	10.3	10.2
	.995	22.8	18.3	16.5	15.6	14.9	14.5	14.2	14.0	13.8
	.999	47.2	37.1	33.2	31.1	29.8	28.8	28.2	27.6	27.2
6	.025	0	.03	.07	.11	.14	.17	.20	.22	.23
	.05	0	.05	.11	.16	.20	.23	.25	.28	.30
	.90	3.78	3.46	3.26	3.18	3.11	3.05	3.01	2.98	2.96
	.95	5.99	5.14	4.76	4.53	4.39	4.28	4.21	4.15	4.10
	.975	8.81	7.26	6.60	6.23	5.99	5.82	5.70	5.60	5.52
	.99	13.7	10.9	9.78	9.15	8.75	8.47	8.26	8.10	7.98
	.995	18.6	14.5	12.9	12.0	11.5	11.1	10.8	10.6	10.4
	.999	35.5	27.0	23.7	21.9	20.8	20.0	19.5	19.0	18.7

df for denominator	Percentile	df for numerator								
		10	12	15	20	24	30	60	120	∞
1	.025	.14	.15	.16	.17	.17	.18	.19	.19	.20
	.05	.20	.21	.22	.23	.23	.24	.25	.26	.26
	.90	60.2	60.7	61.2	61.7	62.0	62.3	62.8	63.1	63.3
	.95	242	244	246	248	249	250	252	253	254
	.975	969	977	985	993	997	1,001	1,010	1,014	1,018
	.99	6,056	6,106	6,157	6,209	6,235	6,261	6,313	6,339	6,366
	.995	24,224	24,426	24,630	24,836	24,940	25,044	25,253	25,359	25,464
	.999	605,620	610,670	615,760	620,910	623,500	626,100	631,340	633,970	636,620
2	.025	.18	.20	.21	.22	.23	.24	.25	.26	.27
	.05	.24	.26	.27	.29	.29	.30	.32	.33	.33
	.90	9.39	9.41	9.42	9.44	9.45	9.46	9.47	9.48	9.49
	.95	19.4	19.4	19.4	19.4	19.5	19.5	19.5	19.5	19.5
	.975	39.4	39.4	39.4	39.4	39.5	39.5	39.5	39.5	39.5
	.99	99.4	99.4	99.4	99.4	99.5	99.5	99.5	99.5	99.5
	.995	199	199	199	199	199	199	199	199	200
	.999	999.4	999.4	999.4	999.4	999.5	999.5	999.5	999.5	999.5
3	.025	.21	.22	.24	.26	.27	.28	.30	.31	.32
	.05	.27	.29	.30	.32	.33	.34	.36	.37	.38
	.90	5.23	5.22	5.20	5.18	5.18	5.17	5.15	5.14	5.13
	.95	8.79	8.74	8.70	8.66	8.64	8.62	8.57	8.55	8.53
	.975	14.4	14.3	14.3	14.2	14.1	14.1	14.0	13.9	13.9
	.99	27.2	27.1	26.9	26.7	26.6	26.5	26.3	26.2	26.1
	.995	43.7	43.4	43.1	42.8	42.6	42.5	42.1	42.0	41.8
	.999	129.2	128.3	127.4	126.4	125.9	125.4	124.5	124.0	123.5
4	.025	.22	.24	.26	.28	.30	.31	.33	.34	.36
	.05	.29	.31	.33	.35	.36	.37	.40	.41	.42
	.90	3.92	3.90	3.87	3.84	3.83	3.82	3.79	3.78	3.76
	.95	5.96	5.91	5.86	5.80	5.77	5.75	5.69	5.66	5.63
	.975	8.84	8.75	8.66	8.56	8.51	8.46	8.36	8.31	8.26
	.99	14.5	14.4	14.2	14.0	13.9	13.8	13.7	13.6	13.5
	.995	21.0	20.7	20.4	20.2	20.0	19.9	19.6	19.5	19.3
	.999	48.1	47.4	46.8	46.1	45.8	45.4	44.7	44.4	44.1
5	.025	.24	.26	.28	.30	.32	.33	.36	.37	.39
	.05	.30	.32	.34	.37	.38	.40	.42	.44	.45
	.90	3.30	3.27	3.24	3.21	3.19	3.17	3.14	3.12	3.11
	.95	4.74	4.68	4.62	4.56	4.53	4.50	4.43	4.40	4.37
	.975	6.62	6.52	6.43	6.33	6.28	6.23	6.12	6.07	6.02
	.99	10.1	9.89	9.72	9.55	9.47	9.38	9.20	9.11	9.02
	.995	13.6	13.4	13.1	12.9	12.8	12.7	12.4	12.3	12.1
	.999	26.9	26.4	25.9	25.4	25.1	24.9	24.3	24.1	23.8
6	.025	.25	.27	.29	.32	.33	.35	.38	.40	.41
	.05	.31	.33	.36	.38	.40	.41	.44	.46	.48
	.90	2.94	2.90	2.87	2.84	2.82	2.80	2.76	2.74	2.72
	.95	4.06	4.00	3.94	3.87	3.84	3.81	3.74	3.70	3.67
	.975	5.46	5.37	5.27	5.17	5.12	5.07	4.96	4.90	4.85
	.99	7.87	7.72	7.56	7.40	7.31	7.23	7.06	6.97	6.88
	.995	10.2	10.0	9.81	9.59	9.47	9.36	9.12	9.00	8.88
	.999	18.4	18.0	17.6	17.1	16.9	16.7	16.2	16.0	15.7

df for denominator	Percentile	df for numerator								
		1	2	3	4	5	6	7	8	9
7	.025	0	.03	.07	.11	.14	.18	.20	.22	.24
	.05	0	.05	.11	.16	.20	.24	.26	.29	.30
	.90	3.59	3.26	3.07	2.96	2.88	2.83	2.78	2.75	2.72
	.95	5.59	4.74	4.35	4.12	3.97	3.87	3.79	3.73	3.68
	.975	8.07	6.54	5.89	5.52	5.29	5.12	4.99	4.90	4.82
	.99	12.2	9.55	8.45	7.85	7.46	7.19	6.99	6.84	6.72
	.995	16.2	12.4	10.9	10.1	9.52	9.16	8.89	8.68	8.51
	.999	29.2	21.7	18.8	17.2	16.2	15.5	15.0	14.6	14.3
8	.025	0	.03	.07	.11	.15	.18	.20	.23	.24
	.05	0	.05	.11	.17	.21	.24	.27	.29	.31
	.90	3.46	3.11	2.92	2.81	2.73	2.67	2.62	2.59	2.56
	.95	5.32	4.46	4.07	3.84	3.69	3.58	3.50	3.44	3.39
	.975	7.57	6.06	5.42	5.05	4.82	4.65	4.53	4.43	4.36
	.99	11.3	8.65	7.59	7.01	6.63	6.37	6.18	6.03	5.91
	.995	14.7	11.0	9.60	8.81	8.30	7.95	7.69	7.50	7.34
	.999	25.4	18.5	15.8	14.4	13.5	12.9	12.4	12.0	11.8
9	.025	0	.03	.07	.11	.15	.18	.21	.23	.23
	.05	0	.05	.11	.17	.21	.24	.27	.29	.31
	.90	3.36	3.01	2.81	2.69	2.61	2.55	2.51	2.47	2.44
	.95	5.12	4.26	3.86	3.63	3.48	3.37	3.29	3.23	3.18
	.975	7.21	5.71	5.08	4.72	4.48	4.32	4.20	4.10	4.03
	.99	10.6	8.02	6.99	6.42	6.06	5.80	5.61	5.47	5.35
	.995	13.6	10.1	8.72	7.96	7.47	7.13	6.88	6.69	6.54
	.999	22.9	16.4	13.9	12.6	11.7	11.1	10.7	10.4	10.1
10	.025	0	.03	.07	.11	.15	.18	.21	.23	.25
	.05	0	.05	.11	.17	.21	.25	.27	.30	.32
	.90	3.29	2.92	2.73	2.61	2.52	2.46	2.41	2.38	2.35
	.95	4.96	4.10	3.71	3.48	3.33	3.22	3.14	3.07	3.02
	.975	6.94	5.46	4.83	4.47	4.24	4.07	3.95	3.85	3.78
	.99	10.0	7.56	6.55	5.99	5.64	5.39	5.20	5.06	4.94
	.995	12.8	9.43	8.08	7.34	6.87	6.54	6.30	6.12	5.97
	.999	21.0	14.9	12.6	11.3	10.5	9.93	9.52	9.20	8.96
12	.025	0	.03	.07	.11	.15	.19	.21	.23	.26
	.05	0	.05	.11	.17	.21	.25	.28	.30	.33
	.90	3.18	2.81	2.61	2.48	2.39	2.33	2.28	2.24	2.21
	.95	4.75	3.89	3.49	3.26	3.11	3.00	2.91	2.85	2.80
	.975	6.55	5.10	4.47	4.12	3.89	3.73	3.61	3.51	3.44
	.99	9.33	6.93	5.95	5.41	5.06	4.82	4.64	4.50	4.39
	.995	11.8	8.51	7.23	6.52	6.07	5.76	5.52	5.35	5.20
	.999	18.6	13.0	10.8	9.63	8.89	8.38	8.00	7.71	7.48
15	.025	0	.03	.07	.12	.16	.19	.22	.24	.27
	.05	0	.05	.11	.17	.22	.25	.28	.31	.33
	.90	3.07	2.70	2.49	2.36	2.27	2.21	2.16	2.12	2.09
	.95	4.54	3.68	3.29	3.06	2.90	2.79	2.71	2.64	2.59
	.975	6.20	4.77	4.15	3.80	3.58	3.41	3.29	3.20	3.12
	.99	8.68	6.36	5.42	4.89	4.56	4.32	4.14	4.00	3.89
	.995	10.8	7.70	6.48	5.80	5.37	5.07	4.85	4.67	4.54
	.999	16.6	11.3	9.34	8.25	7.57	7.09	6.74	6.47	6.26

df for denominator	Percentile	\multicolumn{9}{c}{df for numerator}								
		10	12	15	20	24	30	60	120	∞
7	.025	.25	.28	.30	.33	.35	.36	.40	.42	.44
	.05	.32	.34	.37	.40	.41	.43	.46	.48	.50
	.90	2.70	2.67	2.63	2.59	2.58	2.56	2.51	2.49	2.47
	.95	3.64	3.57	3.51	3.44	3.41	3.38	3.30	3.27	3.23
	.975	4.76	4.67	4.57	4.47	4.42	4.36	4.25	4.20	4.14
	.99	6.62	6.47	6.31	6.16	6.07	5.99	5.82	5.74	5.65
	.995	8.38	8.18	7.97	7.75	7.65	7.53	7.31	7.19	7.08
	.999	14.1	13.7	13.3	12.9	12.7	12.5	12.1	11.9	11.7
8	.025	.26	.28	.31	.34	.36	.38	.41	.43	.46
	.05	.33	.35	.38	.41	.42	.44	.48	.50	.52
	.90	2.54	2.50	2.46	2.42	2.40	2.38	2.34	2.32	2.29
	.95	3.35	3.28	3.22	3.15	3.12	3.08	3.01	2.97	2.93
	.975	4.30	4.20	4.10	4.00	3.95	3.89	3.78	3.73	3.67
	.99	5.81	5.67	5.52	5.36	5.28	5.20	5.03	4.95	4.86
	.995	7.21	7.01	6.81	6.61	6.50	6.40	6.18	6.06	5.95
	.999	11.5	11.2	10.8	10.5	10.3	10.1	9.73	9.53	9.33
9	.025	.26	.29	.32	.35	.37	.39	.43	.45	.47
	.05	.33	.36	.39	.41	.43	.45	.49	.51	.53
	.90	2.42	2.38	2.34	2.30	2.28	2.25	2.21	2.18	2.16
	.95	3.14	3.07	3.01	2.94	2.90	2.86	2.79	2.75	2.71
	.975	3.96	3.87	3.77	3.67	3.61	3.56	3.45	3.39	3.33
	.99	5.26	5.11	4.96	4.81	4.73	4.65	4.48	4.40	4.31
	.995	6.42	6.23	6.03	5.83	5.73	5.62	5.41	5.30	5.19
	.999	9.89	9.57	9.24	8.90	8.72	8.55	8.19	8.00	7.81
10	.025	.27	.30	.33	.36	.38	.40	.44	.46	.49
	.05	.34	.36	.39	.43	.44	.46	.50	.52	.55
	.90	2.32	2.28	2.24	2.20	2.18	2.16	2.11	2.08	2.06
	.95	2.98	2.91	2.84	2.77	2.74	2.70	2.62	2.58	2.54
	.975	3.72	3.62	3.52	3.42	3.37	3.31	3.20	3.14	3.08
	.99	4.85	4.71	4.56	4.41	4.33	4.25	4.08	4.00	3.91
	.995	5.85	5.66	5.47	5.27	5.17	5.07	4.86	4.75	4.64
	.999	8.75	8.45	8.13	7.80	7.64	7.47	7.12	6.94	6.76
12	.025	.28	.30	.34	.37	.39	.41	.46	.49	.52
	.05	.34	.37	.40	.44	.46	.48	.52	.55	.57
	.90	2.19	2.15	2.10	2.06	2.04	2.01	1.96	1.93	1.90
	.95	2.75	2.69	2.62	2.54	2.51	2.47	2.38	2.34	2.30
	.975	3.37	3.28	3.18	3.07	3.02	2.96	2.85	2.79	2.72
	.99	4.30	4.16	4.01	3.86	3.78	3.70	3.54	3.45	3.36
	.995	5.09	4.91	4.72	4.53	4.43	4.33	4.12	4.01	3.90
	.999	7.29	7.00	6.71	6.40	6.25	6.09	5.76	5.59	5.42
15	.025	.28	.31	.35	.39	.41	.43	.49	.51	.55
	.05	.35	.38	.42	.45	.47	.50	.54	.57	.59
	.90	2.06	2.02	1.97	1.92	1.90	1.87	1.82	1.79	1.76
	.95	2.54	2.48	2.40	2.33	2.29	2.25	2.16	2.11	2.07
	.975	3.06	2.96	2.86	2.76	2.70	2.64	2.52	2.46	2.40
	.99	3.80	3.67	3.52	3.37	3.29	3.21	3.05	2.96	2.87
	.995	4.42	4.25	4.07	3.88	3.79	3.69	3.48	3.37	3.26
	.999	6.08	5.81	5.54	5.25	5.10	4.95	4.64	4.48	4.31

df for denominator	Percentile	1	2	3	4	5	6	7	8	9
		df for numerator								
20	.025	0	.03	.07	.11	.16	.19	.22	.25	.27
	.05	0	.05	.12	.17	.22	.26	.29	.31	.34
	.90	2.97	2.59	2.38	2.25	2.16	2.09	2.04	2.00	1.96
	.95	4.35	3.49	3.10	2.87	2.71	2.60	2.51	2.45	2.39
	.975	5.87	4.46	3.86	3.51	3.29	3.13	3.01	2.91	2.84
	.99	8.10	5.85	4.94	4.43	4.10	3.87	3.70	3.56	3.46
	.995	9.94	6.99	5.82	5.17	4.76	4.47	4.26	4.09	3.96
	.999	14.8	9.95	8.10	7.10	6.46	6.02	5.69	5.44	5.24
24	.025	0	.03	.07	.12	.16	.20	.23	.25	.28
	.05	0	.05	.12	.17	.22	.26	.29	.32	.34
	.90	2.93	2.54	2.33	2.19	2.10	2.04	1.98	1.94	1.91
	.95	4.26	3.40	3.01	2.78	2.62	2.51	2.42	2.36	2.30
	.975	5.72	4.32	3.72	3.38	3.15	2.99	2.87	2.78	2.70
	.99	7.82	5.61	4.72	4.22	3.90	3.67	3.50	3.36	3.26
	.995	9.55	6.66	5.52	4.89	4.49	4.20	3.99	3.83	3.69
	.999	14.0	9.34	7.55	6.59	5.98	5.55	5.23	4.99	4.80
30	.025	0	.03	.07	.12	.16	.20	.23	.26	.28
	.05	0	.05	.12	.17	.22	.26	.30	.32	.35
	.90	2.88	2.49	2.28	2.14	2.05	1.98	1.93	1.88	1.85
	.95	4.17	3.32	2.92	2.69	2.53	2.42	2.33	2.27	2.21
	.975	5.57	4.18	3.59	3.25	3.03	2.87	2.75	2.65	2.57
	.99	7.56	5.39	4.51	4.02	3.70	3.47	3.30	3.17	3.07
	.995	9.18	6.35	5.24	4.62	4.23	3.95	3.74	3.58	3.45
	.999	13.3	8.77	7.05	6.12	5.53	5.12	4.82	4.58	4.39
60	.025	0	.03	.07	.12	.16	.20	.24	.26	.29
	.05	0	.05	.12	.18	.23	.27	.30	.33	.36
	.90	2.79	2.39	2.18	2.04	1.95	1.87	1.82	1.77	1.74
	.95	4.00	3.15	2.76	2.53	2.37	2.25	2.17	2.10	2.04
	.975	5.29	3.93	3.34	3.01	2.79	2.63	2.51	2.41	2.33
	.99	7.08	4.98	4.13	3.65	3.34	3.12	2.95	2.82	2.72
	.995	8.49	5.80	4.73	4.14	3.76	3.49	3.29	3.13	3.01
	.999	12.0	7.77	6.17	5.31	4.76	4.37	4.09	3.86	3.69
120	.025	0	.03	.07	.12	.16	.20	.24	.27	.29
	.05	0	.05	.12	.18	.23	.27	.31	.34	.36
	.90	2.75	2.35	2.13	1.99	1.90	1.82	1.77	1.72	1.68
	.95	3.92	3.07	2.68	2.45	2.29	2.18	2.09	2.02	1.96
	.975	5.15	3.80	3.23	2.89	2.67	2.52	2.39	2.30	2.22
	.99	6.85	4.79	3.95	3.48	3.17	2.96	2.79	2.66	2.56
	.995	8.18	5.54	4.50	3.92	3.55	3.28	3.09	2.93	2.81
	.999	11.4	7.32	5.78	4.95	4.42	4.04	3.77	3.55	3.38
∞	.025	0	.03	.07	.12	.17	.21	.24	.27	.30
	.05	0	.05	.12	.18	.23	.27	.31	.34	.40
	.90	2.71	2.30	2.08	1.94	1.85	1.77	1.72	1.67	1.63
	.95	3.84	3.00	2.60	2.37	2.21	2.10	2.01	1.94	1.88
	.975	5.02	3.69	3.12	2.79	2.57	2.41	2.29	2.19	2.11
	.99	6.63	4.61	3.78	3.32	3.02	2.80	2.64	2.51	2.41
	.995	7.88	5.30	4.28	3.72	3.35	3.09	2.90	2.74	2.62
	.999	10.8	6.91	5.42	4.62	4.10	3.74	3.47	3.27	3.10

df for denominator	Percentile	df for numerator								
		10	12	15	20	24	30	60	120	∞
20	.025	.29	.33	.36	.41	.43	.45	.52	.55	.58
	.05	.36	.39	.43	.47	.49	.52	.57	.60	.64
	.90	1.94	1.89	1.84	1.79	1.77	1.74	1.68	1.64	1.61
	.95	2.35	2.28	2.20	2.12	2.08	2.04	1.95	1.90	1.84
	.975	2.77	2.68	2.57	2.46	2.41	2.35	2.22	2.16	2.09
	.99	3.37	3.23	3.09	2.94	2.86	2.78	2.61	2.52	2.42
	.995	3.85	3.68	3.50	3.32	3.22	3.12	2.92	2.81	2.69
	.999	5.08	4.82	4.56	4.29	4.15	4.00	3.70	3.54	3.38
24	.025	.30	.33	.37	.41	.44	.47	.53	.57	.61
	.05	.36	.40	.44	.48	.50	.53	.59	.62	.66
	.90	1.88	1.83	1.78	1.73	1.70	1.67	1.61	1.57	1.53
	.95	2.25	2.18	2.11	2.03	1.98	1.94	1.84	1.79	1.73
	.975	2.64	2.54	2.44	2.33	2.27	2.21	2.08	2.01	1.94
	.99	3.17	3.03	2.89	2.74	2.66	2.58	2.40	2.31	2.21
	.995	3.59	3.42	3.25	3.06	2.97	2.87	2.66	2.55	2.43
	.999	4.64	4.39	4.14	3.87	3.74	3.59	3.29	3.14	2.97
30	.025	.30	.34	.38	.43	.45	.48	.55	.59	.64
	.05	.37	.40	.44	.49	.52	.54	.61	.65	.68
	.90	1.82	1.77	1.72	1.67	1.64	1.61	1.54	1.50	1.46
	.95	2.16	2.09	2.01	1.93	1.89	1.84	1.74	1.68	1.62
	.975	2.51	2.41	2.31	2.20	2.14	2.07	1.94	1.87	1.79
	.99	2.98	2.84	2.70	2.55	2.47	2.39	2.21	2.11	2.01
	.995	3.34	3.18	3.01	2.82	2.73	2.63	2.42	2.30	2.18
	.999	4.24	4.00	3.75	3.49	3.36	3.22	2.92	2.76	2.59
60	.025	.31	.35	.40	.45	.48	.52	.60	.65	.72
	.05	.38	.42	.46	.51	.54	.57	.65	.70	.76
	.90	1.71	1.66	1.60	1.54	1.51	1.48	1.40	1.35	1.29
	.95	1.99	1.92	1.84	1.75	1.70	1.65	1.53	1.47	1.39
	.975	2.27	2.17	2.06	1.94	1.88	1.82	1.67	1.58	1.48
	.99	2.63	2.50	2.35	2.20	2.12	2.03	1.84	1.73	1.60
	.995	2.90	2.74	2.57	2.39	2.29	2.19	1.96	1.83	1.69
	.999	3.54	3.32	3.08	2.83	2.69	2.55	2.25	2.08	1.89
120	.025	.32	.36	.41	.46	.50	.53	.63	.70	.79
	.05	.39	.43	.47	.53	.56	.60	.68	.74	.82
	.90	1.65	1.60	1.55	1.48	1.45	1.41	1.32	1.26	1.19
	.95	1.91	1.83	1.75	1.66	1.61	1.55	1.43	1.35	1.25
	.975	2.16	2.05	1.95	1.82	1.76	1.69	1.53	1.43	1.31
	.99	2.47	2.34	2.19	2.03	1.95	1.86	1.66	1.53	1.38
	.995	2.71	2.54	2.37	2.19	2.09	1.98	1.75	1.61	1.43
	.999	3.24	3.02	2.78	2.53	2.40	2.26	1.95	1.77	1.54
∞	.025	.32	.37	.42	.48	.52	.56	.68	.76	1.00
	.05	.39	.43	.48	.54	.58	.62	.72	.80	1.00
	.90	1.60	1.55	1.49	1.42	1.38	1.34	1.24	1.17	1.00
	.95	1.83	1.75	1.67	1.57	1.52	1.46	1.32	1.22	1.00
	.975	2.05	1.94	1.83	1.71	1.64	1.57	1.39	1.27	1.00
	.99	2.32	2.18	2.04	1.88	1.79	1.70	1.47	1.32	1.00
	.995	2.52	2.36	2.19	2.00	1.90	1.79	1.53	1.36	1.00
	.999	2.96	2.74	2.51	2.27	2.13	1.99	1.66	1.45	1.00

Appendix C—Areas for the (Z) Distribution

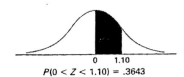

$$P(0 < Z < 1.10) = .3643$$

z	.00	.01	.02	.03	.04	.05	.06	.07	.08	.09
0.0	.0000	.0040	.0080	.0120	.0160	.0199	.0239	.0279	.0319	.0359
0.1	.0398	.0438	.0478	.0517	.0557	.0596	.0636	.0675	.0714	.0753
0.2	.0793	.0832	.0871	.0910	.0948	.0987	.1026	.1064	.1103	.1141
0.3	.1179	.1217	.1255	.1293	.1331	.1368	.1406	.1443	.1480	.1517
0.4	.1554	.1591	.1628	.1664	.1700	.1736	.1772	.1808	.1844	.1879
0.5	.1915	.1950	.1985	.2019	.2054	.2088	.2123	.2157	.2190	.2224
0.6	.2257	.2291	.2324	.2357	.2389	.2422	.2454	.2486	.2517	.2549
0.7	.2580	.2611	.2642	.2673	.2704	.2734	.2764	.2794	.2823	.2852
0.8	.2881	.2910	.2939	.2967	.2995	.3023	.3051	.3078	.3106	.3133
0.9	.3159	.3186	.3212	.3238	.3264	.3289	.3315	.3340	.3365	.3389
1.0	.3413	.3438	.3461	.3485	.3508	.3531	.3554	.3577	.3599	.3621
1.1	.3643	.3665	.3686	.3708	.3729	.3749	.3770	.3790	.3810	.3830
1.2	.3849	.3869	.3888	.3907	.3925	.3944	.3962	.3980	.3997	.4015
1.3	.4032	.4049	.4066	.4082	.4099	.4115	.4131	.4147	.4162	.4177
1.4	.4192	.4207	.4222	.4236	.4251	.4265	.4279	.4292	.4306	.4319
1.5	.4332	.4345	.4357	.4370	.4382	.4394	.4406	.4418	.4429	.4441
1.6	.4452	.4463	.4474	.4484	.4495	.4505	.4515	.4525	.4535	.4545
1.7	.4554	.4564	.4573	.4582	.4591	.4599	.4608	.4616	.4625	.4633
1.8	.4641	.4649	.4656	.4664	.4671	.4678	.4686	.4693	.4699	.4706
1.9	.4713	.4719	.4726	.4732	.4738	.4744	.4750	.4756	.4761	.4767
2.0	.4772	.4778	.4783	.4788	.4793	.4798	.4803	.4808	.4812	.4817
2.1	.4821	.4826	.4830	.4834	.4838	.4842	.4846	.4850	.4854	.4857
2.2	.4861	.4864	.4868	.4871	.4875	.4878	.4881	.4884	.4887	.4890
2.3	.4893	.4896	.4898	.4901	.4904	.4906	.4909	.4911	.4913	.4916
2.4	.4918	.4920	.4922	.4925	.4927	.4929	.4931	.4932	.4934	.4936
2.5	.4938	.4940	.4941	.4943	.4945	.4946	.4948	.4949	.4951	.4952
2.6	.4953	.4955	.4956	.4957	.4959	.4960	.4961	.4962	.4963	.4964
2.7	.4965	.4966	.4967	.4968	.4969	.4970	.4971	.4972	.4973	.4974
2.8	.4974	.4975	.4976	.4977	.4977	.4978	.4979	.4979	.4980	.4981
2.9	.4981	.4982	.4982	.4982	.4984	.4984	.4985	.4985	.4986	.4986
3.0	.4987	.4987	.4987	.4988	.4988	.4989	.4989	.4989	.4990	.4990

Appendix D—Price/Value Schematic

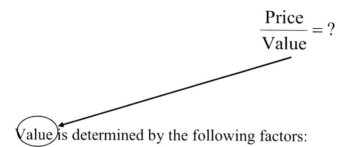

$$\frac{\text{Price}}{\text{Value}} = ?$$

Value is determined by the following factors:

- Rebates
- Applications
- Image
- Brand
- Quality
- Desire
- Promotions
- Service
- Tax Factors
- Longevity
- Financing
- Guarantees
- Training
- Residual

$$\frac{PRICE}{VALUE} = SATISFACTION$$

Satisfaction must be ≤ 1.0.

Appendix E—Competitive Intelligence

Academic and Trade Journals

American Journal of Economics and Sociology

American Statistical Association Journal

Business Education Forum

Business Ethics Quarterly

Business Review

Econometrica

Journal of Economics and Business

Review of Business and Economic Research

Academy of Marketing Science Journal

American Demographics

Barron's National Business and Financial Weekly

Business

Business Horizons

Business Marketing

Business Week

California Business Education Journal

California Management Review

Chain Store Age-Executive

Columbia Journal of World Business

Communication Week

CPA Journal

Decision Sciences

Direct Marketing

Forbes

Fortune

Harvard Business Review

Industrial Marketing

Internet Business Journal

Journal of Business Research

Journal of Advertising

Journal of Advertising Research

Journal of Banking and Finance

Journal of Business Ethics

Journal of Business Logistics

Journal of Business Research

Journal of Consumer Affairs

Journal of Consumer Marketing

Journal of Consumer Research

Journal of Forecasting

Journal of Global Marketing

Journal of High Technology Management and Marketing Research

Journal of Macromarketing

Journal of Marketing

Journal of Marketing Education

Journal of Personal Selling and Sales Management

Journal of Public Policy and Marketing

Journal of Purchasing and Materials Management

Journal of Retailing

Journal of Services Marketing

Journal of Telecommunications

Journal of the Academy of Marketing Science

Logistics Spectrum

Marketing News

Marketing Science

Merchandising

Nation's Business

Northern California Executive Review

Purchasing

Retail Week

Sales and Marketing Management

Value Line

Wall Street Journal

Public Documents

American Statistics Index

Business and Economics
Census of Retail Trade
Census of Wholesale Trade
Consumer Information Catalog
Consumer Price Index
Consumer Price Index News
Consumer Spending Update
Catalog of Copyright
Durable Goods Manufacturers' Shipments and Orders
Economic Indicators
Exports of Merchandise
Federal Trade Commission Bulletin
Imports of Merchandise
International Affairs
Marketing Moves: GPO
Population Estimates
Producer Price Index
Retail Trade Sales and Inventories
Statistical Abstract
Survey of Current Business
Women's Wear Daily

Information Services

Dunn & Bradstreet Market Identifiers
Guide to U.S. Government Publications
Non-Store Marketing Report (Sroge)
Simmons Media/Marketing Service
Standard Rate and Data (media)
Survey of Current Business
Wall Street Journal Index

Computer Data Bases

AdTrack (St. Paul, MN)
Dialog Information Services, Inc. (Palo Alto, CA)

Dow Jones News/Retrieval (Princeton, NJ)
Mead Data Central (Dayton, OH)
Mediamark Research, Inc. (New York, NY)
Newsbank (New Canaan, NJ)
News Net (Bryn Mawr, PA)
Nexis (Dayton, OH)
Vu Text (Philadelphia, PA)

Books

How to Find Information about Companies: The Corporate Rate Intelligence Source Book (8th edition, Washington D.C.: Washington Researchers, Ltd. 1991).

Directory of On-Line Data Bases (New York: Cuadra/Elsevier, 1992).

Competitor Intelligence: How to Get It; How to Use It (New York: John Wiley & Sons, 1985).

Trade Associations

Advertising Research Foundation (New York, NY)
American Advertising Federation (Washington, D.C.)
American Marketing Association (Chicago, IL)
American Society of Transportation and Logistics (Lock, Haven, PA)
Association of National Advertisers (New York, NY)
Direct Marketing Association (New York, NY)
General Merchandise Distributors Council (Colorado Springs, CO)
International Association of Sales Professionals (New York, NY)
Marketing Research Association (Rocky Hill, CT)
Marketing Science Institute (Cambridge, MA)
National Association of Wholesaler-Distributors (Washington, D.C.)
National Purchasing Institute (Bethesda, MD)
Public Relations Society of America (New York, NY)
Retail Advertising and Marketing Association (Chicago, IL)

Appendix F—Problem Set

Problem Set

Each page of the following pages in this appendix provides a practice problem in a different market application environment. First, a primary research problem, next a forecasting problem, then a pre-product life cycle problem, a positioning problem, a distribution problem, a break-even problem, and, last, a profit maximization problem.

Do not work these applications by computer algorithm. They have been written to be simple enough to do by hand. That is precisely the point. (If you like, use a hand held calculator for four-function calculations and square root only.)

Today many students of these quantitative marketing methods are quite capable to "keystroke" them into a software package and observe the result. The problem is that students are often painfully incapable of determining if the answer is, in fact, correct or incorrect.

Gratefully, these quantitative routines are consistent. If we can learn to work a fairly simple problem, understanding the variables and their relationship to one another, then we can depend on a computer to solve complicated problems and be confident to know a correct answer when we see it. Also , if the answer is incorrect, we know enough about the procedure to observe the inter-relationship among the variables and find/correct the error in the procedure.

The following exercises are by no means the majority of quantitative marketing techniques. But they are among some of the most popular and powerful and do offer an opportunity to try your own personal skill after observing and reading about their use in the previous articles. Be certain to show all work/steps required to reach the solution so that if your answer is incorrect you will be able to easily find the "culprit" and effect a true solution.

Work the final solution of each problem assigned to you on the back side or "solutions" side of the page. The book has a perforated binding so that you can easily tear out the page when assigned and turn it in to be graded.

SAMPLE SIZE CALCULATION (A primary research application)

Following is a "Pilot Sample Distribution of Attitude Responses" to a single psychographic Ho: based on utiles of agreement and disagreement. From these pilot data, calculate the appropriate sample size of respondents for a survey of the population from which the pilot sample was drawn.

Utiles (coded "x" values)

	x	f	fx	$(x-\bar{x})$	$(x-\bar{x})^2$	$f(x-\bar{x})^2$
STA	5	16				
SLA	4	10				
UND	3	2				
SLD	2	1				
STD	1	3				

Solve this primary research problem for "n" using the following formula. Explain the meaning of your answer.

$$S = \sqrt{\frac{\sum f(x-\bar{x})^2}{n}} \qquad \hat{\sigma} = S\sqrt{\frac{n}{n-1}} \qquad n = \frac{Z^2\hat{\sigma}^2}{e^2}$$

where:

Z = The number of standard deviations from the mean

$\bar{x}$ = The mean of the customer responses collected

$\hat{\sigma}$ = Estimate of the variability in the entire national target market of respondents

e = The error interval tolerated above or below the average response of the actual population respondent

S = The standard deviation of the pilot sample responses

Confidence level = .90 and error about the mean = .10.

Do your sample size calculations and solution here:

REGRESSION ANALYSIS (A forecasting application)

Following are sales demand data and coding for five months of a new product life cycle.
Using bivariate regression analysis, determine the initial product life cycle trend line.
Provide a graphic and quantitative solution for the sixth month (August) forecast to
management. **Also, calculate the "R" value of your solution.**

Month	X	Y	$\hat{Y}$
MAR	1	8,000	
APR	2	9,000	
MAY	3	10,000	
JUN	4	13,200	
JUL	5	14,750	

Where: $\hat{Y} = a + bX$

and

$$a = \frac{(\sum Y)(\sum X^2) - (\sum X)(\sum XY)}{N(\sum X^2) - (\sum X)^2}$$

$$b = \frac{N(\sum XY) - (\sum X)(\sum Y)}{N(\sum X^2) - (\sum X)^2}$$

Y

X

Do your regression analysis and solution here:

EXPECTED VALUE
(A Pre-Product Life Cycle Application)

Following is the first quarter potential for three new products. The pre and posterior probability of events have already been established and their respective payoffs have been forecast in the business analysis phase of the pre-product life cycle (PPLC).

Product A has a 50% chance of surviving the PPLC. If it survives, there is a 20% chance of deep market penetration and a payoff of $300,000, or an 80% chance of minimum market penetration and a $20,000 payoff. If the product fails the PPLC, there is a negative cost incurred of $5,000.

Product B has a 60% chance of surviving the PPLC. If it survives the PPLC, it has a 70% chance of moderate market penetration and a payoff of $40,000. If it passes the PPLC, it also has a 30% chance of a failed market at a cost of $2,000. If Product B does not pass the PPLC (it has already been announced to selected media), it has a negative effect on brand loyalty at a cost of $5,000.

Product C has a 30% chance of surviving the PPLC. If it survives the PPLC, it has a 30% chance of deep market penetration and a payoff of $300,000. If it survives the PPLC, it also has a 70% chance of moderate market penetration and an $18,000 payoff. If it fails to pass the PPLC (the product has been pre-announced in major markets), there is negative brand loyalty at a cost of $15,000.

Also consider producing no new product in your decision process.

1. Clearly draw, label, and prune the decision tree analysis for this decision.
2. Perform backward stochastic induction.
3. Determine the expected value of Products A, B, and C.
4. Use the Bayesian Decision Rule to make a market management recommendation.
5. **In addition**, construct a payoff table. A payoff table is not required to reach the graphic solution.

Do your decision analysis and solution here:

Multidimensional Scaling (A positioning application)

Following is a three-dimensional grid.   Plot the personal computer data based on your observation of current market price, hardware quality, and software availability.   also, around the respective three-dimensional position (point), indicate the vendor's market share.

Note: Each axis in the diagram is, in reality, orthogonal to the other axes (90°).

Evaluate and position the following products:
2
Apple iMac
Dell XPS
HP Pavilion
Compaq A17

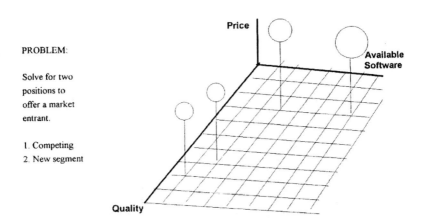

PROBLEM:

Solve for two positions to offer a market entrant.

1. Competing
2. New segment

(Defend your decision in prose and document your sources.)

Do your multidimensional scaling solution here:

PERT ANALYSIS (A distribution application)

$$T_e = \frac{T_o + [T_m(4)] + T_p}{6}$$

From the following two-path PERT program, determine the probability of successful contract fulfillment for product physical distribution if the contract time (T_S) is 35.5 hours.

$$V = \left[\frac{T_p - T_o}{6}\right]^2 \qquad\qquad Z = \frac{T_s - \sum T_e}{\sqrt{\sum V}}$$

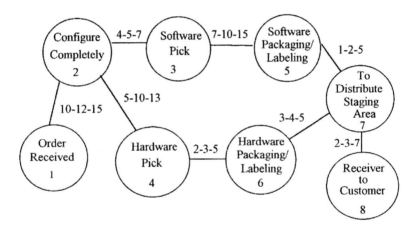

1. Solve the above network problem.
2. Explain in prose the operational steps required for management to complete a PERT network.

Do your PERT analysis calculations and solution here:

BREAK-EVEN (A unit and dollar application)

Milo Bender Associates has developed the 586MF (Mighty Fast) personal computer. The company is an OEM seller of technology. MBA has decided that the retail price point for the new 586MF should be $5,000. This price does not include software or any maintenance agreement.

1. Determine the 586MF Break-even point in units.

2. Determine the 586 MF break-even point in dollars.

$$BE_{(units)} = \frac{650,000 + 500,000 + 150,000 + 200,000}{5000 - 1700 - 1500 - 200 - 100}$$

$$= 1000 \text{ units}$$

$$BE_{(dollars)} = \frac{650,000 + 500,000 + 200 + 150,000 + 200,000 + 100}{5000 - 1700 - 1500 - 200 - 100} \times 5000$$

$$= \$5,000,000$$

The product will be shipped FOB the client's location.

Costs of production include rent ($650,000), capital equipment payment (one-half million dollars), labor ($1,700), raw materials ($1,500), utilities (200), insurance ($150,000), plus general O&A ($200,000), and freight ($100). VC per units?

(continued on the next page)

3. Provide a legend for formulae variables.

Varible cost — raw materials 1,500

labors   1,700

utility   200

freight   100

Fixed cost   rent + cost of production 650,000

cap equip cost   500,000

Insurance   180,000

general OdA   200,000

SP   retail price   5000

4. Briefly explain in prose the meaning of a B/E calculation.

$$\frac{FC}{sp-VC}$$

B/E = no profit, no lose

In order to make up fix cost, we use UC-VC as marginal profit per units to calculate units needed to B/E.

LINEAR PROGRAMMING (A profit maximization problem)

In the "cola wars" Jolt has decided to experiment with two new and different formulas, Super Jolt Plus and Diet Jolt both new offerings will sold in bottles only. As a consultant to Jolt's market manager you are asked to recommend the best combination of production to maximize profit given the following proprietary information.

It takes two hours to bottle one gross of Super Jolt Plus, and it takes one hour to label them. It takes three hours to bottle one gross of Diet Jolt, and it takes four hours to label them. The company anticipates making $10 profit on one gross of Super Jolt Plus and $20 profit on one gross of Diet Jolt. Without having to spend additional money for capital goods, the bottling department has 20 hours available and the labeling department has 15 hours of excess capacity. How many gross of Super Jolt Plus and how many gross of Diet Jolt would you recommend to maximize your client's profit?

Let 'X' be the number of gross of Super Jolt Plus and 'Y' be the number of gross of Diet Jolt.

Provide the maximizing and constraint functions as well as a graphic solution. (Use the back of this page to provide tableau and calculations.)

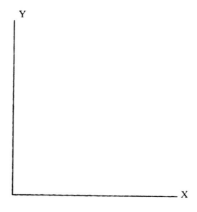

Do your linear programming tableau and calculations here:

Appendix G—Code of Ethics

American Marketing Association

Members of the American Marketing Association (AMA) are committed to ethical professional conduct. They have joined together in subscribing to this Code of Ethics embracing the following topics:

Responsibilities of the Marketer

Marketers must accept responsibility for the consequences of their activities and make every effort to ensure that their decisions, recommendations, and actions function to identify, serve, and satisfy all relevant publics: customers, organizations, and society. Marketers' professional conduct must be guided by

1. the basic rule of professional ethics: not knowingly to do harm;
2. the adherence to all applicable laws and regulations;
3. the accurate representation of their education, training, and experience; and
4. the active support, practice, and promotion of this Code of Ethics.

Honesty and Fairness

Marketers shall uphold and advance the integrity, honor, and dignity of the marketing profession by

1. being honest in serving consumers, clients, employees, suppliers, distributors, and the public;
2. not knowingly participating in conflict of interest without prior notice to all parties involved; and

3. establishing equitable fee schedules including the payment or receipt of usual, customary, and/or legal compensation for marketing exchanges.

_____

Note: Code of Ethics reprinted with permission, American Marketing Association (AMA), Chicago, IL.

Rights and Duties of Parties in the Marketing Exchange Process

Participants in the marketing exchange process should be able to expect that

1. products and services offered are safe and fit for their intended uses;
2. communications about offered products and services are not deceptive;
3. all parties intend to discharge their obligations, financial and otherwise, on good faith; and
4. appropriate internal methods exist for equitable adjustment and/or redress of grievances concerning purchases.

It is understood that the above would include, *but is not limited to,* the following responsibilities of the marketer:

In the area of product development and management,

- disclosure of all substantial risks associated with product or service usage
- identification of any product component substitution that might materially change the product or impact on the buyer's purchase decision
- identification of extra-cost added features.

In the area of promotions,

- avoidance of false and misleading advertising;
- rejection of high-pressure manipulations or misleading sales tactics;
- avoidance of sales promotions that use deception or manipulation.

In the area of distribution,

- not manipulating the availability of a product for purpose of exploitation;
- not using coercion in the marketing channel;
- not exerting undue influence over the reseller's choice to handle a product.

In the area of pricing,

- not engaging in price fixing;
- not practicing predatory pricing;
- disclosing the full price association with any purchase.

In the area of market research,

- prohibiting selling or fund raising under the guise of conducting research;
- maintaining research integrity by avoiding misrepresentation and omission of pertinent research data;
- treating outside clients and suppliers fairly.

Organizational Relationships

Marketers should be aware of how their behavior may influence or impact on the behavior of others in organizational relationships. They should not demand, encourage, or apply coercion to obtain unethical behavior in their relationships with others, such as employees, suppliers, or customers.

1. Apply confidentiality and anonymity in professional relationships with regard to privileged information;
2. Meet their obligations and responsibilities in contracts and mutual agreements in a timely manner;
3. Avoid taking the work of others, in whole, or in part, and represent this work as their own or directly benefit from it without compensation or consent of the originator or owner;
4. Avoid manipulation to take advantage of situations to maximize personal welfare in a way that unfairly deprives or damages the organization of others.

Any AMA members found to be in violation of any provision of this Code of Ethics may have his or her Association membership suspended or revoked.

Appendix H—Memory or Critical Thinking?

Many students approach learning without giving much thought to study habits. If these habits are not good ones or have never been fully developed, learning will not result, no matter how much time the individual spends poring over the material or concept. Students need to remember that merely reading and highlighting is <u>not</u> studying. What they are doing is simply reading and highlighting.

Our objective should be to acquire knowledge, not simply to memorize a lot of relatively useless facts for an exam. The facts learned from short-term memory "exercises" are quickly forgotten and never really integrated in a meaningful way into one's knowledge base. There is no magic to acquiring true knowledge. It is based on the simple tenets of critical thinking.

Memory = Recall   →   **Result**: "I remember that."

Skill= Understanding →   **Result**: "I know what to do."

Application= Performance→ **Result**: "I can use my skill to accomplish a specific task."

Formulae:

Memory = Exposure   (easily lost or forgotten)

Skill + Application = Knowledge (retained knowledge base)

Memory + Skill + Application = **CRITICAL THINKING**

Many students believe that any test question that requires more capability than memory is "tricky" or designed to fool them. These students are very frustrated because no matter how much time they spend reading, re-reading, and memorizing, the result is still only at an "exposure" level; they have not yet reached a level of true knowledge. In business and industry, this same kind of effort is not rewarded. Result (critical thinking) is rewarded.

A simple how-to approach to develop/improve critical thinking skills.

There is good news and bad news here. The good news is that we do not have to be "rocket scientists" to improve our study habits and ability to think. The bad news is that most of us have many years of bad study habits (counting on memory work only) which must be broken, and this "retraining" is hard work. Also, to develop knowledge, one must be willing to spend efficient, dedicated time, focused specifically on increasing the ability to think critically and to truly understand the information.

There are many ways to approach critical thinking. Following is one "how-to" approach that has helped many of my students who wanted to improve their study habits and were looking for a step-by-step "map" to follow. In the process, their goal was to change their weak study habits and break through the "glass ceiling" that memory learning alone creates to real knowledge.

When working with new written material, I suggest that you read it more than once.

First Reading:

Take it easy here. Relax, sit back and leisurely read the material. We're not reading for content or for memory this time. Read deliberately, but do not allow yourself to go back and re-read any passages or underline or make any notes—just read to the end for a general understanding of the topic to be studied. DO NOT SKIM.

Second Reading:

Now, take your highlighter or pencil and underline the most important points in the material (only terms, topics, concepts—not sentences). While you are selecting the most important items, also keep a dictionary right next to the text. Each time you read a word that is unknown or unclear to you, look up its definition. (Also use your Glossary and Index here.) This will insure that you do not miss any important information. Such dictionary work will increase your vocabulary, and we are now beginning the "efficiency" portion of critical thinking: you are in the process of creating one enhanced copy of the material to be further studied. Each time you look up a word, circle it in the text, draw a line into the margin, and write out a short definition that you will now see each time you read the passage. Continue through the material in this manner.

Now you will begin to really benefit from the efficiency of focusing on the most important material. The goal is to end up with an efficient format to study from, rather than reading and re-reading hundreds of paragraphs and scores of pages. In an attempt to memorize the chapter material, many students recopy the text, write outlines, identify terms on a separate sheet of paper, prepare note cards, etc. and spend a copious amount of time, only to find that in the end their study was not efficient. They never really integrated all that they attempted to study, and they had so many sources of information, including all those they created as well, that they ended up more overwhelmed and confused than anything.

Preparing for an Examination

Now re-read your highlighted material, as well as the definitions of the vocabulary words you looked up. For each area that has been highlighted or underlined, practice writing three levels of test questions—one that tests only memory ability; one that tests skills acquired concerning the concept; and one that tests your ability to apply the concept.

Preparing in this way will be a far more effective method to be sure that knowledge is retained and that you are ready for the examination. Once you have written these questions, they can now serve as your "study guide" to further prepare you for the examination. ("Notes" pages have been provided for you periodically throughout the book so that you can write your own study questions.) Also see Appendix I—"Make Your Study Time Effective"—to improve your knowledge and study efficiency. Appendix J provides specific review questions to help assure the reader that s/he is building the proper market knowledge base (memory, skill, and application) in the foundation articles of this book.

Taking detailed lecture notes is very important in a classroom or lecture setting. Capable speakers, trainers, and faculty will have greater knowledge, education, and experience than will be found in any single textbook. Students will not easily find these additional enhancements to the course in any other way. Benefiting from their presentation requires a daily written account of whiteboard material, examples, and media deliveries. As a student or professional, it will be your responsibility to capture and learn these remarks.

There is no doubt that these steps require hard work and are quite time-consuming. No one ever said that acquiring knowledge and an education came easily. If you are looking for the path of least resistance, it is readily found. Just look for classes known for awarding high grades, that are also known to contain little content, that are taught by personally popular professors, and you too can be one of those graduates who only understand one-syllable words, still count on fingers and toes, and who, if lucky, will at some point find a job working at a fast food franchise rather than owning one.

Appendix I—Make Your Study Time Effective

Excerpted by permission from: *Make Sense Out of College*, by Susan G. Thomas (amazon: Charleston, 2010).

Study, Don't Just Passively Read

Far too few students really understand what it means to actually study, and you do want to use your study time wisely, so read on because this is an extremely important section. Let me describe first what studying is <u>not</u>. It is not a quick skim of the chapter at 11 o'clock at night. It's also not reading coupled with heavy use of a highlighter. That approach doesn't put the chapter's contents into your brain and doesn't help at all with your actually understanding what you've read. Studying is also not about taking notes from the book, essentially writing or typing pages and pages of facts directly from the chapter in hopes of putting it to memory. Studying is also not about creating an outline of the assigned chapter.

All of the above methods, which you see used all the time (just walk through the library on a Saturday and look at how people are studying), are inefficient and ineffective and therefore pretty much a waste of your study time. They are what I would call "busy work." Doing any of them makes you <u>think</u> you are getting somewhere, but you really aren't. You're simply avoiding doing the most important (but probably most difficult) aspect of true studying—attempting to really <u>understand</u> what you read.

<u>Build your general vocabulary</u>. A very important part of studying is to understand the meaning of all the words used in your textbooks. Circle every word you don't know the meaning of and look up its definition. Keep a small paperback

dictionary in your backpack for this purpose. Look up the word you don't know the meaning of and write its definition in the margin of your book. If you hear your instructor use a word you don't know, write it in the margin of your notes, and look it up after class. For a while you may feel like you're doing this constantly, and maybe you will be, but the payoff will be well worth it. If you're serious about getting the most out of studying, you will be consulting this dictionary several times. If you continue to look up and memorize the definitions of all words that you don't know as you encounter them in your assigned readings, you will increase your vocabulary tremendously. As you start to naturally use these same words in everyday conversation, you will begin to sound like the educated person you are becoming.

<u>Work to understand, not just memorize, key terms.</u> Let's talk for just a minute about memorization, when it should be used and when it shouldn't be used in a course. It should be used far less often than you think, but it does have its place at times. It must be used in courses that contain important names, places, and dates. You've already memorized several important dates just to get through high school history courses—1492, 1776, etc. Another situation where memorization is key to passing a course is in foreign language study, where students must put into memory hundreds of nouns, adjectives, adverbs, and verbs, not to mention the conjugated forms of common verbs, as well as idiomatic expressions that every language has.

There is no other way to get a language into your brain other than rote memorization. Math courses are another subject area that needs some memorization because advanced math, at least, seems to be built on formulas. I know that many high school teachers tell students they don't need to memorize these formulas; they can just look up some math fact or formula if they need it when and if the time comes. I would say this is bad advice. If you want to look and act like an educated person, you have to have a certain amount of knowledge and facts literally at your fingertips.   Let me give you an example.

When I taught Business Communications and we were to the point in the course where we were discussing employment—resumé and cover letter writing, as well as interviewing, I talked with several recruiters visiting campus at the time to find out what they looked for in our students during the interview process.   One interviewer told me that one of the questions he asks candidates is to quickly estimate the square footage of the room they're in. This happened to be a question asked by an interviewer of Business majors, so maybe he wanted to test math skills and felt they were important for the job; or maybe he believed knowing simple math formulas and how to work them were an indication of a bright student, whatever their major was.   I'm not sure which, but he did expect students to remember, obviously, the formula for square footage, quickly eyeball the dimensions of the room in round numbers, do the math in their heads, and quickly spit out a close approximation.

To see how well my students would have done in this exercise, I presented the same problem to them in class the following day—I asked them to calculate the square footage of our classroom in their heads, right then.   To my shock, I had just <u>one</u> student out of 30 who had memorized the formula for square footage (length x width) and who was then able to compute almost instantaneously the correct answer for the square footage of our classroom. Since most of the other students just gave me a blank stare when I presented them with the problem, I asked them why they couldn't do the problem.

Most told me their math teachers in high school had told them they didn't need to memorize any formulas; they could just look it up in a book or, these days, "Google it" if they ever needed any formulas, or other factual information for that matter. I hope you can see from this true story how impractical such an approach to learning is—that in the real world you will often not have time to "look up" every important fact you will be expected to know.   So for some of the important basics and to avoid severe embarrassment on the job and in other settings, put some of the math (and other) basics to memory right now!

Realistically, then, for some courses, some of your study time will be devoted to memorization, but studying needs to be far more than this. It really needs to be centered on learning and understanding the concepts presented in your textbook and class lectures. Yes, there are key terms presented in most every chapter, and, given their straightforward presentation, it would seem that if you just memorized these key terms and their definitions, you'd be prepared enough for the next exam. Don't be fooled, however, by the simple, straightforward appearance of definitions.   They contain so much information about the subject matter that you must truly understand these terms to have a hope of understanding the course subject. And don't assume that you really understand these terms simply because you can memorize the few words or sentences that define them.

Let me give you an example of what I mean when I say you need to understand the term, not just memorize its definition. Let's take a key term from an *Introduction to Marketing* text chapter as an example.   Chapter One is entitled, "Marketing: Creating and Capturing Customer Value."   In this first chapter, one of the key terms listed and described is "demarketing." As a student in this Marketing course, this would likely be a term you have never heard of before. The author defines "demarketing" as "a company's efforts to purposely reduce demand." Seems simple enough.   But just memorizing these words doesn't guarantee that you understand at all what the term "demarketing" means or how it's applied in the real world.

Look at the words that make up the definition of "demarketing."   You see the word "demand" within the definition. If you were to look up "demand" in a general dictionary, you would find its meaning to be "to ask for boldly or urgently." In Marketing, however, the term "demand" has a very different and field-specific meaning. You will now need to look back to an earlier page in this same chapter to see how the author defines "demand" in a Marketing sense. On a previous page, he states that the term "demand" means "a human want backed by buying power." Do you know what the term "buying power" means in Marketing as well? I think you can see how many layers deep we can go just to understand one key term. Think of this multi-layered process as "unwrapping" or "unpacking" a term's definition.

So if you're studying key terms correctly, you're studying them for true understanding. You will find yourself flipping back and forth often between pages within a chapter (or to other parts of the book, maybe to a glossary in the back) to find definitions of definitions, so to speak, as well as explanations of even more basic terms. Given this need to constantly be flipping back and forth within a chapter's pages to really study and learn, I think it's safe to say that students who are simply slowly turning the pages one by one in the textbook as they read are not really studying at all; simply taking in one sentence after another cannot possibly create understanding. So before you think you understand the definitions of the key terms, be sure you look up the meanings of any of the terms used to define the key term, until you understand every word and term in the definition.

When you start to get this proactive in your studying, you will find that your understanding of the subject matter will start to grow rapidly. This is part of what active learning is: getting personally involved with the content in the textbook, searching out information you don't understand, and finding the connections between the concepts discussed. Real studying, then, is a lot like detective work because it is all connected— your job is to find out how.

<u>Work to develop skill with the concepts and the knowledge of how to apply the concept.</u> A textbook is big on presenting terms and their definitions. But this is just laying the groundwork for

what lies ahead. They eventually want to move you to the next level—a level of understanding that will make you able to actually use the course content in real-world situations. It's probably easiest to see how this is meant to unfold by looking at studying a foreign language course. First you must put to memory hundreds of nouns, adjectives, adverbs, verbs, and verb forms—you first must build a knowledge base to work from.

This constitutes the memorization part of the course. These are the "tools" you need to put into your brain's database, so to speak, before you can move to the next phase of learning the language—that of actually reading, writing, and speaking the new language, in other words, the application phase of the course. This is where you decide when and how to select from hundreds of words and verb forms, as you face various communication situations.

You will soon realize that it is actually much easier to remember course content if you truly understand it. With memorization, even if you are successful in the short run to put the chapter's key terms and definitions into your short-term memory for the exam, you won't have the ability to apply what you've memorized other than in the one narrow example presented in the book. If you're presented with a slightly different situation on the exam, you're sunk, because you don't really understand the tool (term) and how it's applied.

A math example probably works best here to illustrate. I used to give my students a writing assignment that first required them to apply the mathematical formula to determine the "break-even" point in a business scenario. Given the cost of a piece of equipment that helps to produce a certain product, how many months will it be before this piece of equipment has, in effect, paid for itself, or, in other words, the cost to the company to purchase this equipment has been recouped through sales? Once the students arrived at their answer to the first part, I then asked them to tell me in words what would happen to the answer (months to break even) if, for example, we increased the cost of the equipment.

To do this, the student must understand the nature of the different variables in the break-even formula and how they relate to and directly impact each other. You estimated you could buy the equipment for $10,000, but it actually ended up costing you more than that. What, then, happens to the time to payback? The answer is, payback takes longer. If you decrease A, that is, you were able to buy the equipment for less than the $10,000 you estimated, then what would happen to time to payback?

The answer is, if you decrease the cost of the equipment, time to payback is shorter. It is important that students understand these relationships because "break-even" calculations involve only estimates, and they can turn out to be wrong. Sales might not be as large as was estimated; other costs not even initially considered might enter the picture, so reality might play out differently than the manager's forecast.

All of these elements are boiled down into a formula called "the break-even formula," but, as you can see, there's a whole picture behind the numbers that needs to be understood—to see how the numbers relate to each other and how changing just one variable will change the answer. Students get used to plugging in numbers into formulas to get answers for tests, but often times they don't really understand the elements in the formula and how the elements relate to each other.

<u>Mark up your book for understanding.</u> When you're attempting to really understand what you're reading, the best advice I can give you is focus, focus, focus. Stay with every sentence and be sure every one makes sense to you. One thing that will help you start to internalize the information is to mark up the textbook in a meaningful way as you read. By the way, I know students sometimes don't want to mark in their books because a "clean" one brings a higher price at the end of the semester

when they sell their books back to the campus bookstore; however, the difference in buyback price isn't all that much in the scheme of your life, and you stand to gain a great deal in learning and an improved grade by marking your book in ways that help you to learn the material. You need to make the material your own, so mark it in a way that helps you learn. Just please don't be stingy with your pen!

However, you do want to resist doing too much underlining and highlighting, so before you are tempted to underline something, read the entire paragraph, then choose only a few words to mark, the most important words or point made in that paragraph. In fact, try to isolate the most important sentence in that paragraph. If the writer is a good one, the most important sentence will usually be the first one, often called the "topic sentence." Don't count on that, but it's usually laid out that way, with the remaining sentences added to support and flesh out the topic sentence.

Important information is often bold-faced or underlined for the student. These "signposts" help, so pay particular attention to these. Going over the paragraph more than once in this way also will help you to learn the material, whereas a single, superficial reading does almost no good, even if you highlight or underline as you go.

Develop your own marking methods. The problem with highlighting only or underlining only is that such notation gives all the information equal value. So it's helpful to find a way to mark really important statements. Using asterisks (*) to mark points that are really, really important is often helpful. You could also number in the margin if some sort of a list or priority is given in the paragraph. You could even highlight in a couple of different colors, or use red ink to circle very, very important terms or numbers. In other words, use other means beyond the typical yellow highlighter and black ink underlining to build visual cues for information that's particularly important. Not all of it is of equal importance, so make your text notations visually reflect that.

<u>Study with the next exam in mind</u>. Since all of your study efforts are leading up to an exam, always keep in mind as you study how your instructor might test you on the assigned reading. Some of the questions could be drawn from the key concepts and terms. These would be simple "recall" questions. A more difficult question would expect you to understand the key definitions in the chapter but take them a step further by applying them in some way to a real-world situation. This would be termed an "application" type question.

Let me go to the Instructor's Test Bank for the Marketing textbook I referred to earlier and give you an example of a simple recall question, as well as a challenging question that would be used to test the student's understanding of chapter terms. Here's the easy one involving only recall: *"Which of the following is central to any definition of marketing?"* This multiple-choice question has five possible answers. If you had memorized the book's definition of what Marketing is, you could then easily spot the correct answer among the five choices given. The chapter had stated that "Marketing is managing profitable customer relationships." Recalling that short definition would be enough to get this question right, because only one answer choice of the five possible answers even mentions the word "customers." If you've memorized the definition, you will have no problem seeing the correct answer here.

Now let's look at an example of a question that is considered to be a challenging one, that is, one that involves additional thinking, based on understanding what you've read, not just memorization: *"To avoid traffic gridlock in large metro areas, a community might use _____ to discourage travelers from driving during peak commuting hours."* The reason this is considered a "challenging" question is because the answer can't be found in any specific sentence in the chapter; in other words, arriving at the right answer involves more than simple and straightforward recall. It involves the student's understanding of the various terms presented in the chapter. In this case, the term "demarketing" is the correct answer.

Had the question asked, "What is the correct definition of "demarketing?" it would have been a simple recall question type. But in this case, the student has to know the definition of "demarketing" to even have a chance at getting this question right. He also has to understand <u>when</u> demarketing would likely be used, in what kind of scenario in the marketplace?

According to the textbook, "demarketing" is "the act of seeking fewer customers and reducing demand for a product or service." So you need to understand under what conditions companies might actually try to do this, try to seek fewer customers, something that appears counterintuitive to most Marketing goals! When might a company want to use the technique of demarketing and actually reduce customer demand? The answer is when reducing demand alleviates problems for the company, which is stated in the chapter. In this chapter, the author presented a couple of examples of when the "tool" of demarketing has been used—in Yosemite National Park to help reduce the overcrowding problems they typically have during the summer, although it doesn't state what they did specifically to reduce the crowds.

The concept was also applied by a utilities company to reduce demand for electricity when overuse of utilities occurred during peak hours (in very cold weather or very hot weather). Perhaps this was done by charging higher rates during peak hours. Had simple recall been the objective here, the question might have been, "Which national park used demarketing for its overcrowding problems one summer?" Simple. "Yosemite National Park." No reasoning required here, just recall.

Let's get back to our challenging test question: *"To avoid traffic gridlock in large metro areas, a community might use _____ to discourage travelers from driving during peak commuting hours."* This question brings up a real-world situation you didn't study about at all in the chapter—the idea of traffic gridlock. So here's where true understanding of the term comes in.   You would be expected to realize that traffic gridlock is a business problem not unlike overcrowding in the national park or overuse of utilities during peak hours. You need to be able to connect information you know to new information and realize how it fits. Thus, the student should choose the same Marketing tool to deal with traffic gridlock as the text suggested to solve the congestion problem in Yosemite National Park and to alleviate the overuse of utilities during peak hours, and that is "demarketing."

It is with questions like these that true understanding is tested. So if you understand what the term "demarketing" means and when it would be applied in the marketplace, you would then be able to recognize the term "demarketing" as the correct answer. The other answer choices were far off the mark and could have easily been eliminated if you had true understanding of the chapter's concepts. As you can see, then, understanding requires you to be able to go beyond what has simply been provided in the chapter and to be able to reason your way through new but similar situations given to you on an exam.

<u>Take short study breaks</u>. Many students, once they finally get started studying, like to put in marathon sessions without a break; however, your brain needs a brief break from intense concentration about every hour or so to remain alert. So take a 5- or 10-minute break every hour and walk around, but be careful about where you take this break, or you could end up blowing off the last half of your scheduled study time when you run into friends who are on their way to the pub and ask you to join them. Go to the restroom, go get a drink of water at the drinking fountain, walk up and down a couple of flights of stairs in the library, but walk where you're least likely to run into people you know. After 10 minutes, your brain should feel refreshed and ready to get back to work.

Page 433

Get answers to questions you have. Since you'll be studying with a focus on the upcoming exam, be sure you put question marks in the margins next to information in the textbook that you do not understand. Then listen for your instructor's explanation of these confusing points in the lecture over this chapter. If you don't get an explanation you can understand or your instructor doesn't even mention the point you're confused about, you're going to need to probe further. If you're brave, ask your question during lecture, especially if your instructor asks the class if they have any questions.

If you're not brave enough to raise your hand and ask, then ask him after class or schedule time during office hours to go in personally to get an explanation. The point is, do not let your questions go unanswered, assuming it's probably not an important point anyway and so probably won't be asked about on the exam. Clarify any questions as you go. If you let gaps in your understanding remain, you will pay a price for it later in missed test questions and, worse yet, in not truly understanding the course material for which you are now held responsible. If this course is a prerequisite for others you will be taking, it's even more important that you get a good understanding of the material. So clear up every question all along the way. You'll be glad later that you did.

By the end of several study sessions and after related class lectures, you should have no area left in the assigned material that you don't understand. If you've been putting in serious study time every week since the first day of class, you should be more than prepared for the first test. You will have given your brain time to absorb the material gradually, which is the best way to learn anything—in small doses, slowly over time. Many students, however, attempt to prepare for exams in one crash session, reading all the chapters the night before the midterm.

The human brain simply can't take in that much material that quickly and remember it, so it's highly unlikely students who do this can retain as much as they need to from the assigned chapters and lectures. And if they've missed class lectures as well, they are cruising toward a "D" or an "F" on the exam because true understanding—that which takes time to get—won't be there. On the other hand, students who start studying for the first exam from the day of the first reading assignment in the ways I have suggested above are miles ahead of the other students. If you will follow this approach to studying, you will not need to pull any all-nighters and you will have a solid understanding of the information you've been assigned. You will be more than ready for the next exam.

Appendix J—Study Questions

The following sample questions are included here to help you check your understanding of the concepts presented in all the articles in this book. Answers to all questions can be found at the end of Appendix J. At the end of each question is indicated the type of question it is (*i.e.,* m = memory type, s = skill type, and a = application type).

"Marketing Mix: The Fundamentals"

1. Social responsibility is more a legal issue than an ethical one. (S)

a. true
b. false

2. The marketing mix elements are each equally important when positioning a product. (S)

a. true
b. false

3. The "Four P's" of a marketing mix are   (M)

a. product, price, promotion, and profit
b. promotion, production, price, and people
c. potential customers, product, price, and personal selling
d. product, place, promotion, and price
e. production, personnel, price, and physical distribution

4. "Positioning" is a marketing management aid which shows   (M)

a. how closely existing products match customers' ideal preferences
b. where proposed and/or present brands are located in a market, as seen by customers
c. if some products are viewed as very similar
d. all of the above
e. two among a, b, c are correct

5. The size of a competitor's market is measured by   (S)

a. critical mass
b. share
c. penetration
d. The answer is not among a, b, or c
e. two among a, b, and c are correct

"Forecasting for Market Management"

6. In a regression application, if the B value is high and the R value is both positive and high, this result will influence   (S)

a. X
b. not enough information to determine any relationship

7. Y values are dependent in the regression equation.   (M)

a. true
b. false

8. Major downswings in a product demand curve may be seen when an R value changes from positive to negative (assume "x" variable is equal to time).   (S)

a. true
b. false

9. The application of $Y = a + bX$ attempts to predict a "diffusion of innovation curve" (line).   (A)

a. true
b. false

10. "b" values measure the weight of the dependent variable in a regression solution. (S)

a. true
b. false

11.   If a respondent to a questionnaire gave an invalid answer due to fatigue an frustration, what source of invalidity would have occurred?   (A)

a. evaluation apprehension
b. testing effect
c. maturation
d. expectancy
e. the correct answer is not among a, b, c, or d

12. Elton Mayo discovered interview invalidity in the form of   (M)

a. a halo effect
b. a self-fulfilling prophecy
c. the Pygmalion effect
d. the Hawthorne effect
e. none of the above are correct

13. Which of the following contribute to invalid responses?   (M)

a. instrumentation decay
b. maturation
c. the Hawthorne Effect
d. two of the above are correct
e. all among a, b, and c are correct

14. The greatest source of invalidity in test instruments is/are   (M)

a. interviewer cheating
b. non-standard measures
c. neither a nor b is correct
d. both a and b are equally correct

15. Which of the following interview invalidities is/are related to fatigue? (M)

a. evaluation apprehension
b. maturation
c. instrumentation decay
d. time syndrome
e. two above are correct

"Managerial Market Economics"

16. If the marketing manager raises the price of a product and consumers continue to purchase the item, consumer demand is said to be (S)

a. elastic
b. inelastic
c. at equilibrium
d. saturated

17. A shift in funds flow from M_3 to M_2 indicates (S)

a. greater liquidity
b. less liquidity
c. this change does not affect liquidity

18. Which of the following contemporary economists advocates government control and economic regulation? (M)

a. Friedman
b. Galbraith

19. Which two gross national product variables are of greatest concern to the market manager? (M)

a. "C" and "I"
b. "C" and "S"
c. "G" and "I"
d. a different combination

20. If a shift in funds flow occurs from M_2 to M_3, the marketing manager should anticipate which of the following consumer behaviors? (A)

a. short-term spending
b. short-term saving
c. long-term spending
d. long-term saving

Page 440

21. Which of the following should first be considered during the business analysis stage of the PPLC?   (M)

a. ROI
b. hurdle rate
c break even
d two among a, b, and c are correct
e. a, b, and c are correct

22. Decision theory helps the market manager to   (M)

a. select the most profitable product/service to offer
b. consider various levels of market penetration
c. both a and b are correct

23. Legal issues should be considered first in the _____ area of the new product model.   (M)

a. product development
b. commercialization
c. business analysis
d. correct area is not among a, b, or c

24. The "hurdle rate" concept includes   (M)

a. return on investment
b. risk

c. both of the above

d. neither a or b is correct

25. The value of the following product event fork for Product 1 is   (A)

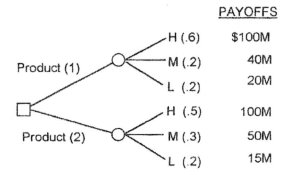

PAYOFFS

	Product (1)	H (.6)	$100M
Product (1)		M (.2)	40M
		L (.2)	20M
		H (.5)	100M
Product (2)		M (.3)	50M
		L (.2)	15M

a. $14 m

b. $68 m

c. $ 6.8 m

d. need more information to calculate

e. the answer is not among a, b, c, or d

"Physical Distribution—An Application"

26. In a PERT application, the critical path is determined by the   (S)

a shortest path

b. longest path

c. average of shortest and longest path

d. summation of variance

27. If the Z calculated for a PERT program is .41, what is the probability of success?   (S)

a. 41%

b. 82%

c. .91%
d. none of the above

28. The formula for variance in PERT programming utilizes two constants among the numerator and denominator.   (S)

a. true
b. false

29. In an expected time calculation, can the distribution of times be skewed?   (S)

a. yes
b. no

30. A PERT chart is most likely to be useful for   (M)

a. evaluating the shape of the target market's response function to the marketing mix
b. forecasting sales
c. scheduling the implementation of the marketing plan
d. setting the marketing budget
e. mapping out the firm's competitive position

"Pricing Strategies"

---

31. Why is price reduction a poor first choice as a pricing tactic?   (S)

a. it may reduce profit
b. consumers may not remain loyal at a lower price
c. it could produce a downward price spiral in the market
d. all above are correct reasons
e. only two among a, b, and c are correct

32. A proactive pricing strategy is best for which of the following?   (M)

a. market leader
b. all firms should be proactive in pricing their products
c. reactive strategies are best for the market leader
d. none above are accurate

33. At a price of $10, we sell 10 items. We cut the price to $8 each and sell 15 items. From that we conclude that demand for the item is   (A)

a. price inelastic
b. price unrelated
c. price elastic
d. none of the above

34. Luxury automobiles would be an example of cost-oriented pricing.   (S)

a. true
b. false

35. Among the assumptions made before a price reduction decision are: (S)

a. competitors will also reduce price
b. consumers will demand more product at the lower price
c. current customers will remain loyal at the lower price
d. both a & b are correct
e. both b & c are correct

"Research: A Marketing Must"

36. Research information eliminates the risk involved in making market decisions.   (M)

a. true
b. false

37. The discount rate discussed in "Research: A Marketing Must" deals with   (M)

a. cost
b. accuracy
c. value
d. tax writeoff
e. two among, a, b, c, d, are correct

38. Secondary research should always be done before primary research.   (M)

a. true
b. false

39. Good secondary research sources include   (M)

a. public documents
b. trade journals
c. relevant historical data
d. all of the above
e. all but one among a, b, and c are correct

40. According to the article, "Research: A Marketing Must," the evaluation of secondary data should include an analysis of   (M)

a. the discount rate
b. the prime rate
c. the funds rate
d. management's heart rate
e. none of the above

"Sampling"

41. The larger a population of consumers is, the greater number of them that must be sampled.   (S)

a. true
b. false

42. In the formula for sample size, which variable relates to differences among respondents' answers?   (M)

a. z score
b. confidence interval
c. standard deviation
d. none of the above

43. Which of the following statements is/are true regarding $n = \dfrac{z^2 \hat{\sigma}^2}{e^2}$?   (S)

a. the greater the confidence level, the greater the "n"
b. the smaller the e^2, the smaller the "n"
c. $\hat{\sigma}^2$ is an estimate
d. all above are true
e. only two among a, b, and c, are true

44. Census data is calculated based on sound techniques of probability.   (M)

a. true
b. false

45. In order to determine a confidence level from a "z" table value of .4750, you would use which of the following?   (S)

a. subtraction
b. addition
c. division
d. a "z" table

"Segmentation"

46. A market segment is any group toward which we direct marketing effort.   (S)

a. true
b. false

47. How many "tests" for applying a market segment strategy were discussed in lecture? (M)

a. two
b. one
c. six

d. four
e. three

48. In practical application, Roger's diffusion of innovation curve has six standard deviations.　　(M)

a. true
b. false

49. In practice, the Diffusion of Innovation Curve is　　(S)

a. a standard curve
b. skewed to the left
c. skewed to the right
d. a, b, and c are all possible
e. none among a, b, or c, is correct

50. A soft-drink manufacturer has only one advertising theme, which is "It refreshes everyone." That is an example of　　(A)

a. a target market
b. a market segment
c. both a & b
d. neither a nor b

"Marketing Problems, Goals, and Constraints"

51. Together Taylor, Herzberg, Schien, and Drucker contributed to the market management decision matrix presented in lecture.　　(M)

a. true
b. false

52. The management area of freedom model presented in class refers to the degrees of freedom from the 'f' distribution.   (S)

a. true
b. false

53. The most difficult step in the decision process model is   (M)

a. defining the problem
b. selecting alternatives
c. developing alternatives
d. taking action
e. the correct answer is not among a, b, c, or d

54. Which of the following is not a potential management constraint to decision making?   (S)

a. time
b. raw material
c. technology
d. budget
e. all of the above are potential management constraints

55. Intermediate objectives help assure more efficient resource management "on our way" to meeting a marketing goal.   (S)

a. true
b. false

"Web (www) Sales and Telemarketing"

56. Telemarketing   (M)

a. has low start-up expenses
b. can expand company sales territory
c. produces average industrial orders of $800
d. two above are correct
e. a, b, and c, are correct

57. Telemarketing applications can provide   (M)

a. database information
b. market research
c. add-on sales
d. two above are correct
e. a, b, and c are correct

58. Telemarketing is another term for telephone sales.   (M)

a. true
b. false

59. It is essential that top management endorse telemarketing in order for such a program to be successful.   (M)

a. true
b. false

60. Which companies can benefit from a telemarketing program?   (M)

a. large
b. medium
c. small
d. two above are correct
e. a, b, and c are correct

"Understanding Market Communications"

61. The following formula calculates the number of inventory credits:

$$[B/C + (A/B \times 100)] \times 0.4$$

a. true
b. false

62.
$$_nC_r = \frac{n!}{r!(n-r)!}$$ was applied in your reading to evaluate communication   (S)

a. costs of advertising
b. reading grade level (i.e., Gunning Fog Index)
c. potential among individuals/groups to miscommunicate
d. This formula was not used in the readings or lecture on communication
e. This formula was used but was not applied to communication

63. Both encoding and decoding messages are affected by the receivers of a market communication.   (M)

a. true
b. false

64. Which of the following best illustrates communication "noise"?   (A)

a. a TV ad is recorded at a higher volume than is used for most TV programs
b. a political candidate rides through town in a car with a loud speaker, asking pedestrians to vote for her
c. magazine sales reps telephone consumers to offer low-priced subscriptions
d. a motorist doesn't see a billboard because a passing truck blocks it from view

65. Mothers Against Drunk Drivers (MADD) is an example of which type of public? (S)

a. legal public
b. general public
c. special interest public
d. the answer is not among a, b, or c

"Channels and Physical Distribution"

66. Physical distribution includes employees such as agents and wholesalers.   (M)

a. true
b. false

67. The general definition of physical distribution is "members or people in a logistics network."   (M)

a. true
b. false

68. Company A produces specialty toys aimed at reaching a group of "yuppie" parents whose taste in products shifts quickly. To secure the feedback information Company A needs to best meet its customer's needs, the company would be best served by which distribution channel?   (A)

a. manufacturer⟹ wholesaler⟹ retailer⟹ consumer
b. manufacturer⟹ agent⟹ retailer⟹ customer
c. manufacturer⟹ retailer⟹ consumer
d. manufacturer⟹ consumer

69. Demand pull may be accomplished by increasing sales commissions.   (S)

a. true
b. false

70. Manufacturer A makes wheels for new cars; Manufacturer B makes cake mix, shortening, and detergents. Which of the following is most likely a true statement?   (A)

a. "A" will market through a longer channel than will "B"
b. "A" will market through a shorter channel than will "B"
c. We do not have enough information to select either of the above answers

"Advertising, Promotion, and Publicity"

71. The acronym "AIDA" stands for attitude, interest, desire, and action   M)

a. true
b. false

72. The primary "job" of promotion is to sell.   (S)

a. true
b. false

73. The primary job of advertising is to

a. inform
b. educate
c. both a and b are correct   (S)

74. After the decision is made to either buy or not buy a product, dissonance occurs in either case. (A)

a. true
b. false

75. Publicity can be

a. paid or unpaid
b. positive or negative
c. both a and b are correct (M)

"Two Plus Two Equals Three". [sic]

---

76. According to this article, quantitative solutions are more legitimate than prose analyses. (M)

a. true
b. false

77. Universities have not effectively combined "word" courses with "number" courses. (M)

a. true
b. false
c. This is not a concept discussed in the article.

78. The article's graphic of a circular matrix visually demonstrates (M)

a. synergy
b. exclusion
c. asymmetry
d. none of the above is correct.

"Business Writing and Academic Writing"

---

79. According to this article, business readers (managers) don't have to read the reports or memos you submit to them. (M)

a. true
b. false

80. In order to make your writing in business more effective, you would   (A)

a. be as concise as possible yet still be clear
b. don't necessarily give your best work the first time; write a first draft and see what your manager has to say about it
c. do not write politically for business; this is business, not politics
d. All of these answers would make your business writing more effective.

81. Unlike "due dates" for assignments in college which usually give students plenty of time to complete, due dates in business can sometimes be unreasonably short. (S)

a. true
b. false

82. In business, audiences will likely have the same or greater subject knowledge than you do as a presenter. (M)

a. true
b. false

83. Some business documents are kept virtually "forever."   What business and legal implications does this have?   (A)

a. trailing liability for you, the writer
b. trailing liability for your company
c. your work remains your own intellectual capital
d. only two above are correct
e. a, b, and c are correct

"Effective Oral Presentations"

84. Which of the following would make your oral delivery more effective?   (S)

a. take as much time as you need to get your points across.
b. don't use notes or your business audience won't think you know what you're talking about.
c. When gathering information for your presentation, collect more material than you plan to use or think you will need.
d. only two above are correct
e. a, b, and c are all correct

85. As a presenter, your primary goals should   (S)

a. build a case
b. build a relationship
c. build a reputation
d. two above are correct

e. a, b, and c are all correct

86. It is important to plan delivery strategy to include a consideration for the age and power differences between you (the presenter) and your audience members.

a. true
b. false

87. "Hecklers" and "snipers" are equally dangerous.   (S)

a. true
b. false

88. It is OK to be defensive when someone challenges your delivery, because doing so will make you appear more confident.   (S)

a. true
b. false

"Multiple Regression and Factor Analysis

89. The weight that an independent variable has in the regression equation is determined by   (S)

a. a criterion variable
b. a variable intercept
c. a coefficient
d. a power
e. the answer is not among a, b, c, or d

90. The strength of correlation between a dependent variable and an independent variable is measured by R value.   (S)

a. true
b. false

91. Factor analysis is a data reduction route.   (M)

a. true
b. false

92. R factor analysis is used to measure relationships.   (M)

a. true
b. false

93. Interpreting a factor matrix would conclude that a factor load of -.50 and +.50 would be of equal value in correlation.   (A)

a. true
b. false

"A Primary Research (VMS) Application"

---

94. The acronym "VMS" stands for   (M)

a. value management system
b. voice mail service
c. various method skills
d. vertical management system
e. none above are correct

95. The measurement of attitude object is based on calculations of both belief and attitude characteristics.   (S)

a. true
b. false

96. In a regression formula, b_2x_2 would indicate that there were at least four variables being considered.   (S)

a. true
b. false

97. The standard deviation in this application is approximately   (M)
a. one utile
b. two utiles
c. three utiles
d. four utiles
e. five utiles

98. The indicated propensity to subscribe to VMS was   (M)

a. 30% to 45%
b. 45% to 60%
c. 60% to 75%
d. 70% to 85%
e. over 90%

"The Retail Lease vs. Purchase Decision"

---

99. Earliest lease transactions occurred in the year   (M)

a. 2000
b. 2000 B.C.
c. 2000 A.D.
d. 1900
e. 1800

100. The alternative minimum tax amount is based solely on net income.   (M)

a. true
b. false

101. Leasing or purchasing digital technology to tell time rather than analog would be an example of

a. obsolescence
b. supercession

102. A sale and leaseback agreement allows the lessee to free working capital. (S)

a. true
b. false

103. The National accumulation of leases by the year 2011 was   (M)

a. $100 billion
b. $150 billion
c. $200 billion
d. $1.0 trillion
e. $1.3 trillion

"Student Writing Weaknesses in Marketing"

---

104. The sample size of students for this study was   (M)

a. 2000
b. 3500
c. 700
d. 200
e. 350

105. The writing grade average of undergraduate student in this study was   (M)

a. B+
b. B-
c. C+
d. C-
e. D+

106. The Harvard Business Review article, "Who's Got the Monkey?" refers to (M)

a. following around in the classroom
b. foolish responses to questions
c. problems in employee delegation
d. having the correct answer
e. the manager having the weakest employee

107. Which of the following were demonstrated to reduce effective student writing in marketing   (M)

a. poor mechanics
b. not writing succinctly
c. not following instructions accurately
d. delegating upward
e. all of the above

108. Having students rewrite assignments to improve their grade actually makes the students weaker.   (M)

a. true
b. false

"Writing Weaknesses in Business Deliverables"

---

109. What did the article say were the main reasons student writing is weak upon graduation from college?   (M)

a. faculty give too many conflicting suggestions as to how students can improve their writing
b. students don't do enough writing in college
c. faculty tend not to correct errors in student writing so students don't know how to improve
d. a, b, and c are all correct
e. b and c are correct

110. What do employers complain is a major writing weakness in the graduates they hire?   (M)
a. Students' spelling is poor.
b. Students have a problem getting to the point quickly.
c. Students' business documents lack political skill.
d. Students' grammar is poor.
e. Students take too long to complete writing assignments.

111. A student's ability to think coherently, logically, and analytically depends mostly on what?   (M)

a. the student's writing skill level

b. the student's reading grade level
c. the student's major in college
d. the size of a student's knowledge base

112. The ability to explain fully and clearly is often undeveloped when students graduate from college. Why is this? (M)

a. faculty sometimes "fill in the blanks" automatically when they read student papers and so don't force students to learn to write clearly.
b. topics given to students for papers in their classes are often too broad in scope to be able to cover all parts thoroughly.
c. students are told there are no right or wrong answers for the assignment, so they are free to develop ideas however they choose.
d. students are told that creativity in their writing is more important than the techniques of writing.

113. What are two things that can confuse a writer's ability to judge accurately in a situation? (M)

a. preconceived ideas
b. past negative experiences
c. a co-worker's opinion
d. prejudices
e. both a and d are correct

"Functional vs. Dysfunctional Interaction"

---

114. The fundamental reasons to fund this consultancy was (S)

a. force management
b. retirement
c. salary
d. training
e. none above is correct

115. In this case, the principal attempted to manage (S)

a. the outcome
b. the consultants
c. both a and b are correct
d. none above are correct

116. Departmental executives saw Pauline as (S)

a. a change agent
b. excellent manager
c. mettling in their affairs
d. a political climber
e. two above are correct

117. The consultants gained access to employees without positioning by the principal. (M)
a. true
b. false

118. The consultants in this case (M)

a. were not able to provide an effective deliverable
b. were not given unfettered access
c. suffered delays of access
d. two above are correct
e. all above are correct

Answers to Sample Questions

1. b
2. b
3. d
4. d
5. b
6. a
7. a
8. a
9. a
10. b
11. c
12. d
13. e
14. b
15. e
16. b
17. a
18. b
19. b
20. d
21. e
22. c
23. d
24. c
25. e
26. b
27. d
28. b
29. a
30. c
31. d
32. a

33. c
34. b
35. e
36. b
37. e
38. a
39. d
40. a
41. b
42. c
43. e
44. b
45. b
46. b
47. e
48. a
49. d
50. d
51. b
52. b
53. d
54. e
55. a
56. e
57. e
58. b
59. a
60. e
61. b
62. c
63. a
64. d
65. c
66. b
67. b
68. d
69. b
70. b
71. b
72. a
73. c
74. a
75. c
76. b
77. a
78. a
79. a
80. a

81. b
82. b
83. e
84. c
85. d
86. a
87. b
88. b
89. c
90. a
91. a
92. b
93. a
94. b
95. a
96. b
97. a
98. d
99. b
100. a
101. b
102. a
103. e
104. c
105. e
106. c
107. e
108. a
109. e
110. b
111. d
112. a
113. e
114. a
115. c
116. e
117. a
118. e

Appendix K—Marketing Arithmetic

Marketing Arithmetic

Return on Investment (ROI):

$$\frac{\text{Net Sales}}{\text{Investment}} \ \text{or} \ \frac{\text{Net Profit Before Taxes}}{\text{Net Sales}} \ \text{or} \ \frac{\text{Net Profit Before Tax}}{\text{Investment}}$$

Percentage Mark-up:

Based on Cost

$$\% = \frac{\text{Selling Price} - \text{Cost}}{\text{Selling Price}}$$

Based on Sales Price

$$\% = \frac{\text{Selling Price} - \text{Cost}}{\text{Cost}}$$

Cost of Goods Sold (COGS): $\% = \dfrac{\text{Cost of Goods Sold}}{\text{Net Sales}}$

Price Elasticity $= \dfrac{Q/DQ}{P/DP}$ or $\dfrac{Q_1 - Q_2 / Q_1 + Q_2}{P_1 - P_2 / P_1 + P_2}$

Gross Profit Margin $= \dfrac{\text{Sales} - \text{Cost of Goods Sold}}{\text{Sales}}$

Net Profit Margin $= \dfrac{\text{Profit After Taxes}}{\text{Sales}}$

Markdown $\% = \dfrac{\text{Original Selling Price} - \text{Reduced Selling Price}}{\text{Original Selling Price}}$

$$\text{Break-Even Units} = \frac{FC*}{SP - VC} \qquad \text{Break-Even Dollars} = \frac{FC*}{1 - (VC/SP)}$$

*or change the numerator to FC+P in order to obtain a given profit level

$$\text{Inventory Turnover} = \frac{\text{Cost of Goods Sold}}{\text{Inventory}}$$

Economic Order Quantity $\qquad EOQ = \sqrt{2SO/ip}$

where:

S = annual quantity sold in units
O = cost of placing an order
i = carrying cost as a percent of selling price
p = dollar price per unit

$$\text{Current Ratio} = \frac{\text{Current Assets}}{\text{Current Liabilities}}$$

$$\text{Quick Ratio} = \frac{\text{Current Assets} - \text{Inventory}}{\text{Current Liabilities}}$$

Finance Charge = down payment + [installment payment (# of periods)] - cash price

$$\text{Rate of Interest} = \frac{\text{Finance Charge}}{\text{Principal x Term of Financing}}$$

Index

extended warranty, 291

F

F test, 45
Facebook, 162
factor analysis, 40, 41, 55
factor loadings, 41, 42, 43
factor matrix, 43
feedback, 295
financial analysis, 379
financial lease, 168
fixed costs, 110
following instructions, 251
Ford, 161
forecasting, 26
Fortune 500, 33, 50
Four P Approach, 141
fraudulent leads, 164
freight policies, 211
frequency analysis, 71
frequency distribution, 10, 82
Friedman, Milton, 105
F-statistic, 38

G

Galbraith, Kenneth, 105
GATT, 128
General Motors, 105, 161
Georgia Pacific, 163
GNP figures, 107
goal orientation, 147
good will, 159
goodwill, 193
Google, 165
GPS promotion, 165
grammar, 249
gross national product, 111
guesswork, 241
Gunning, Robert, 289

H

Halo Effect, 60
hasty generalization, 275
Hawthorne Effect, 60
hedging words, 284
Hewlett-Packard, 22, 120
history, 60

Hope, Bob, 187
human asset, 191, 353
hurdle rate, 109, 168, 191
Hyundai, 207

I

identifiability, 137
image, 193
income statement, 168
independent variable, 22, 23
independent verification, 280
industry boycotts, 297
inferential statistics, 19
inferential statistics, 10, 13
inferential statistics, 74
Institute of Retail Management, vii
institutional ethics, 151
instrumentation decay, 60
Intel, 125
international monetary fund, 106
Internet marketing, 163
Internet sales, 160
interval variable, 37
invalidity, 59
inventory policy, 211
investment per sale, 155
investment tax credit, 172
invisible hand, 102
IP (Internet Protocol), 164
Isaac, Stephen, 63
ITC, 171

J

Jack-in-the-Box, 121
judgment, 272
Justice Department, 201

K

knock-off, 201
knowledge base, 267
Kraft, 191

L

laissez-faire, 102
lead times, 261

P

packaging, 196
packaging applications, 212
patent, 202
path, 216
penetration, 108, 111
Pepsico, 163
Pepsi-Cola, 124
perception, 279
perceptions, 280
performance appraisals, 281
personal opinion, 242, 279
personal selling, 291, 294
personal values, 151
pessimistic time, 216
Phillip Morris, 191
physical distribution, 193, 196, 205
pilot sample, 16
Place, 142
point estimate, 79
point-of-purchase displays, 294
politics and power, 261
poor mechanics, 237
poor organization, 273
poorly developed ideas, 270
pop-ups, 165
positioning, 150, 291
PPC (pay per click), 163
preconceived ideas, 282
prejudice, 282
pre-product life cycle, 191
price, 115, 145
price spiral, 117
price tactics, 122
price war, 118
price, bundling, 129
price, cheaper goods, 122
price, discounts, 126
price, distribution innovation, 125
price, intensive advertising, 124
price, manufacturing cost reduction, 126
price, penetration, 121
price, prestige goods, 123
price, product innovation, 125
price, product proliferation, 124
price, push vs. pull, 129
price, reduction, 126
price, skimming, 120

price, superior services, 123
pricing, 191
pricing, cost-oriented, 118
pricing, demand-oriented, 120
pricing, mark-up, 119
primary research, 53, 72
prime drive time, 294
principal component factor analysis, 43
probable cause, 276
Procter and Gamble, 125
Product, 142
product "landscape", 376
product attributes, 55
product development, 192
product mix, 193
product positioning, 377
product pricing, 377
product testing, 193
product, place, time, utility, 143
production facilities, 210
pro-forma budget, 157
Program Evaluation Review Technique, 215
promotion, 146, 196
promotional pricing, 291
promotional strategy, 55, 195
propensity, 27, 35, 70, 74, 191
psychographic market, 35
psychographic model, 35
psychographics, 35
Psychographics, 377
psycholinguistic scaling, 33
psycholinguistics, 37
public, 296
purchase, 168
purchasing, 168

Q

Q factor analysis, 41
Q technique, 42
qualified buyers, 158
quality, 295
quality assurance, 194
quality control, 194
question
    recall, 431

questionnaire, 56

test instruments, 292
testing effect, 60
textbook marking methods, 430
time limit, 269
time management, 216
Touche-Ross and Co., 1
trade associations, 296
trade shows, 294
trademark, 193
Troy-Built, 206
Twitter, 162
type I error, 40

U

U.S. Chamber of Commerce, 1
UCLA, 160
uncertainty, 175, 215
unnecessary information, 270
unwarranted assumptions, 278
UPI, 296
upper path, 222
UPS, 125
USX (U.S. Steel, Inc.), 1

V

validity, 59, 271
value of perfect information, 351
values, 295
variability, 15
variable cost, 110
variance, 218, 223
Vicom/IT, Inc., vii
vocabulary, 423

W

Wall Street Journal, 289
Walmart, 161
warehouse facilities, 210
Wealth of Nations, 102
web browsers, 164
webmarketing, 163
Weinstock's, 207
Wendy's, 121
Western Electric Company, 63
wholesaler, 206
WilTel, 117
writing succinctly, 238
WYSIWYG, 298

X

X Generation, 131

Y

Yahoo, 165
YouTube, 162

Z

Z calculated, 224
Z table, 218, 224
Z value, 14
Zaltman, Gerald, 59, 65
zero defect, 193

Endnotes

[1]Vincent Bugliosi, *Outrage* (New York: W.W. Norton and Co., Inc., 1996), 52.

[2]Terrence E. Deal and Allen A. Kennedy, *Corporate Cultures: The Rites and Rituals of Corporate Life* (New York: Addison-Wesley Publishing Company, Inc., 1982), 94-95.

[3]Scott Adams, *The Dilbert Future* (New York: Harper Collins Publishers, Inc., 1997), 1.

[4]Jay Conrad Levinson, *Guerilla Marketing* (Boston: Houghton-Mifflin Company, 1984), 3.

[5]Kaiser Fung, Numbers Rule Your World: *The Hidden Influence of Probabilities and Statistics on Everything You Do* (New York: McGraw-Hill Company, 2010), 155.

[6]Donald R. Cooper and Pamela S. Schindler, *Marketing Research* (New York: McGraw-Hill Irwin, 2006), 465.

[7]For a more detailed presentation of validity, see "Interview Invalidity" in this book.

[8] For more complete discussions of successive stages in consumer behavior research and application, see "Multiple Regression and Factor Analysis in Psychographic Research" in this book.

[9]Derek F. Abell, "Strategic Windows," *Journal of Marketing* (July 1978):   21-26.

[10]J. H. Adler, J. G. Mellenbergh and D. J. Hand.   *Advising on Research Methods: A Consultant's Companion* (Huizen: Johannes Van Kessler Publishing, 2008)

Page 473

[11]David M. Levine, David Stephan, Timothy C. Krehbiel, and Mark L. Berenson, "Statistics for Market Managers" (Upper Saddle River: Prentice Hall, 2005), 300

[12]Bo Allen (2008) and Charmaine Kenny (2005), "Statistical Analysis," Random.org.

[13]David M. Levine, David Stephan, Timothy C. Krehbiel, and Mark L. Berenson, *"Statistics for Market Managers,"* (Upper Saddle River: Prentice Hall, 2005), 299

[14]The sampling discussed in this article is an application from a large but finite population.

[15]Lawrence L. Lapin, *Statistics: Meaning and Method* (New York: Harcourt, Brace, and Jovanovich, Inc., 1980), 278.

[16]Ken Black, *Business Statistics for Contemporary Decision Making* (Hoboken, NJ: John Wiley & Sons, Inc., 2010) 469.

[17]Nie, Norman H., et. al. *SPSS: Statistical Package for the Social Sciences* (New York: McGraw-Hill Book Company, 1975).

[18]Robert R. Johnson. and Bernard R. Siskin, *Elementary Statistics for Business* (North Scituate, MA.: 1980), 488-94.

[19]By comparing the relative size of the "b" values, the market manager can determine which of the independent variables will have the greatest influence on customer demand—these variables that have the greatest impact on the customer should be used for the "boiler plate" of the promotional strategy.

[20]Iver E. Bradley and John B. South, *Introductory Statistics for Business and Economics* (Hinsdale, NY: 1981), 317.

[21]David R. Anderson, Dennis J. Sweeney, Thomas A. Williams, Jeffrey D. Camm, and Kip Martin, *Quantitative Methods for Business* (Mason, OH: South-Western Cengage Learning, 2010) 208.

[22] Ken Black, *Business Statistics for Contemporary Decision Making* (Hoboken, NJ: John Wiley & Sons, Inc.), 520-521.

[23]Fred N. Kerlinger, *Behavior Research: A Conceptual Approach* (New York: Holt, Rinehart, and Winston, 1979), 169.

[24]Fred N. Kerlinger and Elazar J. Pedhazur, *Multiple Regression in Behavioral Research* (New York: Holt, Rinehart, and Winston, 1973), 30.

[25] William D. Wells, "Psychographics: A Critical Review," *Perspectives in Consumer Behavior* eds. Harold H. Kassarijian and Thomas S. Robertson (Glenview: Scott, Foresman, and Co., 1973), 181-182.

[26]$A_o = \Sigma\ B_i, a_i$ where: A_o = the attitude toward some object (the product or service); B_i = the strength of the respondent's belief that the attitude object has a particular attribute, a_i. The positive or negative evaluation aspect of the respondent's attitude toward the attribute, and R = the number of beliefs. Both the dotted line in the attitude schematic and the added comma in the attitude formula indicate a departure from Fishbein. B_i and a_i should be regressed separately over "Y" in order to determine anomalies in the psychographic measurement. See Martin Fishbein, "The Search for Attitudinal Behavior Consistency," in *Perspectives_in Consumer Behavior* ed. Harold H. Kassarjian and Thomas S. Robertson (Glenview: Scott, Foresman, and Co., 1973), 212-213.

[27]Michael H. Walizer and Paul L. Wiener, *Research Methods and Analysis: Searching for Relationships* (New York: Harper and Row, 1978), 38.

[28]Stephen Isaac and William B. Michael, *Handbook in Research and Evaluation* (San Diego: Robert R. Knapp, 1976), 100.

[29]Charles Osgood, "Some Effects of Encoding Upon Style of Encoding," in *Style and Language*, T.A. Sebeok, ed. (Cambridge, MA: MIT Press, 1960).

[30]See "Voice Mail—A Primary Research Application," Appendix A. Also see *Psychographics of Telephone Shopping* (San Francisco: Alchemy Press, 1982), Appendix B.

[31]David Freedman, *"Statistical Models Theory and Practice"* (Cambridge University Press, 2005).

[32]David A. Freedman, *Statistical Models: Theory and Practice*. (Cambridge University Press, 2005).

[33]Joseph F. Hair Jr. Rolph E. Anderson, Ronald L. Tatham, *Multivariate Data Analysis* (New York: Macmillan Publishing Company, 1987), 37.

[34] University of Redlands, Institute for Professional Development, "Business Statistics," Redlands, California, 1979.

[35]Jagdish N. Sheth, "Application and Evaluation of Multivariate Data Techniques," University of Illinois Professional Development Seminar, Chicago, IL, Winter 1984.

[36]Fred N. Kerlinger and Elazar J. Pedhazur, *Multiple Regression in Behavioral Research* (New York: Holt, Rinehart, and Winston, 1973), 37.

[37] David A. Freedman, "Statistical Models and Causal Influence: A Dialogue with the Social Sciences" (Cambridge University Press, 2010).

[38] David W. Stewart, "The Application and Misapplication of Factor Analysis in Marketing Research," *Journal of Marketing Research,* Vol. 18 (February 1981), 51-62.

[39] Valentine Appel and Kenneth Warwick, "Procedures for Defining Consumer Market Targets. (New York: Grudin/Appel Research Corporation, 1969) in *Perspectives in Consumer Behavior* (eds. Harold H. Kassarijian and Thomas S. Robertson (Glenview: Scott, Foresman and Co., 1973).

[40] Joseph F. Hair Jr., Rolph E. Anderson, Ronald L. Tathum, *Multivariate Data Analysis* (New York: Macmillan Publishing Company, 1987), 249-255.

[41] Vincent De Champs, "New Revenues from New Technologies," California Telephone Association Conference, Monterey, CA, November 1988.

[42] Jerry L. Thomas, *Psychographics of Telephone Shopping* (San Francisco: Alchemy Press, 1982.) For a complete application, methodology, result, and analysis of a substantial psychographic data collection, read this citation. (See the Preface of this book.)

[43] Robert Vitale, Joseph Giglierano, Waldemar Pfoertsch, *Business to Business Marketing and Practice* (Upper Saddle River: Pearson, 2011), 126.

[44] Roger A. Kerin, Steven W. Hartley, William Rudelius, *Marketing* (New York: McGraw-Hill Irwin, 2011), 19.

[45]David A Aaker and George S. Day, *Marketing Research*, (New York: John Wiley and Sons, 1990), 40.

[46] Donald R. Cooper and Pamela S. Schindler, *Marketing Research* (New York: Mc-Graw Hill Irwin, 2006), 765.

[47]Funding for this primary research study was provided by Voice Technology, Inc., Dallas, TX, and Onaclov Telephone Company, Mercury, CA.

[48]W. Dal Berry, "Voice Mail: A Revolution in Communications," Telephone Engineering and Management, September 1, 1987.

[49]Martin F. Parker, *The Practical Guide to Voice Mail* (Berkeley: McGraw-Hill, 1987), xi-xii.

[50]Voice Systems, Inc., "Voice Mail Evolution or Revolution," *Telecarrier*, May, 1986.

[51]Interview with Vincent J. Deschamps, Vice President, Voice Technology, Inc., Dallas, Texas, August 5, 1987.

[52]Jerry L. Thomas, *Psychographics of Telephone Shopping* (San Francisco: Alchemy Press, 1982), 17-19. See also Martin Fishbein, "The Search for Attitudinal Behavior Consistency" in *Perspectives in Consumer Behavior*, ed. Harold H. Kassarjian and Thomas S. Robertson. (Glenview: Scott, Foresman, and Co., 1973), 212-13.

[53]In this study, the attitude object is voice mail offered by Onaclov Telephone Company.

[54]For this study, Onaclov Telco's management determined not to collect or calculate evaluative aspect data.

[55]The broken line in this figure reflects evaluative aspect. Onaclov TELCO management decided not to collect evaluative aspect data

[56]Hypotheses to be studied were drafted with Victor A. Silveira, Director of Marketing and Customer Service, Onaclov Telephone Company.

[57]The actual regression formula used in this study was $Y = a + b_1 X_1 + b_2X_2 +...+ b_{12}X_{12}$.

[58]Fred N. Kerlinger, *Behavior Research: A Conceptual Approach* (New York: Holt, Rinehart, and Winston, 1979), 169.

[59]Critics argue that "R" values of less than .7 or so, are not predictive. When combined with corroborating evidence of supporting frequency, ANOVA, "Q" factor analysis, eigenvalues, and communality measures, certain lower "R" values can be proven capable of prediction. (See Jagdish N. Sheth in "Multiple Regression and Factor Analysis in Psychographic Research." Also see the XY correlation schematic presented in that same article.)   See David Freedman, *Statistical Models, Theory, and Practice* (Cambridge University Press, 2005).

[60]Gary Armstrong and Philip Kotler, *Marketing: An Introduction* (Upper Saddle River, 2009), p. 456.

[61] Brian Sussman, *Climategate* (Washington, D.C.: WND Books, 2010), ix.

[62]George S. Clason, *The Richest Man in Babylon* (Metairie, LA: Megalodon Entertainment, 2010), 8.

[63]Damodar N. Gujarati and Dawn C. Porter, "Essentials of Econometrics," (New York: McGraw-Hill Irwin, 2010), 1.

[64]Philip Kotler and John A. Caslione, *Chaotics* (Amacom: New York, 2009), 12.

[65]The break-even illustrations are drawn from David W. Cravens and Charles W. Lamb, *Strategic Martketing Management: Cases and Applications* (Homewood, IL: Richard D. Irwin, Inc., 1990), 31,33.

[66]Larry Schweikart, *Seven Events that Made America America* (80 Strand London: Sentinel, 2010), 11.

[67]George W. Bush, *Decision Points* (New York: Crown Publishers, 2010), 447.

[68] Dhruv Grewal and Michael Levy, *Marketing* (New York: McGraw Hill, 2012), 538.

[69]William M. Pride and O. C. Ferrell, *Marketing* (Mason, OH: South-Western Cengage Learning, 2012), 169.

[70] Dhruv Grewal and Michael Levy, *Marketing* (New York: McGraw-Hill, 2010), 154-5.

[71]Charles W. Lamb, Joseph F. Hair, Jr., and Carl McDaniel, *Marketing* (Mason, OH: South-Western, 2012), 179.

[72]William D. Perreault, Jr., Joseph . Cannon, and E. Jerome McCarthy, *Basic Marketing* (New York: McGraw-Hill, 2011), 35-36.

[73] *Ibid.*, 16.

[74]*The DMMA 2006 Statistical Fact Book*, Direct Mail Marketing Association (June 2006), 50.

[75]Malcom Gladwell, *The Tipping Point* (New York: Little Brown and Company, 2002), 273.

[76] See the topic of "Sales Exchange" in the article in this book entitled, "Managerial Market Economics" for the three requirements necessary to complete a market "transaction."

[77] Lloyd Wood, "Great Moments in email History," *U.S. News & World Report* (22 Mar 1999).

[78] "Worldwide Online Population Forecast, 2006 to 2011," JupiterResearch (2006).

[79] "Top 50 Internet Advertisers," Media Value (September, 2009).

[80] Laura Lake, "Explore the Benefits of Marketing Online," *About Guide*, *The New York Times* (November 2010).

[81] "Social Networking 101," Consumer Reports, February 2011, 8.

[82] J. Conboy, "The 10 Worst Predictions for 2010." AOL News, December 2010.

[83] David Kirkpatrick, *The Facebook Effect* (New York: Simon and Schuster, 2010), 374.

[84] Chris W. Sharp, "Minimizing Internet Marketing Risks," Sharpnet Solutions (November 2010).

[85] *Ibid.*

[86] "Blogs and Chatrooms Pose Risks Despite Coveted Demographics," Kris Oser, *Advertising Age* (August 2005).

[87] Aaron Wall. www.SEObookarchives.com.

[88]Price Waterhouse Coopers, "IAB Internet Advertising Revenue Report," 2010.

[89]T. M. Clark, *Leasing* (London: McGraw-Hill Book Company, 1978).

[90]Robert E. Pritchard & Thomas J. Hindlelang, *The Lease/Buy Decision* (New York: Amacom, 1980).

[91]_____. "Changes in Lease Accounting: What Should the Retail Industry Know About It?" Equipment Leasing and Finance Association, 2011.

[92]Robert E. Pritchard & Thomas J. Hindlelang *The Lease/Buy Decision (*New York: Amacom).

[93]See also the post 1984 through 1992 addendum to this article.

[94]Tax Reform Act (TRA) of 1986, Public Law, October 22, 1986.

[95]Jonathan Weisman and John D. McKinnon, "Obama to Push Tax Break," *The Wall Street Journal* (September 6, 2010).

[96]Marks, Barry S., & John W. Stone III. "Look Before You Lease —Equipment Leasing in the 80s" *Business*, 31 (4), 9-11, 13 (1981).

[97]Richard F. Vancil, ed. (1970). *Financial Executive's Handbook* (Homewood, IL: Dow-Jones Irwin).

[98]See *Retail Lease Versus Purchase Decision*, citation in the Preface of this book.

[99]See Appendix D, Price/Value Schematic.

[100] To Mr. Kurt Rohrs, Master of Business Administration candidate, San Jose State University, appreciation is expressed for the research contribution he made to the addendum of this article.

[101] Karen Floersch, "A New Life on Lease," *Business Week*, November 16, 1987, 48.

[102] _____. "Facts and Fancies about Leasing Office Equipment," *The Office*, October 1987, 45, 53.

[103] Karen Floersch, "A New Life on Lease," *Business Week*, November 16, 1987, 48.

[104] *Ibid.*

[105] Paul F. Hughes, "The Benefits of Equipment Leasing," *Metal Center News*, May 1991, 3-4.

[106] Karen Floersch, "A New Life on Lease," *Business Week*, November 16, 1987, 48.

[107] Kenneth R. Sheets, "Firms Now Lease Everything But Time," *U.S. News and World Report,* August 14, 1989, 46.

[108] Karen Floersch, "A New Life on Lease," *Business Week,* November 16, 1987, 48.

[109] _____ "Credit Firms Flounder as Leasing Attracts Tax-Ridden U.S. Companies," *Business International* , June 1, 1987, 171-172.

[110] _____ "Approach to Sham Transactions Approved by CA-9," *Journal of Taxation,* December 1990, 392.

[111]Ralph L. Benke & Charles P. Baril, "The Lease vs. Purchase Decision," *Management Accounting,* Mar 1990, 43.

[112]Ralph L. Benke & Charles P. Baril, "The Lease vs. Purchase Decision," *Management Accounting,* Mar 1990, 43.

[113]Karen Floersch, "A New Life on Lease," *Business Week*, November 16, 1987, 49.

[114]Karen Floersch, "A New Life on Lease," *Business Week,* November 16, 1987, 52-53.

[115]Jim Bald, "Can Leasing Fleet Vehicles Boost Profits?" *Beverage Industry*, January 1992, 1.

[116]Jim Bald, "Can Leasing Fleet Vehicles Boost Profits?" *Beverage Industry,* January 1992, 2.

[117]Sandra Sopko, "Is Leasing Equipment Better Than Buying It?" *The Office,* March 1992, 77.

[118]Sandra, Sopko, "Is Leasing Equipment Better Than Buying It?" *The Office*, March 1992, 41.

[119]Ralph L. Benke & Charles P. Baril, "The Lease vs. Purchase Decision," *Management Accounting,* Mar 1990, 46.

[120]Sandra Sopko, "Is Leasing Equipment Better Than Buying It?" *The Office,* March 1992, 41.

[121]David E. Kerestes, "Leveraged Equipment Leasing Retains Its Tax Advantages, But a Taxpayer Must Be at Risk," *Taxation for Accountants,* June 1990, 362.

[122]Timothy G. Haight & Kenneth J. Smith, "Equipment Leasing Limited Partnerships Continue to Provide Tax Savings," *Taxation for Accountants*, May 1988, 296-300.

[123]Julie Pace, "Obama to Call for Business Investment Tax Breaks," *The Associated Press* (September 7, 2010).

[124]David Herszenhorn, "Senate GOP Digs In to Keep Tax Cuts," *The New York Times* (September 13, 2010).

[125] _____. "Changes in Lease Accounting: What Should the Retail Industry Know About It?" Equipment Leasing and Finance Association, 2011.

[126]William M. Pride and O.C. Ferrell, *Marketing* (Mason, OH: South-Western, 2012) 348-355.

[127]Charles W. Lamb, Joseph F. Hair, Jr., and Carl McDaniel, *Marketing* (Mason, OH: Southwestern, 2012), 181-3.

[128]Everett Rogers, *Diffusion of Innovations* (5th ed.) (New York: Free Press, 2003).

[129]Arthur O'Sullivan, *Economics: Principles in Action* (Upper Saddle River: Pearson Prentice Hall, 2003), 81-82.

[130] CSX Corporation, "How Tomorrow Moves," 2011.

[131]David Anderson, Dennis J. Sweeney, Thomas A. Williams, Jeffrey D. Kamm, and Kipp Martin, *Quantitative Methods for Business* (Mason, OH: South-Western, 2010) 583-589.

[132]T_o, T_m, and T_p specify a continuous beta probability distribution. The distribution may be symmetrical or skewed (to the right or to the left).

[133] The weighting of the T_m variable is a fundamental underpinning of the original statistical design by Booz, Allen and Hamilton, Inc.

[134] Monroe C. Beardsley, *Thinking Straight* (Englewood Cliffs: Prentice-Hall, Inc., 1975), 1.

[135] *Ibid.*, 2.

[136] Benjamin B. Wolman, ed., *Dictionary of Behavioral Science* (New York: Van Nostrand Reinhold Company, 1973), 366.

[137] Circular Matrix adapted from Richard N. Farmer and Barry F. Richman, "A Model in Research in Comparative Management," *California Management Index*, 4, No. 2 (Winter 1964), 58.

[138] Teresa L. Flateby, "Maximizing Campus Responsibility for the Writing Assessment Process," *About Campus*, Wiley Company Periodicals, Inc., 2005.

[139] Vera Labat & John Bilorusky, "Knowledge-Building in Everyday Life," Improvement of Post-Secondary Education, U.S. Department of Education, 2003.

[140] Linda P. Rosen, Lindsay Weil, & Claus Von Zastrow, "Quantitative Literacy in the Workplace: Making It a Reality," *Quantitative Literacy*, 2001.

[141] Teresa O'Regan & Karmen Mackenzie, "Writing to Express Not to Impress," *Essays: Writing in the Disciplines*, 2005.

[142] William Oncken, Jr., & Donald L. Wass, "Who's Got the Monkey?" *Harvard Business Review*, 1974.

[143] Mike McHugh, Teaching Children to Follow Directions, *Homeschool Helps*, 2007.

[144]William Oncken, Jr., & Donald L. Wass, "Who's Got the Monkey?" *Harvard Business Review*, 1974.

[145]Rajesh Setty, "Ways to Distinguish Yourself," *Life Beyond Code*, 2005.

[146] Holly Blackford, "A Baker's Dozen of Student Writing Problems, *Rutgers Wire.*

[147] A nonscientific judgment sample, stratifying industry segments of Finance, Retail, Public Administration, Manufacturing, and Technology recruiters yielded the following results. Each of the purpose and environment dimensions enumerated in this article was measured on a 10-point interval scale of importance in the decision to hire. When tabulated across all dimensions, the degrees of importance ranged from 7.5 to 9.3, with a mean of 8.5 and a standard deviation among responses of 0.49. While these metrics may be considered anecdotal, the professional opinions come from national corporate recruiters, each having between 10 and 30 years of hiring experience.

[148]National Association of Colleges and Employers, *Job Outlook*, 2009 Survey (www.NACEweb.org).

[149]Gloria Collins, "Struggling for Words: Commas, Hyphens, and Quotation Marks, "ed. Jody Ulate, www. SJSU.edu/wsq.

[150]For greater applied detail, see Jerry L. Thomas, "A Study of Student Writing Weaknesses in Marketing: Does Anybody Know It, Care, or Have a Solution?" *Conference Proceedings*, Marketing Educators' Association Conference, April 23-25, 2009.

[151]Jerry L. Thomas, "Improving Student Writing Weaknesses in Business Deliverables," Sabbatical Leave, San Jose State University, March 2005, 1-24.

[152]Dale Carnegie, *How to Win Friends and Influence People* (La Vergne, TN: BN Publishing, 2010) 25.

[153]See "Managerial Market Economics—The Fundamentals" in this book for a discussion of transaction requirements.

[154]See Tom Peters, "20 Ideas on Service," from *Executive Excellence*, (Palo Alto: TPG Communications, 1991), 3-5.

[155]Susan G. Thomas, *Grammar and Punctuation Essentials for Business Communication* (Cincinnati: South-Western Publishing Co., 1992).

[156]William D. Perreault, Jr., Joseph P. Cannon, and E. Jerome McCarthy, *Basic Marketing* (New York: McGraw-Hill, 2011), 367.

[157]Dale Carnegie, *How to Win Friends and Influence People* (La Vergne, TN: BN Publishing, 2010) 40.

[158]Tom Waits, Singer, Songwriter.

[159]William D. Perreault, Jr., Joseph P. Cannon, and E. Jerome McCarthy, *Basic Marketing*   (New York: McGraw-Hill, 2011), 366.

[160]David Anderson, Dennis J. Sweeney, Thomas A. Williams, Jeffrey D. Kamm, and Kipp Martin, *Quantitative Methods for Business* (Mason, OH: South-Western, 2010) 235-236.

[161]David Anderson, Dennis J. Sweeney, Thomas A. Williams, Jeffrey D. Kamm, and Kipp Martin, *Quantitative Methods for Business* (Mason, OH: South-Western, 2010), 3.

[162] Edgar H. Schein, *Organizational Culture and Leadership* (Sloan Fellows Professor of Management Emeritus at MIT's Sloan School of Management).

187-204

205-213; 215-219

155 - 166